"A valuable resource for both the lay audience and clinicians alike, *My Mother, My Mirror* offers a thoughtful and engaging perspective on mother-daughter relationships in all of their complexity. Laura Arens Fuerstein provides a route for mothers and daughters to examine and re-evaluate the beliefs that serve to keep them bound in self-defeating distortions. She is a compelling storyteller, and her examples, drawn not only from her clinical work, but from works of fiction, biographies, and mythology, provide vivid and engaging illustrations that bring theory to life. Notably, she refrains from blaming mothers (who, after all, are recipients of their own psychic inheritance), and ultimately helps to promote a freer and more authentic sense of self."

> —Melinda Parisi, Ph.D., psychologist and program director of the University Medical Center at Princeton Eating Disorders Program

"*My Mother, My Mirror* offers a fresh look at the feelings of inadequacy so common in women. Few self-help books contain the intellectual and clinical sophistication informing this lively, readable work. Laura Arens Fuerstein translates the jargon of contemporary psychoanalysis and psychological science into images and metaphors that resonate poignantly with deeply felt female experience. With this contribution, her therapeutic skills reach far beyond her clinical office and give readers new opportunities to grow into their best selves."

> —Nancy McWilliams, professor at Rutgers Graduate School of Applied and Professional Psychology

"As a breast surgeon, I have a privileged window into women's body-related self-images, and get a very good idea of their inner strengths. Those with a realistic view of themselves seem to adjust more easily to physical changes that may result from surgery. As Laura Arens Fuerstein writes, the overemphasis placed on female beauty is partly attributed to the media and our culture's focus on youth and glamour, but its deepest causes often lie in our mothers' distorted views of themselves that they unwittingly pass on to their daughters. *My Mother, My Mirror* is a highly engaging book that offers women a clear and unique approach to shedding the emotional baggage that maintains these distorted views."

> —Alisan Goldfarb, MD, Mount Sinai School of Medicine Department of Surgery, in New York City

"In *My Mother, My Mirror*, Laura Arens Fuerstein uses her long experience as an analytic clinician and teacher of psychotherapy to help us recognize and change distortions in our views of ourselves. These distortions are born of distortions in our mothers' views of themselves when we were children. With her firm base in psychodynamics, she demonstrates how to use free writing and other creative activities that engage the senses, as well as literature and mindfulness, to shift toward a truer self-image and greater fulfillment. The book is groundbreaking in that it lifts the mother-daughter relationship guilt trip, while at the same time inspiring us to grow by facing anger, preserving love, and avoiding blame."

> —Susan Gutwill, MSW, psychotherapist and member of the board and teaching staff of the Women's Therapy Center in New York City

# my mother, my mirror

*Recognizing and Making the Most of*
*Inherited Self-Images*

## LAURA ARENS FUERSTEIN, PH.D.

NEW HARBINGER PUBLICATIONS, INC.

Distributed in Canada by Raincoast Books

Copyright © 2009 by Laura Arens Fuerstein
     New Harbinger Publications, Inc.
     5674 Shattuck Avenue
     Oakland, CA 94609
     www.newharbinger.com

*The Tell-Tale Heart* by Laura Arens Fuerstein, ©2007, originally published in *Mind-Body Problems*, edited by Janet Schumacher Finell, is reprinted here with the permission of the Rowan & Littlefield Publishing Group.

Cover design by Amy Shoup; Text design by Michele Waters-Kermes; Acquired by Melissa Kirk; Edited by Karen O'Donnell Stein

Library of Congress Cataloging-in-Publication Data

Fuerstein, Laura Arens.
 My mother, my mirror : recognizing and making the most of inherited self-images / Laura Arens Fuerstein.
  p. cm.
Includes bibliographical references.
ISBN-13: 978-1-57224-569-3 (pbk. : alk. paper)
ISBN-10: 1-57224-569-7 (pbk. : alk. paper)
1. Self-perception in women. I. Title.
BF697.5.S43F84 2009
153.7'5--dc22
    2008052424

FSC
**Mixed Sources**
Product group from well-managed
forests and other controlled sources
Cert no. SW-COC-002283
www.fsc.org
© 1996 Forest Stewardship Council

11  10  09

10 9 8 7 6 5 4 3 2 1

First printing

To
Mark,
Michael,
and Eric

The human understanding is like a false mirror, which, receiving rays irregularly, distorts and discolors the nature of things by mingling its own nature with it.

—Francis Bacon, *Aphorisms*

# contents

CHAPTER 12

# acknowledgments

This book and I were nourished by the support, inspiration, time, talent, and wisdom of many incredibly caring people. I am so deeply grateful to them.

Thanks to my family members for all the ways they have cared for me. Those deceased are Arthur Arens, Ruth Arens, Lillian Kutlow, and Joseph Weiss. I thank my other family members for always being there and rooting for me throughout the development of the book, from pre-conception to birth: Robert Arens, Jeannette Aronow, Carol Fuerstein, Millie Gold, Bobbi Lewis, Harvey Lewis, David Lewis, Dina Lewis and the rest of the Lewis family, Mally Netter, and Sandi Rudin.

Thanks to Herb Strean, my teacher, mentor, and friend, now deceased, who validated and inspired me and sparked my writing career.

Thanks to the following friends and colleagues: Carol Lefelt provided her steady support, insight, and teaching talent to help me find my voice and gain the courage to use it. The prowess, expert counsel, and encouragement of my agent and friend Britt Carlson produced wonders. My editor, Melissa Kirk, believed in me and the book and made it happen. All my other editors at New Harbinger generously gave me their time and the rewards of their efforts. Heather Mitchell, my literary agent, graciously offered her treasured insights and kind presence. Charles Salzberg supported me and freely provided me with his expertise and wisdom. Lorraine Gallagher, Ed Lowenstein, Mona Phillips, and Nina Williams formed a primal core of sustenance, validation, clarity of vision, and valuable feedback on the many drafts they read, frequently on the spot. Susan Berlin, Ellen Deck, Kay Fracher, Marc Geller, Daniel Goldberg, Marjorie Gutman, Paula Warhaftig, and Andrea Zanko sustained me with a limitless flow of encouragement, treasured input, and an unfailing belief in me. Janet Black, Cris Grapa, Joelle Hofbauer, and Linda Yellin bestowed me with their excitement for me, their creative insight, and their invaluable responses to drafts, often at a moment's notice. Nancy McWilliams graciously gave her precious time and kind support. Susan Gutwill warmly reached out and cheered me on. Bill Berlin supplied me with valued feedback and introduced me to the viewing audience. Al Shire offered his unfailing kindness and encouragement through the years. Carol Tosone sparked my desire to write a book. Arlene Litwack bestowed me with her abiding positive influence.

Thanks to Carmen Crea Jr., Fran Lee, Miriam Libove, Rabbi Bennett Miller, Audrey Napshen, Janice Victor, and Valeri Weidmann, who generously reached out to me with their support.

Thanks to Peter Skolnick, Joel Stein, Nina Willdorf and Bunny Wong, who freely shared their time and expertise.

Thanks to old and new friends for supporting me and allowing me to blab about the book at various developmental stages: Dee Anderson, Laura Arrue, Sharon Atlas, Addie Baughman, Shelley Block, Ruth Bowers, Evie Braun, Joe Braun, Jerry Carlin, Mark Chernin, Hillary Corburn, Gene Corburn, Karen Dwyer, Tamesin Dyas, Art Factor, Jane Factor, Jeff Fracher, Dave Gallagher, Marjorie Geller, Susan Goldman, Julie Green, Mindy Greenstein, Warren Grover, Beatrix Hamm, Greg Hamm, Elaine Herzog, Greg Herzog, Carol Heydt, Bob Hill, Cindy Hill, Ken Hyman, Tom Johnson, Susan Jurish, Myra Klein, Steven Lefelt, Carol Lerner, Neil Lerner, Louise Levine, Murray Levine, Randy Levy, Barbara Littman, Len Littman, Judith Logue, Ross Macdonald, Sheryl Magaziner, Dennis Marshall, Rita Marshall, Mitchell May, Elizabeth McCandlish, Bob Mollinger, Nynfa Mueller, Richard Nurse, Jay Offen, Jerry Offen, Larry Perfetti, Lori Petrusky, Jan Press, Bob Raymond, Ron Reich, Peter Richman, Lanie Rockman, Andy Rockman, Pat Rockman, Alan Rockoff, Joy Rockoff, Penny Rosen, Anna Ruach, Wendy Saiff, Beth Bass Ehrenworth, Lenore Schiff, Helene Schwartzbach, Denise Sedehi, Rebecca Sedehi, Cathy Siebold, Sandra Sinicropi, Shawn Sobkowski, Howard Stein, Ruth Stein, Beth Stuckey, Kay Tsurumi, Stephen Warhaftig, Marsha Wasserman, Susan Weltman, Judy Wimpfheimer, Kathleen Winrow, Suzie Wise, and Lisa Zablocki.

Thanks to my Wednesday-morning study group members—Wendy Eisenberg, Maureen Hudak, Laurie Martin, Judi Oshinsky, Nancy Robins, and Nancy Schley—for their part in creating the texture and fabric of the book. They steadily cheered me on, courageously revealed their inner processes, and heightened my knowledge of myself.

Thanks to my sons, Michael and Eric, whose unconditional love sustained me throughout my journey. They openly showed their steady belief in me, offered their unerring insights about me, and bestowed me with their much-needed humor—all while dealing with having a mother who is also a therapist and asks her kids (perhaps one time too many), "So how does that make you feel?"

Thanks to my husband, Mark, for nourishing me in measureless ways throughout the long, absorbing process of writing this book. The best I can do is offer glimpses of what he gave me: a limitless flow of support, a clarity of vision, a breadth of wisdom, an untold patience, a magical way of producing a countless number of half-full glasses, and a willingness to drop everything to read yet another draft—all this, while meeting the challenge of being married to a woman who is both a therapist and a writer.

Finally, thanks to all my patients through the years, for giving me the privilege of having a part in their lives, and for revealing their most deeply hidden truths to me—the colorful threads that formed the tapestry of this book.

# introduction

*I knew it was my mother...she looked up. And when she did,*
*I saw my own face looking back at me.*

—Amy Tan, *The Joy Luck Club*

The idea for this book began to grow when Jenny, a thirty-year-old administrative-law attorney, entered my consulting room for the first time and, after whispering hello, told me what had brought her to therapy: "I'm a poster child for insight. I've learned a lot from books about body image, self-image, how to improve your social life, how to be more sensual, how to lift self-esteem, and how to find the right husband. But I can't seem to use what I've learned to change the way I feel when I'm out there hoping some guy will fall in love with me *despite* my nose."

She went on: "The looks thing seems to be a family tradition on my mother's side. My mother told me she had a similar problem around my age, but it was a different part of the body. She didn't like her breasts because they were too small and made her feel like damaged goods. And she compared herself to *her* mother, who had the hourglass figure that society put on a pedestal in those days. I get the feeling my grandmother was kind of obsessed with the body thing too—except with her, it was about feeling superior to other women. My mother said my grandmother made her feel that her "almost-there breasts" were inferior to my grandmother's full ones. She said that as a teen, she remembered my grandmother saying things like, 'Don't you think you should wear a top with a more interesting neckline, to make *that* the focal point?'

"And my mother said she had demons similar to mine about attracting men. She also told me she still feels that way; would you believe it? She never wears sexy lingerie, and I think it's because they'd reveal more of her breasts. I wouldn't be surprised if she and my dad never have sex with the lights on because of my mom's problem. And he always seems turned on by her, even now that she's fifty-five. But it's as if that doesn't matter to her. Only her distorted view of herself counts."

"But the worst part is that I think she has passed body shame on to me. In my case, it's my wide nose that's the problem. She made me so self-conscious about it that I can't feel a guy's eyes on my face without wanting to crawl into a hole. I'm sure he's thinking, 'This woman has great eyes and a nice smile. She'd be attractive if her nose didn't take up her whole face.'"

## discovering the carnival mirror

While listening to Jenny, I recalled visiting an amusement-park fun house as a little girl. I caught an image of myself in a distorted mirror that stood next to a truer one. I kept going back and forth between the two mirrors, transforming myself into a freak at will. At that age I wasn't entirely sure which image was real and which wasn't, so I alternated between giggles and wariness, wondering whether that creature looking back at me was really only make-believe.

"It's as if you're at a fun house, a carnival," I told Jenny. "You're looking into one of those wavy mirrors all the time, and that's giving you a distorted self-image, a carnival-mirror self-image. You see yourself as unattractive, but that view is not correct. I have a hunch that your mom gave you that idea because she had a carnival-mirror self-image too. In truth, you have a body and face that go nicely together. When someone looks at you, they don't zero in on any one feature; they see an overall attractive woman."

Of course, when we've taken something negative about ourselves as the truth throughout childhood, as adults we don't believe anyone who contradicts that image with a positive statement. So Jenny could only see my comments as flattery. I knew it would be some time before her self-image could come closer to the reality of who she was.

As I thought about how I could help Jenny transform insight into change, I also began to think about how often women have important revelations in therapy. But having an insight in the consulting room is much easier than converting it into growth in daily life. This book is intended to help women outside the consulting room transform those insights into real-life change, as well as help the clinicians who treat women with related issues in therapy.

## the kernel of the book

When talking with Jenny, I recalled how I had almost slipped into an old habit while at my dying mother's hospital bedside, before she disappeared into a coma. Still conscious, she'd expressed a wish to go home. Although doctors had said there was nothing we could do but care for her in the hospital and let her die painlessly, for a split second I found myself wondering how I could gratify her wish to go home. What was I thinking? I knew she couldn't go home. I realized that while growing up, I'd often made difficult situations easier for her at key moments, especially when other family members weren't around. And now, I felt lured into that familiar, special-helper role once again.

That day in her hospital room, as on many of my adult days, I was able to stop my reflex response of acting as the helper. In this case I knew that acting on her request would get my mother and me nowhere. It didn't surprise me that insight allowed me control over my behavior. While engaged in therapy for my analytic training many years before, I'd worked through my taking on the make-it-better role with her. That not only helped me grow personally but also furthered my work, because it separated out the "special assistant" from the "therapist."

Besides the positive effect the change had on me as a clinician, it also released creativity that led me to write a number of published papers in my field. But I didn't find my natural voice until after my mother's death, when I started writing about the two of us. And, though I already knew a lot about my childhood relationship with her when she died, I hadn't fully defined it until my own written words ushered me to the roots of the part I played for her. The more I wrote, the more clearly I saw how my mother's self-image had colored mine and led to my living out that role of helper, an idea we'll discuss in more detail in chapter 1. I realized that my mother and I had a sort of hand-me-down carnival mirror, just as Jenny and her mother did.

3

# the carnival-mirror self-image

My awareness of parallels in the development of Jenny's and my own self-image led me to embrace four key concepts I've used in my work with women through the years, guiding them as they've discovered their truer self-image and freed themselves of others' views of them. First, if your mother has a distorted self-image, it's likely she'll view you through her own inaccurate lens—especially if she sees you and herself as one. Second, that view of you, which doesn't match who you truly are, will cause you to also see yourself in a distorted way. Third, when you see that your mother's skewed image of *her*self no longer has to cause your skewed image of *your*self, you gain a truer self-image. Finally, that shift frees you to get more out of your life. (Note: When the term "mother" is used here, it refers to the *childhood mother*—your mother at the time she raised you.)

We might say that each female generation hands a distorted reflection, like the one from the carnival mirror, down to the next. *The carnival-mirror self-image*—a distorted view of the self—passes from grandmother (and often from earlier ancestors as well) to mother to daughter. At times the daughter's distortion obviously resembles the mother's or grandmother's. And at other times it appears quite different, but the common thread lies beneath the surface.

## Remember the Five Mother Mantras

If you are a mother, I imagine that right now you might be having thoughts like, "Did I hug my baby girl enough when she got upset? Maybe my face looked worried when she was having a toddler tantrum; did I convey the idea that her anger would hurt me? When she was ten and began going to sleepovers at friends' houses, did I imply that she was leaving me stranded? Is that why she's not as outgoing as I would like her to be? Have I ruined her self-image for life?"

If you are having these thoughts, you might wonder, "Why should I put myself through another guilt trip?" Those feelings are natural. When you have thoughts like these, take a moment to recall the five "mother mantras," which you will find at the end of this introduction. If you keep these mantras in mind as you read on and journey through the five thought links, I believe your guilt will fade and you'll find growth at the end of the path. See chapter 12 for a discussion of how to turn guilt into growth.

4

## Let's Not Forget Dad and Other Family Members

This book's focus on mothers and daughters does not imply that the mother-father relationship, the father-daughter relationship, and the input of other primary caregivers during your childhood don't also contribute to your self-image, sense of self, and degree of fulfillment. Perhaps your father or someone else played the primary-caregiver role in your childhood. But because the role of mother is universally powerful, it has a unique influence that stands on its own.

## The Female Body Image Reigns

Although I discuss various aspects of the female self-image in this book, I focus most on the body image. For many reasons, this subject hits close to home. Our looks now, our mother's looks then, and our grandmother's looks before that are all critical components of how women value themselves. What I've found is that, if a woman's *body* image is out of focus, the distortion causes ripples in other aspects of her self-image, including how she sees herself in relationships, at work, in social settings, and in her sexuality.

## Mixed-Bag Self-Image

On paper, the self-image may appear black or white, true or distorted. But in most situations it's actually a mixed bag filled with accurate and inaccurate views.

Becky, a thirty-one-year-old retail manager, has a mixed-bag self-image. She has a skewed view of herself at work. She's somewhat controlling with underlings, but she doesn't see it; she thinks she's easy on them. Yet her distorted self-image in the workplace doesn't thwart her success, because having an air of authority in her supervisory position is necessary in order to keep things moving, her employer says. But socially, the distortion works against her, because she's bossy with her friends outside of work. So her controlling ways dampen her enjoyment of life. She's unhappy with lost friendships yet can't see herself needing help; each time a relationship fades, Becky blames it on the friend.

As you can see, the self-image is a mix of perspectives. And the terms we use to describe it, though they may seem definitive, are not absolute; rather than black and white, they are shades of gray. We all view ourselves in ways that don't totally match our innate self or who we can be. The terms "distorted," "inaccurate," "skewed," and "carnival mirror," when used to describe the self-image, simply mean that there's enough distance between how you view yourself and who you would be if you were free of your caregiver's self-image distortions, to make you feel unfulfilled.

## Therapists Can Benefit Too

If you're a therapist who'd like to expand your approaches to treating women with a distorted self-image, you might find this book useful. The strategy is meant to act as a clinical guide, and the concepts underlying it are intended to enhance your store of theory.

Now let's see how the carnival-mirror self-image can be passed from generation to generation.

# three generations inherit the carnival mirror

Colette, a thirty-two-year-old successful career woman with interesting hobbies, good friends, and a nice family, is admired and valued by her community. But when alone, she often doubts herself. Frequently, even after a day full of positive strokes, she berates herself for her pear-shaped body. Because her average-sized hips and thighs are out of proportion with her smallish breasts, she feels inferior to other women.

Colette's mother, Nicole, reinforced that feeling while raising Colette, because Nicole had her own pear shape that made her feel second rate: her thighs, cellulite included, were her main focus. Because Nicole's mother, Eloise, had done the same with her, Nicole entered motherhood primed to view her own daughter as defective if she had the family pear shape. Eloise's focus on her pear shape had its own twist: her "swinging hips" took center stage.

Since Eloise had problems seeing her daughter Nicole as separate from *her*, and Nicole had problems seeing *her* daughter Colette as separate from her, each mother viewed her daughter with the same judging eye she used for herself. Each mother sent the same carnival-mirror message in her own way: "Sorry to say it but you're stuck with the pear-shaped figure handed down through the generations. That's our family 'heirloom.'" The self-image distortion for grandmother, mother, and daughter got locked in place, because each daughter was influenced by her mother to stress one flaw that came to overshadow positive attributes, physical and otherwise.

## One Magnified Flaw Distorts the Self-Image

As a young girl, Eloise had a way with others and was a leader in any group, positive qualities that her mother had undervalued, because she'd placed her daughter's pear shape at center stage. Eloise's daughter, Nicole, had lustrous, wavy hair and talent in ice-skating, qualities that Eloise had undervalued, because she, too, put the spotlight on her daughter's pear shape. Likewise, Nicole's daughter, Colette, had lovely skin and expressive eyes on top of academic prowess, which Nicole undervalued, because she, too, gave the leading role to her daughter's pear shape.

### *side effects of the distortion*

For all three women, their view of themselves didn't reflect all that they truly were. Each daughter had a lot going for her, but her mother couldn't help her appreciate those strengths because the mother couldn't see them in herself. If Eloise had viewed herself more accurately, she would have felt freer to enjoy her own social and leadership qualities, and perhaps use them in gratifying community work or a career. If Nicole had viewed herself more accurately, she would have felt freer to develop and enjoy her ice-skating talent. And if Colette had viewed herself more accurately, she would have felt freer to make the most of her attractive aspects and academic skills, and she would experience less self-doubt in adulthood.

If your childhood mother had a distorted self-image, as these women's mothers did, there's a good chance that you have one too, especially if your mother had trouble seeing you as separate from her—although she most likely had no idea she was passing it on, because she inherited it from her mother. And that distortion keeps you from living a fuller life. As you will read throughout this book, the *five thought links approach* to finding a truer self-image involves letting go of the carnival mirror that your mother passed to you when she raised you.

One major effect of a skewed self-image is that you are held back from living more fully. And because your sense of self is thwarted, you wind up with less fulfillment than you could otherwise have. You might feel generally frustrated, flighty, indecisive, timid, stuck, bored, uptight, uncreative, hyper, or sidelined. Or you might feel held back in one or two specific areas. You might feel that you're missing something in life but don't know what it is.

You can get a sense of whether you have a general satisfaction problem or a more specific one by reading the following remarks by a few individuals about their self-images. Each woman also lets us know how she could have inherited her mother's own way of seeing herself and her life that has held back both mother and daughter.

"A lot of times I just get the blahs and can't ditch them because I don't know how," says Sarri. "Is that because my mother used to feel the same way and said it runs in the family, so I've viewed myself as stuck with her problem?"

"I keep thinking I'll join the health club and lose weight, but I don't," remarks Randy. "I remember that my mother often mentioned the diet she couldn't stay on, the exercise class she couldn't attend, and her flabby body she couldn't stand. Yet she was always on me to take small bites and work off weight after a heavier meal. Did she try to make me into the perfect woman so she could live through me? I guess, deep down I rebel by refusing to exercise and diet—even if that works against me."

Becca says, "I can't have close relationships with men beyond sex. I'm afraid that if they see that I have more needs than I show, they'll reject me, so I remain a mystery to them. I think the pattern might have started when I was a kid and interrupted my mother to ask for help with something. She seemed annoyed a lot of the time, so I kept my needs to myself. She has been to therapy recently and has been able to tell me that she had the same feelings with my grandmother. Maybe I inherited this problem from her."

"I've said I'd love to go to school to learn landscape design since the kids have gotten older, but I just can't get myself to do it," says Lisa. "My mother told me that a career should never overshadow mothering. The funny thing is that she gave up her chance to be an orchestral flutist when she raised me, and regretted it her whole life. Did she send a message that made me view myself as unable to outdo her by going for my dream?"

You might have a self-image distortion resembling Sarri's, Randy's, Becca's, or Lisa's, or you might have your own unique kind. You might know what you need in order to get more out of life, or maybe you don't have any idea how positive change would look. In either case, the five thought links strategy can help you define what "living life to the fullest" means for you, whether you've never been in therapy, are contemplating it, or have experienced therapy before.

Here's a brief sketch of the book's approach.

## the five thought links

We'll fully discuss the strategy in chapters 7 through 11.

**Thought Link 1:** *Parse* your self-image and your childhood mother's self-image so that they are no longer blended together.

**Thought Link 2:** *Face* the buried anger toward your childhood mother that ties you to her and to your self-image distortion.

**Thought Link 3:** *Face* the buried love for your childhood mother that ties you to her and to your self-image distortion.

**Thought Link 4:** *Face* the buried sadness about what your childhood mother never gave you that ties you to her and to your self-image distortion.

**Thought Link 5:** *Blend* previous thought links in order to shift from the carnival mirror to the truer mirror.

## how to read this book

It is my sincere hope that through reading this book you will discover and embrace your truer self-image. In order to get the most out of the book, I recommend reading it from beginning to end. But if you wish to select just the chapters that relate to your situation, keep the following in mind: chapters 1 through 6 offer background knowledge for use with the five thought links presented in chapters 7 through 11. Chapter 12 discusses the way to use the approach as a mother with your own daughter. The Questions for Reflection at the end of each chapter are there to deepen your insights while you are reading the book. The Reading Touch Tools are added questions that relate the themes of each chapter to other books that delve into the issues of mother-daughter relationships.

Whenever I use a woman's name to illustrate a point, for simplicity, I won't call her a "client" or "patient." Just assume that she's been in therapy with me unless I say otherwise. However, the people and situations mentioned in this book are actually composites of real people and events, so it will be only a coincidence if you think you recognize aspects of an actual person or happening. With personal disclosures, I've changed names or places to maintain privacy, but the details are true. The importance of the examples is not in their facts but, rather, in how valuably they illustrate concepts.

## Two Notes About How the Five Thought Links Strategy Works

This approach includes a way to gain insight and then learn how to convert that insight into change in daily life. I want to stress that insight from a book often goes deeper when combined with therapy: a relationship with a trained analytic clinician can give the written word extra power to help create change. (If you seek such a therapist, see page 222 for a list of websites that can lead you to the proper sources.)

In *Train Your Mind, Change Your Brain*, Sharon Begley (2008) refers to the importance of mindfulness, the Buddhist practice of staying in the present moment without judging oneself or taking action, in the burgeoning field of neuroscience. New discoveries about the adult brain's plasticity, specifically its capacity to let us modify the way we view ourselves, point to mindfulness as a basic element of change. Consequently, mindfulness is a key part of the five thought links approach to transforming insight into change.

## A Model Journey

Throughout the book we will join Jenny, a woman in therapy who has journeyed through the five thought links. As we begin the first chapter, we will look at some of my own steps in that journey.

# before you read on, learn the five mother mantras

As you embark on your journey and begin reading, keep in mind the following important points.

## 1. It's All About the Mother in Your Mind

Maybe you're thinking, "But I had a *good* relationship with my mother and this book doesn't apply to me." That may be true, but this book could help you as much as it would a woman who had a negative relationship with her mother, because the book's approach focuses on the *image* of your mother from your childhood—not on your actual mother.

## 2. Mother Blame Goes Out the Window

The book does not point a finger at your mother for causing your problems. Instead, it highlights a hidden pattern passed from mother to daughter that distorts each woman's self-image, and is *unwittingly* passed from mother to daughter.

## 3. Put Yourself in Your Little-Girl Shoes

The book speaks to you mostly as a *daughter*. While reading, you may find that it's easy to shift your viewpoint from that of you as a little girl to that of you as the *mother* of your little girl—and end up with the accompanying guilt trip. Thinking the following words can help you return to the daughter mindset: "As a child I inherited a distorted self-image from my mother, and my daughter inherited it from me. Like my mother, I was unaware I was handing down the carnival mirror to the next female generation."

## 4. Long Live the Good-Enough Mother

"The good-enough mother" is a phrase coined by Donald Winnicott (1994), an analyst who was first a pediatrician. It implies that we can all make tons of mistakes in raising our kids (and most of us do) and they can still grow up to be healthy adults. A daughter's "distorted self-image" refers to one changeable aspect of her; it is not a brand.

## 5. Gray's the Thing in Mothering

The book may seem to give black-and-white messages with no shades of gray, such as, "Your child will have either a truer or distorted self-image, based on whether your mothering is perfect or imperfect." Those messages are simply there for the purpose of explaining the concept of the distorted self-image and how it comes about. But in real life, almost everything related to mothering comes in subtle shades of gray. So there's no need to expect yourself to be a perfect mother or daughter. Just work to accept yourself, your mother, and your daughter as you and they are, and recognize that many of our failings and weaknesses can be either repaired or simply embraced. This book can help you do just that.

PART I

# mothers and daughters, mirrors and viewers

# CHAPTER 1

# the self-image: do I see me as mommy saw me?

*My mother was troubled by my lack of beauty, and I knew it as a child senses these things.*

—Eleanor Roosevelt, *The Autobiography of Eleanor Roosevelt*

*When I entered your hospital room and saw you in a fetal position, comatose and dying, my eyes quickly lit on the translucent cup filled with runny, red Jell-O and the unopened half-pint of skim milk on the food tray beside your bed. Your breathing rumbled out of sync with the ventilator's steady beats. How absurd, Mom—Jell-O and milk for you? The dietitians must have had you on the food chart, dying or not. I lifted your lids like heavy shutters that were closed to block the light. A day before, with your lungs drowning in your own body fluids and you sounding like a deep-sea diver speaking through a mask, you said some of your last words to me: "I want to go home."*

*One last time, I was hearing the call to play that familiar role with you—your special helper at difficult times. But I quickly reminded myself of what the doctors had said, and held back my feelings, because I knew you would die, fight or no fight, in the hospital.*

Soon after my mother died, I wrote the above words, which described the feelings I had just prior to her death. Before any other family members arrived, I sat in her hospital room alone, surrounded by blah green walls and stiff drapes, in a harsh stillness. As I watched her curled up and looking forsaken in the steel bed that seemed to overpower her, I had many thoughts that would pour out of me in the writing I began about us a few weeks later.

As I mentioned in the introduction, years before, while engaged in therapy as part of my training, I'd explored my role as her anointed aide during my childhood. But I hadn't as clearly understood how her self-image had affected mine until she died and I wrote about the two of us. Through my writing I asked myself, more determined than ever before, how I had come to see myself as my mother's special helper during difficult times when other family members were absent. I had to return to my mother's childhood to get the complete answers.

I recalled my mother saying that my immigrant grandmother had a hard life when she first came to this country and lived in a lower Manhattan tenement, where my mother spent her early years. She also mentioned that because my grandfather worked long hours and my grandmother was often tired and preoccupied with her chores and another child, she got the most attention from her mother when she sang—sometimes alone, sometimes with a cousin, and often with her brother's accompaniment on the piano. Giving her mother a lift was a central way that she felt valued as a child.

I realized that my mother had viewed herself as playing a special-helper role for *her* mother, just as I had for mine. How did I get the message that I should play that part? My mother's inaccurate view of herself gave her an inaccurate view of me. Since specialness meant having worth to her when she was a child, it meant the same to her when she was an adult; only instead of getting that feeling of being special by giving her mother a "lift" through singing, she felt it through my attentiveness when she felt upset. Mostly through reading her body language, I learned early on that I could feel important to her by playing the "make-it-better" role. And, although she and other family members gave me strokes in other ways, her nonverbal signs when I acted as a soothing presence became her most powerful messages to me.

Just as she had felt with her mother, I felt particularly valued when creating a change in my mother's mood—from upset to calm. When lightning hit the weeping willow she'd lovingly planted in our yard, or

16

when the school nurse called to say my brother had been bitten by a snake (it turned out to be a harmless garter snake) in the playground, I saw her eyes soften and her posture relax after I came on the scene.

And, although we played different individual parts for our mothers, my mother and I shared a self-image issue: We both felt we should play a certain role in order to feel most valued by our moms. In other words, we each had a self-image distortion because we couldn't see ourselves as we truly were. If we could have, we wouldn't have felt that part of our worth was based on a certain way of being with our mothers. When writing about the issue we had in common, what I learned helped me separate my self-image from hers even more than I had years before.

In my therapy with women, I'd used the concept of related self-image distortions in mother and daughter for many years. But the process had never seemed as vivid as it did now. That clarity, combined with my new creative force and listening to the statements of Jenny, a woman with lots of insight before she entered treatment but no knowledge of how to apply the insight to daily life, led to this book. I felt that women, both in and out of the consulting room, and therapists who treat them, could benefit from her journey that led to her transformation of insight into change.

## the truer self-image leads to the freer self

Jenny's self-image took shape with her mother's self-image distortions pressed into it. A *distorted self-image* connotes a view of your skills, worth, and qualities—physical and otherwise—that greatly differs from your inherent self, if allowed to grow naturally. Additionally, it means not only that we view aspects or the whole of ourselves in a skewed way but also that we make one of our traits decide our whole sense of worth.

This chapter will begin with an introduction to the situation that brought Jenny to therapy. Next, we will explore what the self-image is. Finally, we will consider four key elements that shape the daughter's self-image.

# Jenny in the consulting room

The first moment Jenny walked through the door, I noticed her averted eyes and contained body as she softly said hi. After placing herself squarely in the center of the roomy chair before me, a loud silence filled the space between us while she nervously twirled the glossy ringlets of her auburn hair. Sun rays that streamed in from the window spotlighted her hair's orange-red strands. She timidly uttered her first words of treatment.

"I feel shaky and scared, and often break out with at least one zit when I'm about to enter some dating-scene thing. I feel like I lose the contest with other women in competing for guys. A lot of times I just can't do it and instead stay home and veg. And when I have a chance in bed with a guy I like, I freak. This has been going on for years, and I've tried the whole deal: hypnosis, meditation tapes, tranquilizers, antidepressants, an eye lift. I'm twenty-nine and single, and I think you are my last resort."

## She's a Veteran of Therapy—but Where's the Change?

Jenny had been in therapy in the past and had gained lots of insight about how her childhood relationship with her mother had affected her social and sex life. But the wisdom didn't stop her from freezing up in the bar or bedroom. "I *know* my mother's in the bedroom with me when I'm uptight in bed, but how do I get her *out* of there?!" she asked.

Many times Jenny told me she hated her looks, especially her nose, as noted in the introduction. She feared she'd never marry and have children, because she felt her "man's nose" made her unattractive to men. When she was in bed with a man she really cared about, she would tense up, focusing on how her nose would turn him off. Women she saw as winning the dating game seemed to have smaller noses. Even in middle school, all those popular girls who got the guys had cute little noses. Some of them had had nose jobs, and she said she'd missed the boat by not having the surgery back then because of her fear of doctors.

One day I looked intently at Jenny as she spoke, noticed her dimples when she smiled, and her large deep-brown eyes and curly hair, and I thought about how her nose, framed by other features, fit her face. When I asked where she'd gotten the bad feeling about her nose, she said that her mother, who herself felt unattractive, would often say, "You got Dad's big nose."

So, Jenny had grown up staring at her nose first whenever she looked in the mirror, focusing on the "man's nose" that made her feel less attractive than other girls. She didn't really notice her other features or look at her face as a whole. As a teen she became so self-conscious that she began avoiding social events where the "cute girls with the cute little noses" would be. She was now repeating this pattern on an adult level, feeling inferior to other women and holding herself back in the dating arena.

## Jenny's Mother's View of Jenny

We began to explore Jenny's sense of how her mother, Sonya, viewed her and how that influenced Jenny's view of herself. Jenny realized that if Sonya believed that Jenny's nose made her less appealing to guys than women with cute noses, Jenny believed it too. She tried to understand why her mother's perception of her carried such weight in her self-image. One reason was that she had put her mom on a pedestal from childhood on because she was the one with the clout in the family. Since Jenny's father and two older sisters had given her mother so much power, Jenny did too; her father would say, "If it's not cloudy and Mommy says it's cloudy, then it's cloudy."

And Sonya had made Jenny feel that she should hold beliefs that matched hers in order to win approval. When she was a little girl, if Jenny picked red barrettes and her mother picked blue, there would often be a struggle on mornings before school while her mother plaited her hair:

"You won't look as pretty in the red barrettes, because red doesn't match your dress."

"I don't care if they don't match. I love the red ones. Red's my favorite color."

If Jenny wound up wearing the red barrettes, she paid the price when her mother scowled. Then she'd go off to school resentful and upset, and be distracted from her work. By her teens she'd lost the sense of her own tastes, because they'd gotten so blended with her mother's. In therapy she began to put the pieces together about how her mother's skewed view of herself—like the one Jenny saw in the "carnival mirror" discussed in the introduction—had influenced her skewed view of Jenny.

## Mother's Carnival-Mirror Self-Image Forms Daughter's

By age fifteen Jenny had begun avoiding social events. She also began binge-eating while holed up in her house and thus gained weight. So now her mother's critical comments included her figure too.

"You have to watch those doughnuts. They're going straight from your mouth to your hips." In reality, because Jenny had larger breasts than Sonya, her hips looked nicely proportioned with the rest of her body. But Sonya could only see them as flawed, because she felt that her own feminine hips were out of proportion with what she called her "barely there chest."

By adulthood, Jenny had developed a terrific fear of competing with other women for men's attention. The thought of entering bars and clubs or Internet dating sites, where she would have to post a photo, sent her anxiety soaring. Even if she sent a photograph and a guy seemed interested, she feared he'd lose interest once he saw her nose in real life. If she did face the crowd one night and feel rejected by guys, she'd run home to binge and hide out afterward, just as she had done in her teens.

When she was younger, all Jenny knew was that she was defective because her looks didn't please her mother. In therapy she realized that her mother's critical view of her was rooted in her critical view of herself; her mother had grown up with a distortion in her own self-image. Sonya was raised by *her* mother, Nadia, to feel that anything less than an hourglass figure like Nadia's put a woman at a disadvantage with men.

During Sonya's childhood, Nadia had projected a superior front while probably hiding her sense of low self-worth (we'll discuss Nadia's self-image in chapter 11). She bragged about the numbers of suitors who knocked at her door because of her figure. And when Sonya's breasts turned out to be small, Nadia told her she'd have to work overtime for a "good catch."

## The Carnival-Mirror Heirloom

Over time Jenny realized that, in order to free herself socially and sexually, she'd have to view herself more accurately, as a woman whose nose and hips didn't define her worth and appeal—to men and women. In order to make that shift, she had to discover how Nadia's self-image distortion had influenced Sonya's and how Sonya's had influenced Jenny's.

Once she saw the thought links in that generational chain, her view of herself became more accurate. And Jenny strengthened her conviction that her mother's nit-picking about her looks was influenced by her own distorted self-image rather than an inborn defect in Jenny.

We'll discuss her changes farther on. But now, let's explore how the self-image forms in a general sense, so that you can learn about how accurate or inaccurate yours may be.

# how does the self-image form?

In the following pages, we'll discuss three major influences on the daughter's self-image: the mother's view of herself, the daughter's view of her mother, and the daughter's modeling of herself after her mother.

## The Mother's View of Herself

Each of us has a view of the self, influenced by our mother's view of *her*self, that begins to form at birth. Even before our infant eyes discern the features of our mother's face, her voice and touch send a message that begins to form the way we will see ourselves. Do we hear sweet songs that soothe when we're wet, tired, or hungry—or muted tones offering little promise of something better? Do we feel tender touches when diapered or bathed—or notes of annoyance through a sharp poke or a hard pat?

In attempting to *know* her baby, the attuned mother must *see* her baby. And because in the earliest time of life baby and mother are one, our self-image molds itself around our mother's view of herself. The common gender of mother and daughter intensifies the bond and heightens the impact of her gaze on us. Of course, we must first attach to our mother to gradually gain separateness from her. But at times, the tie becomes rigid, which prevents a gradual separation that leads to a more objective view of oneself.

Since a mother with an inaccurate self-image often feels down on herself, her look into her daughter's eye is even more powerful, more penetrating, more consuming, and more imploring than it might otherwise be. Why? Because she tends to hope for a rebirth, a second chance, through her daughter. And, though the mother's message about herself and her daughter often travels through the mother's gaze into her daughter's eyes, it can also arrive via a subtle facial expression, body shift, or vocal tone. A screeching silence can often send the most powerful cue.

## how the mother's self-image shapes the daughter's self-image

The cycle from mother's self-image to daughter's self-image can play out differently, depending on whether the mother passes on a truer mirror or the carnival mirror.

**The Truer-Mirror Heirloom:** Danielle's story helps show us how the truer mirror cycle works. Danielle's mother, Ilona, never excelled at sports, but that didn't get in the way of her ability to feel good about herself while growing up. Ilona's mother recognized her daughter's musical talent and nurtured her interest in it, furthering her truer self-image. When she became an adult, Ilona's truer self-image led her to learn the guitar and enjoy playing it, resulting in a freer self and more fulfillment.

While raising Danielle, Ilona had enough fulfillment to allow her daughter her own. She didn't need to keep Danielle back from sports just because she hadn't done well in them at Danielle's age. And Ilona also didn't need to live through Danielle by making her achieve in an area that she had achieved in, like music. So instead, when Danielle showed a talent and interest in tennis while growing up, Ilona encouraged her to see her natural ability—supporting her truer self-image. Ilona nurtured that skill, just as *her* mother had nurtured hers. By the time Danielle was a teen, her innate tennis ability had blossomed and she enjoyed the sport, leading to a freer self and greater fulfillment.

**The Carnival-Mirror Heirloom:** Unlike Danielle's mother, Maggie's mother had a carnival-mirror self-image.

> *Mom, it feels as if it's always been this way. Your eyes said*
> *a thousand words telling me how I should act. Your sighs;*
> *tightened lips; wrinkled brow; stiff posture; and thin, polite*
> *voice sent a clear message when I wanted to do what you*
> *never could—feel free to do my own thing. I became you, the*
> *constrained little girl.*

Maggie read me the above words she'd written after a session in which we talked about how much her self-image resembled that of her mother, Brenda. Brenda had grown up believing herself to be strange, because as a child, when she sometimes chose to play alone instead of going to a friend's house, her mother called the wish odd, even though Brenda had many friends and played with them often.

So, as a mother, without being aware of it, Brenda passed on the carnival mirror to her daughter. When Maggie seemed content playing alone in her room once in a while rather than visiting a friend, Brenda would ask, "Are you sure that's what you want to do?" By the time Maggie was a tween, she couldn't enjoy solitary experiences without feeling like a nerd; she had a skewed self-image. If she had had a truer self-image, she would have viewed herself as healthy for feeling good in her own skin and not needing the company of others all the time.

The effect of our mother's self-image on our own often takes root long before our birth.

## *mother's preconception dreams*

As a teen, Barbara, whose mother scrutinized her, pictured the baby she'd give birth to someday as an improved version of herself: blonder, with blue eyes. When Barbara had a daughter with brown, curly hair and brown eyes, she felt disappointed and viewed her daughter with a critical eye, as her mother had done with her.

**Prenatal Pictures, Postnatal Plummets:** In *Our Looks, Our Lives,* Nancy Friday (1999, 20) reinforces the idea that, preceding a woman's pregnancy, parents fantasize about the baby: "There is a shape, a size, a certain sex, a color of hair created from the parents' own lives, what they had, or wish they'd had." This prenatal picture leads to a huge letdown for our mother if she has a carnival-mirror self-image and we don't counter her sense of defectiveness by being an idealized form of herself.

On the flip side, if our mother has the carnival-mirror self-image and we *do* match her fantasy, we may wind up with another type of problem: pressure to be the ideal daughter she needs us to be. This, of course, also leads to the same effect: an inaccurate self-image.

Haley shows how that process plays out. At birth, Haley's thick, black hair made her mother, Irene, joyous, because Irene had been born bald and always had "thin, mousy-brown hair." Irene linked Haley's hair to her sister with thick, black hair, whom she'd always felt inferior to. As a result, throughout Haley's childhood Irene treated her in an idealizing way, as a child without problems. So Irene overlooked any self-doubts her daughter might have expressed in order to deny that she had any flaws.

Haley's hair eventually turned dark brown; however, her mother continued to call it black and pointed to magazine photos of actresses with black hair that "looked just like Haley's." So, because Haley believed that her true looks put her so far from the pedestal that her mother had placed her on, she developed a distorted image of herself as "not good enough." Further, she had to hide her self-image problem from her mother, because she didn't want to disappoint her.

We've seen how the mother's self-image affects how she views her daughter, which then affects how the daughter views herself. Another influence on the daughter's self-image is the way she perceives her mother. Sometimes she sees her pretty accurately, especially when the mother has a truer self-image and doesn't need to camouflage any self-doubt or shame. But when the mother wears a mask while relating to her daughter, the daughter will probably see her as she wants to be seen, not as she truly is.

## Daughter's View of Her Mother

Linda, a woman in therapy for three years, discovered the truth behind her mother's self-righteous, judgmental attitude. Her mother would say gossipy things with conviction based on her own distorted view of the world, not facts: "Well, Jim must have cheated on his wife, so that's why she left him," or "I bet the minister drinks; that's why he's late for services." As a child, Linda believed that her mother must always be right. So Linda's own opinions, even if reasonable, carried little weight in her own mind. As an adult in treatment, she realized that her mother's know-it-all manner actually concealed her insecurity. It took a while before Linda could believe that her own views had value.

A similar experience is described in Rebecca Wells's *Divine Secrets of the Ya-Ya Sisterhood* (1997).

### *a camouflaged mother in fiction*

In Wells's book, the main character, Sidda, has an experience similar to Linda's. Sidda expresses relief when she discovers that her childhood mother, Vivi, was not an actual celebrity but an insecure woman

24

who'd learned to deny childhood wounds by making up "her own solar system...and [living] in its orbit as fully as she could" (1997, 33)

Vivi had grown up with a distorted image of herself as sinful, based on *her* mother's inaccurate view of her as seductive with her father when she was a teen. When Vivi herself grew up to be a mother, she tried to hide her guilt by masquerading as a celebrity who outshone others. The mask caused Sidda to view her mother as a star and to view *herself* as bad if she achieved more than her mother had. "Even winning a spelling bee made me worry, because I never trusted that I could shine without obliterating [mother]" (Wells 1997, 33).

Many women like Linda and Sidda have childhood mothers who veil their insecurities with facades such as specialness, self-sufficiency, brilliance, or lightheartedness. And, because to young children, mothers are all-powerful, the daughters buy their stories and the carnival mirror along with them. So they wind up viewing themselves in skewed ways, as inferior, imperfect, lacking worth, or unable to reach their mothers' achievement levels without hurting them.

We've discussed two key effects on our self-image related to our childhood mother: how she viewed *us* based on her own self-image and how we viewed *her*. The third is how we modeled ourselves after her.

## Daughter Models Herself After Her Mother

One of my sons once pointed out that at certain moments I have a kind of quizzical facial expression that's just like my mother's. I wasn't at all aware I had it until he noticed it. When I tried to replicate it, I was stymied, probably because it goes back to the time of imitation when I was so young that my mother's expressions melded into my own.

### *aping the apes: imitation*

Like other primates, we're social creatures who learn survival-based behavior by imitating our mothers. With our earliest vision we can mimic certain expressions, as Louis Cozolino (2006) states in *The Neuroscience of Human Relationships*. "Mirror neurons," located in the brain's frontal lobes, fire when we view our mother's actions, allowing us to copy these actions. Anger, sadness, disgust, surprise, joy, and fear register on her face through particular ways of moving her eyes, brows, and mouth, all of which we make part of our own.

In *Infant Research and Adult Treatment*, Beatrice Beebe (2002) augments that concept in her discussion of facial mirroring with infants and mothers. Reflecting goes both ways when infants and mothers are facing each other. "The infant represents the experience of seeing the mother's face continuously changing to become more similar to his or her own; the infant also represents the experience of his or her own face constantly changing to become more similar to the mother's face" (98).

We find an illustration in Hope Edelman's (2006) *Motherless Daughters*; she writes about a thirty-three-year-old client who'd been separated from her mother at age three and now, as an adult, had a habit of playing with her hair when under stress. She didn't realize how she was copying her mother until she "remembered her [mother] taking her hair and rubbing it on her face." The client says, "It blew me away, because it was like this hidden, weird thing that I did" (37).

Early imitation of mothers is probably so ingrained that we can't change its imprint dramatically, though we can be aware of its effect on others. If, as infants, we've mimicked our mother's worried look, as adults we might have a similar anxious appearance, which affects the way people relate to us. In turn, their responses shape our self-image.

## *from imitation to modeling*

As you grow, the simpler imitation of your mother shifts to something more complex: *modeling* yourself after her (also, identification). Modeling yourself involves *internalizing* her traits (making them part of your own without trying) and *emulating* her (striving to be like her). Healthy modeling occurs when your mother has a truer image of herself that boosts your truer self-image. Unhealthy modeling occurs when she sees herself in the carnival mirror, which influences you to do the same.

**Modeling That Boosts the Truer Self-Image:** As a child, Sydney loved to watch her mom sew clothes and sing along with the radio. She'd take Sydney shopping to help her pick buttons and trim for dresses she'd make for her. Sydney remembered putting the shiny black and sparkly buttons in circles on a table, and the lacy and cotton eyelet trims in piles. As a teen she asked for sewing lessons, and as an adult she enjoyed quilting. Sydney internalized her mother's pleasure in sewing and emulated her, which motivated her to develop her own sewing skills.

## Modeling That Distorts the Self-Image:

> *I married Craig just to spite Mom, I think. I didn't know it then, but I know it now, and I've been in a crummy marriage for twenty years. When he drinks, I see "loser me" in his glazed-over eyes. She tried to get me to marry a more refined guy than Craig, because she wasn't happy with "farmer Dad," whom she married because she saw herself as a loser too. I went the other way to rebel and wound up with the same husband letdown she had.*

Many women like Susan, whose words are above, model themselves after mothers with self-image distortions. Surprisingly, they may enter treatment feeling that they're nothing like their mothers. These women believe they've chosen a totally different way of life, work, raising kids, or marriage style. But on a deeper level they resemble teens who rebel in an attempt to believe they're separate from their parents. Those adolescents really aren't separate, because they stay tied to home by hanging around and flaunting their defiance. Meanwhile, they defeat themselves by playing hooky, skipping homework, smoking cigarettes, drinking, or using drugs.

We're like the defiant teen when we use *rebel modeling*. Without being aware of it, we fight against being like our mothers with so much passion that deep down we stay connected to them because we make them matter so much in our choices. Like the rebel teen, the daughter defeats herself, because the unconscious tie to her mother compels her to make choices that don't serve her well.

Hope Edelman (2006) underscores this issue in *Motherless Daughters*. She presents a therapist's experience of treating a woman whose mother had taught her to see herself through a negative lens. The therapist says, "'My concern about this woman is that she's so determined to be the opposite of her mother, she's losing the freedom to do what she really wants'" (238).

In that vein, therapist Robert Karen (1998) states in *Becoming Attached* that ironically, when he's treated women who seem to have had conflicted mother-daughter relationships, they reveal powerful modeling after their mothers, "with the result that many of these women feel doomed to the worst aspects of the mother's destiny, including in some cases a bitterness toward men or fate in general" (224).

Whatever the influence, if our childhood mother's own self-image is distorted because she's gazing at the carnival mirror, there's a good chance she'll pass that self-image on to us. That's because during our infancy she represents life or death, which causes us to shape our view of ourselves in a way that we feel will keep her going. Western culture's carnival mirror heightens the effect of the personal mirror we gaze at, just as it did for our female forebears.

# culture's effect on the female self-image

When I recently described this book to a thirty-year-old woman, she quickly asked, "Are you going to talk about how different society was for my sixty-five-year-old mother when she was my age?" I agreed with her that the world has changed a lot for women, and she has many more opportunities than her mother did, but her question highlighted a major point of my book: that the important strides women have made in society haven't dramatically improved our self-image as a group. Despite the progress of the women's movements, mothers and daughters still share a long-lived common bond: we berate ourselves because we don't act and look as we should, according to the culture's ideals.

## Culture Tells Women How to Be

Many women fear how they'll appear to others if they go all out, whether that means being a go-getter when applying for a job position, grabbing a blissful moment of reading on a veranda, eating a savory meal with gusto, or decisively declaring their opinions. In *Women's Eating Problems: Social Context and the Internalization of Culture*, Susan Gutwill (1994) describes a hidden cause of this problem. Mothers absorb society's message that "puts women in charge of meeting needs rather than entitling them to be receivers of emotional care and privilege," which leads to "frustrated desire and smoldering rage...built into... women's everyday experience" (7–8). When the mothers raise daughters, they unwittingly convey a confused message to their little girls that it's okay to need TLC at home, but it's not okay to show that need outside. So the daughters model themselves after the mothers and gain a similar distorted self-image: they're bad if they show desire. Chapter 5 will discuss female desire further.

# Culture Tells Women How to Look

Our entertainment and news media offer a one-stop shop: on one magazine page, a message tells us that we're flawed because we don't resemble the model pictured there, and a few pages later a product ad proclaims that we can look more like her. If our mother bought into that idea while growing up, then we probably did too. And if that's the case, we are, as she was, prone to attempt to avoid negative feelings toward ourselves by trying the external fixes our marketing-based society is more than happy to provide.

When our mothers were young women, maybe there weren't as many eye-grabbing commercials showing first the "before" body—pasty, lumbering, and flabby in the kitchen—followed by the "after" body— bronzed, sultry, and cut on the beach. But instead they may have dealt with the pressure of the Marilyn Monroe, buxom-blonde ideal or the image of Twiggy, the 1960s actress who made ultra-thin seem ultra-in and ultra-straight seem ultra-great.

Scarlett O'Hara's waist-cinching corsets have been exchanged for cutting-edge cosmetics, despite the women's movement's stress on beauty beneath the skin. While our mothers might have given themselves a permanent or tossed and turned while trying to sleep with rollers in their hair, now those of us with enough funds may seek other external routes to self-improvement. While these efforts can produce positive results, they also are often ineffective, painful, or unhealthy. Examples of these attempts include tanning, extreme diets, stomach surgery (which is particularly problematic after the process is done if the patient has not learned about the deeper issue that might cause her to lose control with food), and, more recently, vaginal rejuvenation. But whether or not these physical changes are considered "successful," they can't reshape the woman's *inner* view of herself.

## *cosmetic surgery: two sides of a coin*

Sometimes a reverse situation occurs with external procedures such as cosmetic surgery: some women who can afford such a procedure and could benefit from it won't let themselves have it because they don't feel entitled to it. When women have cosmetic procedures done for the right reasons by the right doctors, the procedures can be a wonderful alternative to waking up every day and feeling awful about their noses, wrinkles, sunken cheeks, or varicose veins. And though no external method, in and of itself, shifts a woman's self-image from distorted to more accurate, it can help her self-esteem along while she works on her deeper issues.

The more we understand our reasons for what we're putting ourselves through, the healthier the process will be for our self-image. If we choose a cosmetic procedure, we have to value ourselves enough to seek the surgeon who will treat us as individuals and help us make the best decision.

There are examples of physicians on both ends of the spectrum. One woman, who appeared on a TV show about facial procedures, had had fifteen nose jobs; only one surgeon had suggested she go to therapy! A woman in treatment with me insisted on "fixing" the circles under her eyes, even when three doctors recommended that she shouldn't. The fourth one gave her the green light, and she had him do the surgery. Another woman in therapy had a scar on her body that she said kept her from having sexual experiences. She could have made it almost invisible with a cosmetic procedure, but she wouldn't, though she wasn't able to say why. It turned out that she had fears about sex and used the scar as a way of avoiding it. She eventually found a compassionate cosmetic surgeon who patiently helped her make the soundest decision based on the medical facts he offered. She came to trust him and went ahead with the procedure, and she felt good about it, while continuing to discuss her underlying sexual fears in therapy.

Another woman, in her fifties, went to a cosmetic surgeon to discuss the possibility of a nose job. The surgeon sensed that, because of her age and personality, if she had the procedure she'd be upset by the change. Because he was sensitive to her feelings, he helped her see why it wasn't a good idea. Six months later she returned to him and had another procedure done that was appropriate and helpful.

So, cosmetic procedures for the right reasons with the right doctors, who care about our feelings and note our individual needs, can be very positive experiences, as long as we're not engaging in them as escape routes from self-loathing. Of course, if we can't afford these approaches, we might feel hopeless. Many of us might ask, "Without a physical metamorphosis, what metamorphosis is there?" So it's important to keep in mind that, although external changes transform body parts, they don't, in and of themselves, make changes that help free us in an enduring way.

## _outside change, inside same?_

The outer solutions don't deal with one of the primary causes of reduced fulfillment: the carnival-mirror self-image. In addition, external changes such as these don't always last. Tightened skin sags, diets plateau, and pills run out of steam. In addition, the woman who hates her appearance lives on, even before the face-lift loses its lift or the tummy tuck gets untucked. Because of the carnival-mirror self-image, she continues to feel dissatisfied with her appearance. And our culture adds extra distorted reflections to our own carnival mirrors. What we really need is to know how that outer influence affects us _internally_, so we don't fall prey to advertising's sales tactics.

If, because of our race or ethnicity, we have darker skin or facial features that differ from those of white women, our cultural experience gets even tougher.

## Double Whammy for Non-Caucasian Women

In _The Bluest Eye,_ Toni Morrison (1994) captures the feelings of Pecola, an eleven-year-old black girl from Ohio in the 1940s. Pecola is so affected by the white culture that she prays for her eyes to be blue. The narrator points to a primary cause of Pecola's problem:

All the world had agreed that a blue-eyed, yellow-haired, pink-skinned doll was what every girl child treasured. "Here," they said, "this is beautiful, and if you are on this day 'worthy' you may have it" (20–21).

Related to Pecola's self-image is the way the white culture, through history, has affected African American mothers' self-images, which in turn influences their daughters' self-images. Leslie Jackson and Beverly Greene (2000) write in _Psychotherapy with African American Women_ about the challenges for those mothers in raising their daughters: "A mother can spend several hours working on her daughter's hair...she may feel that she has a direct, positive impact on something in a world where so many of her actions...result in failure" (175).

Although our culture has opened up a good deal, racially speaking, since Morrison and Jackson and Green wrote their books, many African American girls still grow up with an intensified focus on their hair, eyes, and skin color. And as we've discussed, when a woman stresses one feature over the others, her self-worth centers on that feature and leads to a skewed view of herself.

## Let's Recap

We've discussed how a woman's self-image begins to form at birth, sometimes even before birth, with her mother's fantasies about what her girl will be like. We explored how the mother's own self-image begins to shape the daughter's self-image in three ways while raising her: how she views the daughter, how the daughter views the mother, and how the daughter models herself after the mother. And we discussed a fourth influence on a woman's self-image: Western culture's ideals for women.

Chapter 2 will focus on the childhood mother's enduring influence on her daughter's self-image, through the lingering picture of the "mommy in the mind," the mother image.

### A Note to Mothers of Girls

While reading this chapter you may have said to yourself, "Whew, did I do all that to my daughter?" If you're asking yourself this question, please remember that, if you've inherited a carnival-mirror self-image, you couldn't help relating to your daughter in ways that passed the "heirloom" on to her. Hang in there and wait until you have read the later chapters on the five thought links to see how you can gradually lift the weight of self-blame.

# Questions for Reflection

1. If you think your childhood mother's self-image
   tions, how would you describe them?

2. How do you think those distortions influenced your self-
   image?

3. If you think your mother had a façade that didn't match her
   actual view of herself, how would you describe the façade
   and what was actually behind the facade?

4. Can you describe your own healthy and unhealthy modeling after your mother?

5. If you think your self-image has distortions, what are they
   and how do they squelch your innate skills, strengths, or
   traits?

6. What would "greater fulfillment" look like for you?

## *Reading Touch Tool*

Dorothy Allison's *Bastard Out of Carolina* has a mother-daughter
theme. If you have read or plan on reading the book, your responses to
the questions below can deepen your understanding of how your own
mother-daughter relationship influenced your self-image.

### *Bastard Out of Carolina,* by Dorothy Allison

- How does Anney's self-image influence Bone's?

- Do you see anything like a shared self-image distortion
  between Anney and Bone? How would you describe it?

- How are Anney's and Bone's self-images affected by the
  culture?

# the mother image: mommy in the mind

*The moment she lifted me, I was wrapped in her smell...*
*the scent got laid down in me in a permanent way*
*and had all the precision of cinnamon.*

—Sue Monk Kidd, *The Secret Life of Bees*

One day, a few years after my mother died, I pictured the scene of her death, still vivid in my mind. For a moment I stepped outside myself as daughter and asked myself, as therapist, how my adult image of her compared with my childhood one. My mother, who stood five feet tall, looked even smaller, curled in a fetal position in her metal-framed hospital bed. Yet she, a fragile Thumbelina while dying, had so often seemed a mighty giant during my youngest years.

## what is the mother image?

My image of my mother in adulthood stood in stark contrast with the luminous one I had in childhood. Her importance in that picture from the past made her seem much bigger than she was in reality. Again, the therapist in me began to think about how large and strong a mother— even a mother small in stature—is to a child. My little girl's mind, like the minds of kids universally, made "mother" more powerful than she actually was, because I needed her for survival while growing up.

Only as an adult in therapy did I find out about the little girl in her while she raised me. I discovered how important it was for her to feel special in her own mother's eyes, and how she probably kept that feeling into adulthood, even after my grandmother had died. Though I learned about the child in her and intellectually believed it existed, my sense of her power over me lived on until I changed the picture of her that had stayed in my mind since childhood.

We'll call the enduring sense of the childhood mother the *mother image:* the positive or negative sense of the childhood mother that stays mostly out of awareness throughout life. The sense of her comes through as an image, vocal tone, verbal message, or manner of being touched. When positive, it gives support or solace, which feeds the truer self-image. When negative, it creates discomfort and insecurity, which feeds the distorted self-image. Most of us aren't conscious of the influence the mother image has on us—in an elated or trying moment, during a phase of contentment, or during a crisis.

The contrast between the sense of the mother now and the sense of her in the past that's conveyed by the mother image comes through in Joanne's comments. "How could that frail, seventy-year-old woman whom I helped choose bras and panties yesterday have been a tigress as a mother when I was a kid?! It's absurd that I'm still afraid she'll roar at me. She can hardly speak beyond a murmur."

## mother image: mother's understudy in the unconscious

Even if our mother viewed herself as over-the-top flawed while raising us, our mother image would paint her as the Wizard of Oz, because we depend on her for our survival in our early years. We need her to exude power so that we can feel secure. Of course, as grown-ups we know that she's always been more like what Dorothy finds at the end of the yellow-brick road: a usually well-meaning but flawed human.

## The Mother-Image Message

But the mother image keeps telling us something different, which defies reality, and we believe it (unlike a disturbed person who hears voices, we're unaware of the "voice" of the mother image). That's because she's the enduring stand-in for the mother of our earliest years, imprinted in our memory as mighty in our eyes. Jami's experience shows how the mother image echoes the childhood mother. Jami's mother image seems reserved when she vigorously gets into sports, just as her mother seemed reserved when she got rambunctious as a toddler. (Her mother inherited a discomfort with freedom of motion from her own mother.) So Jami's mother image reinforces the childhood mother's communication that letting herself go might be a no-no and that she should reduce her participation in sports in order to please her mother.

How does that mother-image message reinforce parts of Jami's self-image that were influenced by her mother's input? Since physical activity and receiving warmth from her mother didn't go together for Jami as a toddler, she became less active with her toys. By the time she turned three she wasn't as physically free as she'd been earlier on. Also, since she viewed herself as less desirable when she felt free, her self-image began to form as one who should comply with others' wishes to try to feel lovable. Now, her mother-image message reinforces the one her childhood mother gave her. So, after Jami excitedly enters both a tennis and softball league, she withdraws from tennis, because her mother image tells her, "Don't go overboard with that fun activity."

In chapter 1, we focused on your self-image and how your childhood mother's self-image affected yours. In this chapter we'll explore how she still affects your self-image, but in a different way: through the echo of her in your adult mind, the mother image.

This chapter has four sections. Section 1 discusses how the mother image forms out of realistic and imagined (fantasy) views of the mother. This section also explores the unconscious, the home of the mother image. Section 2 connects your mother image with your self-image. Section 3 considers the unique power of the negative mother image and how important it is to lessen it, in order to gain a truer self-image. Section 4 shows how the above ideas play out in life, through the history of a woman in therapy.

# 1. how does the mother image form?

*When I was in second grade, one day I couldn't find my jacket*
*at dismissal time. I started crying, saying, "My mother's gonna*
*kill me." The teacher took me aside and gazed at me with kind*
*eyes and said, "Do you really think your mother would kill you*
*for losing your jacket?" I recall being calmed by her. God bless*
*her. But looking back, I think that's how I saw my mother when*
*I was seven, even though she really wouldn't kill me. And I think*
*I hold myself back from taking on new challenges today because*
*I still see her that way. Deep down, do I have an imagined fear*
*that she'll kill me if I botch up what I do, like losing my jacket in*
*second grade?*

Leslie's mother image contains parts of who her childhood mother actually was and her *fantasy* of who she was: what her mind made her out to be, from infancy on, based on her actual appearance, habits, personality, and ways of relating to her. Reality and fantasy come together and concoct the mother image that lives on in the *unconscious*: the part of memory outside awareness, which is formed mostly during the time before language could express emotion. The unconscious guides many of our adult feelings and actions, unbeknownst to us.

Mark Solms and Oliver Turnbull (2002) tell us in *The Brain and the Inner World* that the early memory, set into the unconscious while the brain's neural pathways are shaped, later influences relationships. The authors write that, although many of Freud's theories are often challenged today, a group of researchers believes, as Freud did, that the major portion of thought rests in our unconscious. And the unconscious is the storehouse for the mother image. And, as discussed, reality combines with fantasy to create it.

## Fantasy Aspect of the Mother Image

Early in life, especially before we can put feelings into words, our fantasy image of our mother begins to form in our unconscious mind. Sense, thought, and emotional responses to her actual input form the kernels of our fantasies. Each unique mind takes reality and blows it up, shrinks it down, or throws it out of kilter, like Alice's perception of her Wonderland landscape. Our helplessness makes mother's bigness bigger, her power larger, her anger scarier, her limitations more unacceptable. Because negatives in general get magnified at that time for survival reasons (discussed further on), our mother's negatives might also get magnified for survival reasons. Our life or death depends on her. And we don't want to bite the hand that feeds us. (Note: When I use the term "fantasy" in my work, people sometimes take it to mean "mentally ill," because it implies "way out." It's true that sometimes people get too carried away from reality by their fantasies and do become ill or unable to function well. But fantasy is also a normal part of human thought, and serves us in both healthy and unhealthy ways.)

We've seen how fantasy and reality join to form the mother in our mind, the mother image. And the mother image affects our self-image throughout life. This connection isn't meant to say that the earliest time in life is the only time self-image can be shaped or that there are no other significant influences on the self-image besides the early mother. Our narrower focus is simply meant to illustrate points.

# 2. the mother image influences the self-image

While some aspects of the mother image form in later childhood, its core takes shape in our earliest years, when our self-image is also taking shape. That's why the mother image and self-image have a connection. Here's how it happens: Our self-image, while forming, is influenced by our mother's view of us. The mother image stays with us and echoes that view. So our adult self-image continues to be affected by the mother image, just as our childhood self-image was.

When a present relationship stirs a feeling resembling one we had with our childhood mother, our responses echo those we had with her in the past and feed into the self-image, as they did then.

We may sense the mother image giving our childhood mother's straight-ahead look of support or sideways glance of disapproval. We may sense it echoing her words, "I know you can finish the project, because you're good at these things," or "You won't stay with it; I know you." When we're upset now, as adults, we might have the mother image with our mother's soft smile and smell her lentil soup that soothed us as a child. Or, instead, we might have mental snapshots of our childhood mother looking askance while we're trying on a bathing suit that she would have said exaggerated our hips.

The mother image keeps us attached to the self-image that our childhood mother helped create. The positive aspect of the mother image is an offshoot of the mother's own truer self-image and helps form our truer one. The negative aspect is an offshoot of the mother's own distorted self-image and helps form our distorted one.

## Positive Mother Image, Truer Self-Image

You're cranky and don't know why. You just want to be held by your partner, who's tuning you out at the moment. Your sense of the positive mother image calms you, because you experienced your childhood mother as soothing in an ongoing way. So you can quiet yourself. Also, with that input you would have gained a sense of being valued: a sign of a truer self-image. That perception helps you express your need to your partner, because you feel deserving of what you long for and free to ask for it.

But the mother image with a comforting quality when you feel distanced from your partner can transform into one with a very different quality when another kind of interaction occurs.

## Negative Mother Image, Distorted Self-Image

Let's say you're frustrated and angry with your secretary at work. You tell her she's not keeping records well. She becomes silent and then says, "Okay, I heard you," in a monotone that seems to imply that she's putting you down—which makes you more frustrated and angry. Your secretary's silence and monotone voice (even though she likely just feels defensive about her mistakes) remind you of your mother's silence and monotone voice when you felt frustrated and angry as an infant.

In this situation the mother image echoes your childhood mother's reactions. So you can't calm yourself, because you have no modeling for it. You view the secretary's response just as you viewed your mother's response: rejecting when you expressed a type of want she couldn't or wouldn't gratify. That impression contributed to your view of yourself as undeserving of help. In turn, that self-image distortion stops you now from expressing appropriate needs to your secretary.

To gain a truer view of yourself, you need to change the mother image, which is a major theme of the five thought links.

# 3. soften the negative mother image, gain a truer self-image

As I came to understand the causes of my mother's inaccurate self-image, I came to understand the causes of mine. But to change my self-image to a truer one, I had to change the negative part of my mother image that still conveyed a message in adulthood that it had given in childhood: the mother's helper role brings self-worth. How were the negative mother image's signals still influencing me in adulthood? The power of the unconscious and of early negative input is a key part of the answer.

In chapter 1 I discussed one instance when I thought of slipping back into that role in the hospital where she lay dying, when reality said there was nothing to be done. But at other times in my life I've acted upon the mother-image message with others who reminded me of my childhood mother, often in ways not clearly visible. Someone who looked completely different from my mother but had a similar wistful look in her eyes showing she needed a "special helper" could send me, unawares, into that familiar role.

## The Power of the Unconscious

It follows that you need to soften the power of the mother image in order to avoid slipping into those old roles, give yourself truer input, and get away from the distorted input you've received. Often, negative recollections pop out first.

## The Power of Early Negatives

In *The Neuroscience of Human Relationships,* Louis Cozolino (2006) tells us that aspects of the brain developed earliest in life are especially responsive to negative emotional stimuli prior to conscious awareness" (68) for survival reasons. We're wired early on to attend to negative influences because we share with our animal-kingdom cousins the need to be ready for attacks by predators. So, if there are equal amounts of positive and negative experiences with a parent, the negative ones will probably make a deeper mark. That's another reason why the suddenly different and upsetting input that Kimberly, a woman in treatment, received as a toddler came to dominate over positive earlier input, and her mother image reflected that more-negative sense of her childhood mother.

## 4. kimberly changes the mother image to change the self-image

*I have this memory of looking out the window of my house on Cedar Street, wearing some kind of pink, lacy thing. Maybe I was two and a half? I think that was the day I started feeling I wasn't worth much, but I can't tell you exactly why I think that. It's just as if this kind of gray place got set down in my brain somewhere. I have the sense that that was the day my mom went crazy and went to another planet, because my grandfather had a stroke in front of her after she'd tried to get him to eat. She told me later that the stroke reminded her of when she was around three and she saw her baby brother in his crib after he had died of SIDS in his sleep. She'd always felt guilty about his death, because she'd been playing with him before it happened.*

When Kimberly told me this, we were talking about her sense that there must have been some sharp shift in her mother Joyce's nurturing in Kimberly's earliest years. On one hand, the adult Kimberly's mother image gave her a feeling of her mother's coolness and a message that Kimberly wasn't worth her time; she thought that perhaps that sense came from the time when she was a little girl. On the other hand, Kimberly always felt deep down that she could get more love from her mother if she could just find a way to please her. She sensed that that feeling came from the time before her childhood mother's crisis.

She felt that she had once had something with her mother that she lost, but she couldn't say what. While Kimberly was exploring her past, her older cousin said that during Kimberly's infancy Joyce gave her "oodles of love." But after Kimberly's grandfather died, when she was a toddler, Joyce felt guilty and began depriving herself of fun times, as if she suddenly felt unworthy of pleasure. And she gave over the mothering to her husband because she felt she was "bad" and might hurt her daughter if she got too close. Besides, she didn't feel she deserved to enjoy her.

Kimberly had a strong hunch that, without knowing it, Joyce had passed the carnival mirror on to Kimberly, who wound up questioning her worth.

In infancy, Kimberly had a connected mother, which formed a positive mother image. As a toddler, Kimberly had a more distant mother, forming a negative mother image. During her adulthood, Kimberly's mother image showed negative pictures whenever Kimberly doubted her worth. If she thought she wasn't entitled to a gift, for example, the mother image had her childhood mother's far-off look that supported Kimberly's feeling that she lacked worth.

In therapy Kimberly saw that her sense of low worth didn't come from some "gene that put her on the discard pile," as she put it. Instead, her mother's own image of herself as guilty caused her to distance herself from Kimberly as a toddler, which made Kimberly feel cast out. Once Kimberly gained that awareness of the roots of her negative mother image, that image gradually faded and her positive one brightened, which helped her shift from the carnival-mirror self-image to a truer one. Chapter 11 discusses how such a change occurs for any woman with issues like Kimberly's.

In a memoir, *Daughter of the Queen of Sheba,* Jacki Lyden (1997, 20) gives a description of a mother image that makes the negative aspects quite obvious when she writes about her experience while looking into her mentally ill mother's dressing-table mirror: "I felt her stare sear me...something greater than fear clutched at my throat, and I could feel my mother embracing me, invisible...(20)" Although Lyden portrays a discomforting mother image here, there are less-dramatic ways that the negative mother image comes through.

# let's recap

In this chapter we first discussed how the mother image—positive and negative—forms out of bits of fantasy and reality related to the child-hood mother and resides in the unconscious, where it remains a hidden influence on the self-image. Next, we explored how the positive mother image—that echoes another part of the mother—contributes to the daughter's truer self-image. And the negative mother image—that echoes another part of the mother—based on the mother's distorted self-image, contributes to the daughter's distorted self-image. We then learned how your self-image becomes truer when you lessen the unique power of the negative mother image. Finally we discussed how one woman in therapy shifted from a distorted self-image to a truer self-image by reducing the strength of the negative mother image.

In the next chapter we'll home in on the give-and-take between you and your childhood mother, and see how those past interactions influence your self-image now.

## A Note to Daughters

You might now be feeling that if you get farther down the road to connect your self-image issues—whether intimacy problems, lack of assertiveness, negative body image, sexual fears, or social anxieties—with your mother image, you'll have negative feelings toward her that you can't handle. If you do feel that way, try to continue reading through chapters through 11, on the five thought links, before you doubt your ability to face the emotions you have now.

# Questions for Reflection

1.  How would you describe your mother image using senses, emotions, and thoughts?

2.  How does your mother image compare with your actual childhood mother? Is it harsher than she actually was or more ideal?

3.  How does your mother image affect your self-image? If it makes you see yourself in a distorted way, how does the main distortion differ from a truer view of you?

## *Reading Touch Tool*

In *The Secret Life of Bees*, by Sue Monk Kidd, the main character, Lily, experiences an event early in life that forms a mother image revealed in her self-image at different times later in life. If you read the book along with this one or afterward, thinking about the questions below can heighten your insight about your own mother image's effect on your self-image.

### *The Secret Life of Bees*, by Sue Monk Kidd

*   How did Lily take positive parts from her mother image and weave them into other relationships to free her sense of self?

*   What aspect of Lily's view of her mother was revealed in her view of herself?

*   Do any aspects of your mother image resemble Lily's?

## CHAPTER 3

# the mother-daughter relationship: an intricate prism

*I've got what my mother's got. However bloody you're feeling,*
*you can put on the most amazing show of happiness.*
*My mother is an expert at that.*

—Princess Diana in *Diana: Her True Story*, by Andrew Morton

While strolling a beach one late afternoon as the sinking sun teased the sea, I suddenly realized that I'd been lured into a sunset matinee directed by nature's dazzling palette. Entranced with the show of shimmering mauves, melons, honeys, violets, and aquas, I pondered why color has always touched me so deeply. One of my earliest memories includes plucking the turquoise and plum crayons out of the crayon box, calling them my very favorites of the pack, and watching in suspense as the partnered hues contrasted in wavy lines on canary-yellow construction paper.

I realized, while watching sun merge with ocean, that as an adult, even though I'm not actually a painter, I often paint my feelings and thoughts as mental images. At that moment I felt a connection to my mother as I pictured her, eyes widening and body animated, trying out various fabric samples in the house, one on a sofa, another on an ottoman, or leafing through the home-decorating magazines that composed her personal library. For years, a pile of frequently replenished issues of *Better Homes and Gardens* and *House Beautiful* lay in the wicker basket near her armchair, which was covered in a cotton print of periwinkle blue and lemon yellow.

My sunset experience revealed that a good part of my interest in color came from my mother. But it also made me note our differences about those things. My mother loved Renoir's golds, reds, and auburns, while I favor Matisse's aquas, greens, and plums (my childhood crayon choices). Perhaps one of the most obvious areas where our contrasting tastes revealed themselves was in floral paintings. My mother's idea of a beautifully painted iris evoked a realistic bloom with realistic colors: yellow, white, purple, blue, mauve. In contrast, I like to see more of the artist's hand: abstract petals, slanted leaves, fantasy hues.

# know your mother, know yourself

When I consider one part of my mother's positive influence on me, I realize I have taken her interest in tint and hue, and woven it through some fabric of my own to create a self that is like her yet not her. In fact, without my realizing it, this book itself, with its focus on image and perception, seems to be a blend of the two of us: a product of my own creation, run through with threads of her creative sensibilities.

But it's in my role as therapist that my mother's visual sense most reveals its impact. In my work I use language as a tool, of course, but my mental artist's brush best helps me know the people I treat by revealing who they are beneath their words.

I think in pictures when, let's say, I hear Denise speaking of her childhood suburban home, offering a memory of herself as a three-year-old fighting with her older sister over ice cream, or relating a story about her grandmother's immigration from Italy to Ellis Island in the late nineteenth century.

Because of what I've come to know about Denise, my mind's eye makes the home a pearl-gray colonial with black shutters, puts the ice-cream squabble in a pale-green kitchen with beige-and-green tile countertops, and places her mother, wearing a white-and-yellow checked apron, absently staring at a soup pot. Then my mental image of the Ellis Island scene dresses her grandmother in a long and billowy black poplin skirt and mulberry brocade blouse with mandarin collar and puffed sleeves, as she walks off the deck of the cargo ship whose hold acted as her domain at sea. (I know, my imagination here has taken a leap. Who would wear those clothes while living for weeks in a cargo ship?!) Denise's grandmother is vivid and sharp in my mind's eye, with the house, mother, and kitchen dimmer and more in the background, because Grandma was the matriarch, the one who ruled the family roost.

All through the journey of self-exploration required by my field, I've had to explore my mother's influence on me and needed to know myself as well as possible in order to keep my own issues separate from those of the people I treat. Knowing myself means knowing my mother and also knowing my mother *and me.*

## Freer Mother, Freer Daughter

The beach scene drove home powerfully that the colorful way I think in my work reflects a positive aspect of my mother. During my childhood, her visual bent seemed to flow freely out of her to form an element of me, in contrast with her earlier discussed aspect that caused her to try to be something special for her mother, an aspect she'd imposed, mostly unknowingly, on me.

The healthy part of my childhood mother naturally became a healthy part of me, because she didn't foist it on me. It just poured out of her. And because color enlivened her, it enlivened me. That interest of hers must have fed an inborn color sense incubating in me. I think of my mother's creative side as her *flowing traits*, those that emerged from her innate self and were revealed because she viewed herself as good with color; and she actually did have a natural talent with it and enjoyed playing with it.

That idea leads to the focus of this chapter: a more detailed look at your childhood mother's qualities that still influence you. Up to now we've highlighted the self-image and the mother image. In this chapter we'll look at actual interactions between you and your mother that shape the self-image and the mother image. But before that, we'll discuss the entanglements and passions that are unique to the early mother-daughter relationship and that determine its power in the way you see yourself.

# the mother-daughter tango

When I began to think about mother-daughter relationships, I recalled my seventh-grade lunch table. One of my schoolmates, June, would often say, after slowly unfolding the foil wrapped around her sandwich and peering inside with what seemed like dread, "Damn, my mother gave me shit on rye again." Each time, I would think, "How could she say that about her mother? She must not love her mother. I'd never say that about my mother."

It wasn't until I was an adult in therapy that I discovered I did have some anger toward my mother, which I'd hidden under positive feelings. I came to see that June and I were two sides of the same coin. June's "shit on rye" comments probably covered a love for her mother. Expressing feelings at one extreme often means that opposite ones lurk beneath the surface.

Mother-child attachment patterns start getting ingrained from the day of birth. Researchers are observing more and more about how those styles get set into mind and body, particularly during the time before we can speak, because, as discussed in chapter 2, we're genetically programmed for survival. Due to the unique female bond, mother-daughter relating includes complex patterns from those early days. (Many mother-daughter relationships are simpler, but those that lead to the issues discussed in this book tend to be the more complex ones.)

## Intricate Dance Steps

The mother-daughter duo, like a couple dancing the tango, reveals an intense relationship. And as in the tango, while an exquisite, seamless grace is displayed in the partners' intertwining, at times their tightly coiled bodies exude a palpable tension.

Though similar to dance partners in intensity, mothers and daughters have even more interweaving and complex variation in their moves. The relationship swirls, dips, and soars, with poignancy, ambivalence, and passion. The childhood mother's issues easily become the daughter's issues, her needs the daughter's needs, her self-image the daughter's self-image, her sense of self the daughter's sense of self. (You might sum up the relationship when the pair's twists and turns go beyond those in the tango by calling it the "bowl of mother-daughter spaghetti.")

Because of the intricate attachment to our mother before we know we're separate beings, that intricacy weaves into our view and sense of ourselves in adulthood.

# the mother-daughter afghan

I recently looked at an afghan my mother helped me crochet in the later years of her life. Her hands were too arthritic to do more than a couple of model stitches at a time, but the pleasure she got out of teaching me seemed to outweigh whatever encumbrance in her joints she experienced. And I got pleasure from letting her teach me. She felt excited when I'd finished it (so did I, after ripping out a particular part one time too many) and was happy when family members could wrap themselves in it to keep warm. Though I'd chosen the afghan's colors and design, and done most of the work, it was a cocreation in which yarn interwove as did my mother's and my feelings.

I also recalled a childhood experience in which my mother and I worked with yarn that also reflected our relationship. When I was eleven she showed me how to knit a scarf, but I think she felt less patience and joy than she did with the afghan project so many years later, described above. The sense I have now is that my mother viewed the scarf too much as a reflection of herself. She had too large a say in the colors—we had a tiff about them—and too great an investment in the stitches' neatness. Perhaps the scarf was, for her, another way to get special attention, because when I finished it, though she did compliment me, it seemed important to her that others know the part she had played. And it didn't seem as if we really shared the experience as much as we did when we crocheted the afghan together.

## Crocheting with the Mother's Flowing and Imposing Traits

While my mother helped me crochet the afghan, her flowing traits resembled her ways with color. They seemed to flow freely and come from her innate self. Conversely, when she taught me to make the scarf, her manner showed *imposing traits* that seemed to come from some unnatural part of her.

Flowing traits that come from our childhood mother nourish our natural-born self, with all its potential—the *innate*, or *inborn*, *self*—leading to the *freer self.* In contrast, imposing traits weigh down what the innate self could become—leading to the *thwarted self.*

## Flowing Traits, Freer Self

In the earliest time of life we feel at one with our mother. So if she's free with herself, then her freer ways become ours. Her broad and ready smile, animated motions, or quick song and lilt in the voice may give rise to our easy smile, lively walk, or ear for music when we grow up. Her flowing traits allow our inborn qualities to take shape in their own way. We don't have to mold ourselves to her needs or those of others later on. We could say that flowing traits let us take the best from our mother and add our own innate ingredients to it to form our freer self. The freer self's qualities include openness and a leaning toward desire, pleasure, playfulness, sensuality, and sexuality. Donald Winnicott, who learned about children and their mothers as a pediatrician before becoming an analyst, coined the term "true self," found in *The Maturational Processes and the Facilitating Environment* (1994). Its meaning overlaps with part of the definition of the "freer self" as I use it here: spontaneous, creative, and authentic. The freer self leads to the daughter's truer self-image.

## Imposing Traits, Thwarted Self

Similarly, if our mother is often restricted, especially during the time when we don't yet feel separate from her, we easily take in her closed ways and they become ours. Her tight facial expression, contained motions, or flat tone of voice, for example, may give rise to our adult readiness to furrow our brow, contain our movements, or use a monotone voice. Imposing traits prevent inborn qualities from growing in their own way, because they get shaped around mother's, or others' needs later on. Her imposing traits block our path; as a result, our inborn traits get detoured, leading to the *thwarted self.*

## *three generations*

*I have a birthmark on my calf the size of two half dollars put together. I was so conscious of it as a teen that, many times, it kept me from going to the beach. My mother would say that I should go anyway, I think because she felt that that would make me more like all the other kids. But she never really helped me feel better; she'd say, "Oh, just put makeup on it, and no one will notice it." When I gave birth to Tania and she had a facial mark that the doctors said would go away, I didn't believe them, because I thought she'd have the same problem as me, and I was jittery when taking care of her. I discovered recently that my mother had had freckles on her face throughout her teens and that she had hated her freckles because she thought they made her look like a little kid. So maybe that's why she couldn't help me with my problem: she couldn't see me objectively because I reminded her too much of herself, and I, in turn couldn't see Tania objectively because she reminded me too much of myself.*

Of course, people's rudeness about body flaws and our culture's ideals about women's bodies surely had their own part in Cynthia's self-image distortion, described above. But she let her birthmark define her whole self-image, mainly because she saw herself in the carnival mirror passed on by Barbara, her mother. And Cynthia passed it on to her daughter, Tania.

**Imposing traits keep the carnival mirror in the family.** The carnival mirror heirloom had been passed down through three female generations. And imposing traits kept it going. Barbara's distorted self-image, which led her to believe she was unattractive because of her freckles, was placed upon Cynthia, whose birthmark evoked Barbara's feelings about her freckles, which she'd viewed as defects. In turn, Cynthia's distorted self-image in connection with her permanent birthmark was placed upon Tania, whose temporary birthmark evoked Cynthia's feeling about her permanent one.

The imposing traits put upon grandmother Barbara, mother Cynthia, and daughter Tania weighed on their innate selves to form thwarted selves: the sense of self that results when the innate self is affected by the mother's distorted self-image.

## *thwarted self*

*The first night I knew I was pregnant I had a dream of a baby
girl in a bunting giving me a bottle! In real life I was excited
and jittery all at once about pregnancy. I began drinking milk
for the baby and having extra scoops of ice cream to give myself
TLC. But I didn't want people to notice my body, because I was
afraid they'd think I was fat. So I bought clothes that hid my
shape. I didn't really gain that much weight, but I felt like a big
chub from the get-go. Deep down I feared that the baby would
have something wrong with it, like me.*

When Kelly entered therapy, she viewed herself as inferior to many
women she saw every day. Her mother idealized Kelly's younger twin
sisters, because they were very active from birth on, unlike their mother,
who was, as she herself said, "too docile and unassertive." Since Kelly
was a placid baby, she reminded her mother of a part of herself that she
had rejected. So her mother wasn't as attentive to Kelly as she was to the
twins. Kelly grew up feeling second rate next to her sisters, and continued to feel this way later, with other women.

Kelly restricted her own inborn athletic skills, because her distorted
view of herself as inferior held her back in basketball, a sport she excelled
in during informal games with friends. Two girls on the school team,
who engaged in bullying, reminded Kelly so much of her sisters that
she'd fumble when they were near her on defense together.

Kelly's thwarted self wasn't free with competition, pleasure, desire,
sensuality, and sexuality, and, like Donald Winnicott's "false self" (1994),
put a damper on Kelly's spontaneity, creativity, and authenticity.

Like Kelly, Tracy also had a childhood mother with imposing traits.
But Tracy's situation allows us to see how a woman can sometimes
uncover flowing traits hidden beneath imposing traits.

## *flowing traits hidden beneath imposing traits*

Although in her early relationship with her mother, Tracy experienced her mother's imposing traits, she also stored away some positive
flowing traits. During a therapy session, she said that she and her mother
had always fought like cats and dogs; later in the session she mentioned
her love for baking. When I asked where that passion had come from,
her eyes lit up as she said, "Oh, I used to help my mom make holiday

cookies. I loved getting to pick the metal cutter shapes and taking turns putting the doughy blobs of stars and animals on the pan."

There's a contradiction, I thought. Her body language and voice belied her words about the steady bad vibes she had gotten from her mother. Then I realized that, despite their conflicts, Tracy had identified with her mother's pleasure in baking, which furthered Tracy's natural bent toward it.

We've discussed the childhood mother's flowing and imposing traits. Here are two related qualities: *tuned-in traits* leading to the *hug cycle*, and *tuned-out traits* leading to the *boomerang cycle*.

# tuned-in traits: the hug cycle

Four-month-old Anna is as happy as a clam listening to music in her crib. But her diaper's wet, so her mother takes her out of the crib to change her, and she starts to cry, rage, and howl. Because her mother is tuned in to her, she can hug Anna; she soothes her and extinguishes the sparks of her rage by helping her gradually shift into and out of an upsetting situation. Anna's mother holds her close while lifting her from the crib to the dressing table, into a diaper, and back into the crib. Anna is comforted and her rage lessens. She goes from howling to whimpering to smiling. Anna's mother shows tuned-in traits—qualities of a freer self that let her respond well to her baby's needs while her own go to the back burner—that help form the hug cycle.

## Effects of the Hug Cycle

Frustration, rage, comforting, soothed state: this is the *hug cycle*, which leads to security. Neuroscientist Louis Cozolino (2006) writes that security helps shape the "social brain," the aspect of the brain molded by early relationships, particularly before language arrives. Security increases most when a caregiver tunes in to help her infant cope with discomfort.

A more-accurate self-image and a freer feeling grow out of the hug cycle, because we don't have to twist and turn our innate self in order to get love; we know we have it. On the flip side, when an infant has a caregiver who shows many tuned-out traits, the baby experiences the opposite effect of that of the hug cycle: the *boomerang cycle*.

# tuned-out traits: the boomerang cycle

When the caregiver displays *tuned-out traits*, it means she can't over-look her own needs in order to take care of her child's, because she has too many of her own problems, often caused by a carnival-mirror self-image. So as infants we're not comforted enough, which adds to the upset we started out with. I call this chain of events—frustration, rage, lack of comforting, more rage—the *boomerang cycle*, which leads to insecurity. The *American Heritage Dictionary, 4th edition* (2000) defines a boomer-ang effect as "a course of action that backfires…[has] the opposite effect from the one intended." So in the boomerang cycle, the response to the infant's needs essentially backfires.

## Three Carnival-Mirror Generations

Before exploring the boomerang cycle, we need to discuss the infant rage that fuels it. Let's first look at the experience of a grandmother, Cora, who passed the carnival mirror, along with tuned-out traits, on to her daughter, Betty, who in turn passed it on to *her* daughter, Tammi.

### grandma cora's carnival mirror

*You know, I felt guilty yesterday when I saw my daughter, Betty, with Tammi, my granddaughter. Tammi was having a crying jag and Betty couldn't soothe her. She said to me, "Mom, I can't take it."*

*I think that I denied Betty confidence as a mother, because when she was a kid I wasn't on her wavelength. I was too busy trying to act like a perfect, invincible mother, because* my *mother acted like a wimp. I think that as a result Betty grew up comparing herself to me, of course, not knowing that under my superwoman act was a little girl just trying to make up for my mother's weakness. And now she doubts herself as a mother to Tammi.*

## *mother betty's carnival mirror*

In Cora's comments above, she questions her past behaviors—though she had enacted it without awareness—when her daughter, Betty, was a little girl. Cora handed the carnival mirror to Betty, just as Cora's mother handed it to her. Because Cora's mother was so meek and passive, she showed her daughter imposing traits that carried the message, "Don't be like me deep down. Be superstrong so you don't wind up like me, a weakling." So, as a mother Cora put on an all-powerful exterior when Betty was a child. And when Betty grew up and became a parent herself, she felt she'd lose the "best mother" contest with Cora.

Because Betty doubts her maternal skills so much, she unconsciously feels that her baby will be better off if she doesn't get too close to her and "ruin" her with her own defects. So she stays distant from Tammi and doesn't show the warmth she has within her. And Betty often gets irritable with Tammi when she's crying, because the more upset Tammi is, the more she reminds Betty of her own maternal flaws. Tammi absorbs her mother's anger, because she's too young to sense that she and her mother are totally separate, which gives her own upset more oomph and leads her, when she's irritated, to imitate her mother's angry behavior.

## *daughter tammi's boomerang cycle*

We can more clearly see how a caregiver's all-out anger can affect a child's behavior if we think of Tammi as a toddler having a tantrum because she wants candy, like Melanie, the little girl I saw in the grocery the other day. (Note: The example that follows may make you think that showing frustration or anger at your child's tantrums makes you different from "ideal" mothers who control themselves better. That's unrealistic. It's totally common and understandable to act angry in the face of a child's out-of-control tantrums. The example is presented simply, as it is, for clarity only.) Melanie's mother loudly said no, which increased the child's crying; in response, the mother yelled no, louder this time than before. And with the increased yelling, Melanie's crying level heightened too. For Melanie, like Tammi, not only have the decibels increased, but the sources of the carnival-mirror self-image have also increased, because the child's own show of anger creates a sense of harming the caregiver rather than feeling soothed.

## A Cause of the Boomerang Cycle

So how does the boomerang cycle's cause-and-effect pattern work? In *The Brain and the Inner World*, neuropsychologists Mark Solmes and Oliver Turnbull (2002) say that we, like all mammals, have a "basic-emotion command system" (115) for survival that includes four primary emotions: seeking, rage, fear, and panic. They report evidence of signs in the early brain that rage, more than any other emotion, gets triggered by frustration. Frustration is part and parcel of infancy, but, as analyst Heinz Kohut (1977) writes in *The Restoration of the Self*, early frustration increases when caregivers don't help us have a sense of control over our environment. And infant rage is a result.

The boomerang cycle opens the doorway to the opposite of the hug cycle's effects: insecurity, fruitless expressions of anger, and self-sabotage.

## An Effect of the Boomerang Cycle

*I know I'm late for the session. And I really wanted to come in today. I don't get it. Why was I unable to leave work five minutes earlier so I would beat the rush-hour traffic? I'm angry at myself. It doesn't make sense. Maybe I wanted to make you wait because you were five minutes late in calling me from the waiting room the other day. I guess I wanted to get back at you, and I was too afraid to tell you how I felt. So I showed you instead and wound up cutting off my nose to spite my face. My mom would crumple up and look sad if I tried to express any anger to her, so maybe I thought you would too.*

### *Ronda's self-sabotage*

Ronda felt anger in our session and couldn't express it directly for fear of hurting me, the stand-in for her childhood mother. Because her sense of her anger, stemming from infant rage, made it seem more harmful than it actually was, her need to stifle it was stronger than it would otherwise be. So she unwittingly directed it against herself, depriving herself of therapy time. Like Ronda, many women repeat aspects of the boomerang cycle without knowing it. A woman might do this with her actual mother if she is alive. But often they go through it with other people who take the mother's place in their mind, like husbands, partners, lovers, children, cousins, friends, employers—or therapists.

Next, we'll look at the novel *Snow Flower and the Secret Fan* to see how a mother's traits can evoke a daughter's responses, which influence her self-image. Not all the traits or responses that we've explored are included here, but those presented offer a good overall picture of what's been discussed.

# a fictional mother-daughter relationship

*Snow Flower and the Secret Fan,* by Lisa See (2005), describes how, in Chinese culture where foot-binding practices are the norm, a mother's influence on her daughter Lily affects Lily's relationships into adulthood. Since we can't witness what actually occurred during Lily's infancy, we'll use the older Lily's thoughts to support hunches about how her childhood mother's traits might have influenced her self-image and sense of self. Throughout, I'll attach my thoughts about the mother's traits and Lily's responses in parenthesis.

But first, I'd like to add a note about foot binding: Because the painful procedure was commonly accepted in China during the 1800s, the period during which the book is set, we can view Lily's mother's values as culturally induced, just as they were for *her* mother. So she couldn't help but feel that the process was essential for her daughter's well-being, however painful it was. We're not blaming the mother here any more than we would blame a mother for imposing a cultural belief that slim equals beautiful, light skin is the best skin, or a clitorectomy is an essential rite of passage. In most cases, mothers think they're doing the best thing for their daughters. Similarly, female foot binding is a powerful example of how any culture's skewed values can influence a mother's self-image and, in turn, her daughter's self-image.

Early in the story, seven-year-old Lily's feet are bound by her mother, who had been crippled by her own childhood foot binding. The mother puts Lily through the same torturous process and makes her believe it's a good thing to do: "'[Mama said] only through pain will you have beauty. I wrap, I bind, but you will have the reward'" (30).

Despite the pain, Lily believes her mother's mantra that the tinier the feet, the greater the chance of a good marriage. And during the foot binding she begins to see love in the skewed way defined by her mother: "'With her fingers Mama pulled my loose bones back and up against the soles of my feet. At no other time did I see Mama's mother love so clearly…'" (30). When Lily reaches age seventeen, she wonders if her childhood mother's hints of love veiled a self-focused goal of benefiting the family through Lily's bound feet and a future marriage. (Here, and in the paragraph above, the mother is showing imposing and tuned-out traits.)

Lily realizes that as a child she didn't know what to do with her difficult feelings, so she stowed them "deep, deep, deep inside" (125). (We don't know about Lily's infancy, so we can't say to what extent she went through the hug or boomerang cycle. But, witnessing her need to bury anger, we can surmise that she got more of the boomerang than the hug.)

In adulthood, Lily recognizes that she's treated her long-cherished friend, Snow Flower, as her mother treated her as a child—in a self-absorbed way. And Lily also sees that she has expressed her anger in unfruitful ways, as her mother did with her. Lily says, "It was easier for me to begin picking at Snow Flower's faults than to feel the emotions raging inside of me" (221). (Unhealthy modeling is shown in this part of the story.) We can see how Lily winds up sending hostility to the wrong person, her friend, and loses a beautiful relationship. We can surmise that Lily was never able to freely express her resentment toward her mother, because her mother's rigid ways must have squelched her daughter's emotions. (This is a clear example of the boomerang cycle.)

Lily's modeling after her mother involved her mother's inaccurate self-image, which told her that she was worthwhile only with the smallest feet possible. In turn, that modeling would form Lily's own self-image distortion based on the same concept (although, in the cultural context, both the mother's and daughter's self-images were accurate). (Here we see unhealthy modeling.)

Toward the end of the story, Lily talks about herself as a mother who practices foot binding with her daughter, just as her mother did with her. She loves her daughter and suffers along with her, while trying to do the binding in the least harmful way. But Lily knows she's caught in the culture's foot-binding loop, which puts mothers and daughters in their own relationship-binding loop.

"My mother love was very strong...but I also transferred the pain I felt about [my friend] Snow Flower out of my body and into my daughter's feet" (223). We can see that Lily believes, just as her mother did, that foot binding is a loving thing to do. But she also shows awareness of passing its negative aspects to her daughter. (The carnival mirror goes from the second to the third generation.)

# let's recap

In this chapter we explored the early mother-daughter relationship with all its complexity, intensity, and endurance, a relationship that colors our adult self-image. We also discussed how our childhood mother's flowing and tuned-in traits lead to the hug cycle, a truer self-image, and a freer self. And her imposing and tuned-out traits lead to the boomerang cycle, a skewed self-image, and a thwarted self.

In the next chapter we'll discuss what happens when the mother can't support her daughter's separation, because she's too often preoccupied with her own issues.

## A Note for Mothers of Girls

You might be thinking, "Yikes! Were my traits flowing enough for my baby girl? Were they too imposing? Did I give her hugs or throw her boomerangs? Does my grown daughter have an awful picture of me in her head that will harm her self-image for life?" It's natural to think this way, but it means that you've slipped into the "mother" viewpoint again. Try to stay with being the daughter as you read on, and recognize that changes in your self-image are possible and that these can help your daughter's self-image as well.

# Questions for Reflection

1. What signs show you that you might have internalized your childhood mother's flowing traits, such as hobbies, skills, and pleasures?

2. What signs might suggest that you internalized her imposing traits, such as restrictions on fun, sex, or letting go?

3. What revealed her tuned-out traits, such as distraction, flat responses when you were feeling enthusiastic or excited, or just not "getting" you?

4. If you've experienced the boomerang cycle, how do you struggle with anger? Do you beat yourself up with it, or do you ineffectually flail your arms and yell?

# *Reading Touch Tool*

Since *Snow Flower and the Secret Fan* was connected with the themes of this chapter, the questions related to this novel, below, can help heighten your understanding of those concepts. Besides, it's a great read!

## *Snow Flower and the Secret Fan,* by Lisa See

- How might Lily's unexpressed anger toward her mother have come out in her relationship with Snow Flower?

- How might your unexpressed anger toward your childhood mother have emerged in unhealthy ways in adulthood?

- How did the Chinese culture distort the self-images of the mother and daughter in this story? Were there differences in the way each received the input from society that foot binding is desirable and the norm?

- How might our Western culture have affected your self-image and your mother's self-image similarly or differently?

CHAPTER 4

# preoccupied mother and overlooked daughter: narcissus and echo

*What pin-money, what jewels, what carriages you will have!*
*Three daughters married! Ten thousand a year!*
*My dearest child ... I can think of nothing else!*

— Jane Austen, *Pride and Prejudice*

"You seem kind of quiet today. Is there something you're hesitant to talk about?"

Mindy gazes at me for a few moments before speaking. She usually starts talking as soon as she sits down.

"Well, all right. I went out last night with Steve and went to bed with him, and it was great."

She's wearing a turtleneck under a sweater and most of the buttons are closed. Usually she wears a looser style of clothing, with open necks and flowing tops. I wonder, is she showing me that she's a good girl despite enjoying sex with her new boyfriend last night?

"Is that bad, or is it something you feel you have to hide?"

There's more silence as she shifts in the chair. I feel a bit of discomfort as I sense hers. I wonder how I will reach her and still give her the space she seems to need.

"Not exactly. But I think I have to hide that I wanted to go to bed with him and that I enjoyed it."

"Is that a sin?"

"I guess not, but I don't think my mother felt I should enjoy sex. I don't think *she* ever did, because she didn't view herself as deserving of pleasure. She often wore loose flannel shirts that I called 'Paul Bunyan shirts'—no female figure showing. I think she was really hung up about sex. The day I asked her about the birds and the bees, she said nothing, went to the library, and got me a book about how all the barnyard animals do it. Can you believe that she never said a word to me about how humans do it?"

"Well, it's important for us to talk about that. But I'm wondering if there's anything I've said that would make you think I feel that way too."

"No. In fact, you've made it seem okay to talk about basically anything. So I don't get why I feel that I have to hold back about my sex life here."

"Do you think that since your mom didn't approve of your enjoying sex, you need to see me that way too? Then I'd be your mom's substitute and not draw you into unknown territory."

"That might be it. I always had this strange feeling when some adult gave me more freedom than my mom did: on the surface I wanted to break away from the mold, but deep down I was afraid of it. It wasn't just because she nixed my letting go. It was also because if I did I'd be too different from her."

## daughter's individuality, mother's anxiety

In Mindy's treatment over the course of two years, I saw more of the engaging, wide-eyed little girl in her than the elegant young woman. During that time, we discussed how she'd clam up in a session if she'd had "too much" fun, especially sexual fun, in the preceding days. It seemed that she was seeing me as the mother who would disapprove not only of her behavior but also of the separateness it created. After all, I wasn't telling her about my own night out on the town.

Mindy made me think about how her separation from her mother had gotten bogged down by her mother's need to be at one with her. That allowed her mother's self-image distortion—her view of herself as undeserving of sexual pleasure—to become Mindy's, and this kept her distant from her mother.

Mindy's experience is distinguished by an *unhealthy separation*: when the caregiver, because of a distorted self-image, stifles her daughter's natural striving to separate. But, ironically, at the same time, Mindy lacked a true close attachment to her mother, because she was compelled to stay back with her emotionally. The mother in this case had *unhealthy narcissism*: a preoccupation that kept her from enjoying life and recognizing her daughter's needs.

On the other hand, when the mother has a truer self-image and healthy narcissism, she's more fulfilled, so she can tune in to her daughter's needs. She can then further her daughter's natural striving to separate and encourage a true close attachment at the same time (it's "true," because it's by choice).

# daughter's individuality, mother's cheers

The interplay of separateness and connection appears at each developmental milestone. When grasping a toy, the infant connects with the caregiver, who recognizes her sense of agency. When learning to walk, the baby connects with the caregiver, who takes pleasure in her independent act. When learning to talk, the toddler connects with the caregiver, who responds to her expression of needs through words. When the child expands her socializing, she connects with the caregiver, who enjoys her daughter's widening of her own horizons. When the "tween" or teen begins puberty, she connects with the caregiver, who shares in the celebration of her blossoming.

The first part of this chapter will discuss how a mother with a balanced self-focus—healthy narcissism—lets herself enjoy her own interests and supports her daughter's interests too: while she sees her daughter as separate, she also furthers closeness with her. The second part will explore how the mother with unhealthy narcissism doesn't see her daughter as separate, which lets any self-image distortion flow swiftly to her daughter. We'll consider more about how, ironically, even though the daughter is at "one" with her mother, she lacks closeness with her. The last part of the chapter illustrates earlier themes through relationships between famous daughters and their mothers.

## mothers with a healthy self-focus

Megan's mother, Adele, had a passion for ballet as a child and was very talented. However, she viewed herself as unworthy of star attention, so whenever she performed for a large audience, she got shaky on her feet. Eventually she dropped ballet, and as an adult she greatly regretted the loss of her opportunity for success. But because Adele gained insight about herself in therapy, she sees herself and Megan as separate, and doesn't have to push Megan into ballet so that she can live through her daughter's achievements. Adele is now passionate about other interests, and Megan is enthusiastic about modern dance, which Adele supports.

When a mother has Adele's balanced self-focus, she can promote her daughter's separation, as Adele did for Megan, and not pass on the carnival-mirror self-image. The daughter feels connected to her mother as an individual. But, as mentioned previously, there's another type of self-focus in mothers that thwarts daughters' separation and furthers an inaccurate self-image. We find an illustration of this phenomenon in the Greek myth of Narcissus.

## narcissus, a preoccupied mother?

Narcissus, the self-focused lad of ancient myth, is utterly entranced with his reflection in a pond and stares at it so long that he eventually falls dead. While this figure is familiar to many of us, we can easily overlook the nymph Echo in the tale, just as Narcissus overlooks her. Echo has been punished by Zeus's wife, Hera, because the goddess, in her typical over-the-top way, assumes her husband has had an affair with Echo. So Hera sentences Echo to a life in which she has no power to start conversations. She can only use her voice to repeat someone else's comment to her.

Echo desires the handsome Narcissus, but like most ladies of the time, she must wait for the gent. One day she gazes at him adoringly from behind a patch of trees. Thinking his pals are around, he calls out a greeting. Assuming he's addressing *her*, Echo yells back. He then cries out "Come!" not knowing who will appear. Echo, feeling encouraged, steps into the light, repeats "Come!" and opens her arms to him. When Narcissus sees her, he is turned off, because she represents a relationship with someone besides himself. Feeling shot down and ashamed, Echo begins a life of hiding in a dark hollow where the only words she hears are her own, ricocheting back to her.

Though Narcissus is obviously not Echo's mother and doesn't pass his self-image issue on to her, Echo's isolation emerges from her feeling of not being seen. Just as Narcissus's inward gaze makes him overlook Echo, some mothers—particularly those with self-image distortions—tend to have an inward gaze that causes them to overlook their daughters.

## Mother's Inward Gaze

"Overlook" here doesn't have the literal meaning of "not seeing." It has more to do with a mother's not viewing her daughter as an individual with her own needs, thoughts, and feelings. But we're not blaming the mother. She can't avoid squelching her daughter's separation, because she's a woman who never became fully independent of her own mother and winds up substituting her daughter for her mother. In *Prisoners of Childhood*, Alice Miller (1981) expands on that idea. She points out that Narcissus's self-love isn't full, because gazing at himself in the pond prevents him from seeing a whole picture of himself. In addition, Narcissus's love for his own image keeps him too preoccupied to see himself and others; he can't notice Echo as an individual. Similarly, some mothers can't love their daughters for who they are, because they're preoccupied with their own worries and can't see them as individuals. We can have compassion for these mothers, but the fact is that their self-focus makes them unwittingly blend the boundaries between themselves and their daughters. So, for one of these mothers, any self-image issue of hers easily becomes her daughter's self-image issue, as it did for Fay, a woman in therapy with me. When raising Fay, her mother achieved a lot of her goals but viewed herself as mediocre if she didn't reach the highest success. She viewed Fay through the same lens: even if Fay performed well in tennis or on a test, she was only middling in her mother's eyes unless she reached perfection.

So when Fay got excited about an achievement that did not earn her a trophy but gave her a feeling of reward, her mother couldn't reflect excitement back. She viewed the feat as run-of-the-mill, because that's how she would rate her own similar feat. So Fay gradually developed a distorted self-image like her mother's. Fay is an *Echo daughter*: not seen for who she is.

## Echo Daughters' Traits

Because daughters like Fay feel overlooked by their mothers (just as these mothers felt with *their* mothers), they wind up "repeating" a language of emotions that others don't hear, just as the nymph Echo did. Echo daughters have feelings and traits like those that Echo might develop, including loneliness, aloofness, or remoteness.

### *lonely echo*

J. Ralph Audy (1981, 114) writes about how others' presence can increase loneliness: "I have felt something like loneliness more often when among people than when alone—among people with whom I could not communicate (and I certainly do not mean being unable to speak their own language)....I have felt bored, and sometimes painfully lonely and alienated, among people who speak my own native tongue but are 'living in a different world.'"

The "different world" Audy describes is the one the Echo daughter lives in. She feels unknown, not because of physical isolation but because her mother doesn't recognize her emotions, sensibilities, needs, or desires. As Winnicott (1986, 130) writes in *Playing and Reality,* "In individual emotional development *the precursor of the mirror is the mother's face*" (Winnicott's italics).

Let's illustrate this idea. Baby Cassie cries, and her mother responds with a flat expression. Because the mother doesn't show she's tuned in to Cassie's discomfort, Cassie doesn't feel seen. So she's missed a step toward learning about herself through the reflection in her mother's eyes. Cassie has had an Echo daughter's experience: her feelings are unreflected, which makes *her* feel unreflected and alone, even with her mother in the same room.

Tennessee Williams's (1944) play *The Glass Menagerie* reveals the relationship of the self-absorbed mother with her Echo daughter. She's lonely even while she's with her mother, because she has to distance and shield herself from the hurt that closeness with her mother could bring.

In the play, the crippled adult daughter, Laura, escapes from her mother, Amanda, and the outside world through a tiny universe of glass creatures, vulnerable like herself. The play shows what generally happens to any daughter, disabled or not, when her mother is too into herself.

We can greatly empathize with Amanda, if we look below her hard surface to see her own vulnerability. Most mothers with a handicapped child feel hurt because they didn't produce typical offspring, among other reasons. But while we don't judge Amanda, we can imagine how easily her self-image distortion (the message that perfect looks and men equal a woman's worth) can pass on to Laura.

Because Amanda has an inward gaze, she views her daughter as a shining reflection of herself. Though Amanda frets about Laura, she's unable to respond to her needs. While Amanda pushes Laura toward male suitors, she brags about her own popularity with men at her daughter's age:

"Your mother received—*seventeen*!—gentlemen callers! Why, sometimes there weren't enough chairs to accommodate them all..." (148).

Laura's glass menagerie provides a refuge where she feels connected in a way she can't with her mother. The fragility of the glass creatures, so much like her own fragility, allows a relationship that isn't possible with Amanda, mainly because Amanda's own self-doubt makes her need to keep a distance from her daughter's flaws.

"Girls that aren't cut out for business careers usually wind up married to some nice man. Sister, that's what you'll do!"

"But, Mother...I'm—crippled!"

"Nonsense! Laura, I've told you never, never to use that word. Why, you're not crippled; you just have a little defect—hardly noticeable, even" (157)!

Laura's "defect" may remind Amanda too much of her own sense of defectiveness.

Another trait of an Echo daughter is aloofness.

## aloof echo

Early on, Echo daughters learn to avoid the hurt of feeling overlooked by acting as if they don't really need their caregivers. They might fight against getting help with tying shoes at age five or letting their caregivers hold their hands to cross a street at age six, or they may resist being comforted when they fall and scrape their knees. Later, this emotion frequently emerges as aloofness. (I'm not referring to healthy signs of independence.)

**Libby:** Teenager Libby has every hair in place, every ounce weighed, and every outfit perfectly matched. She unintentionally comes off as aloof, as if she doesn't need anyone. One day she complains to her friend Anita that she feels down about gaining two pounds. Because Libby has succeeded *so* well in the past at convincing others that everything was "just fine," Anita can't believe that a couple of pounds could be a real problem. Besides, Libby always looks perfect. Why would she need Anita's sympathy? Anita, like Libby's other peers, only sees her perfection and says, "What are *you* complaining about?" Now Libby feels misunderstood and even more down. So how did Libby come to play her role so well that it works against her?

While raising Libby, her mother, Marianne, needed her daughter to make up for her own sense of inadequacy. As a child Marianne had the carnival-mirror self-image: she viewed herself as unintelligent, when in fact she was bright. Since Marianne's parents discouraged her early artistic endeavors, she rebelled by underachieving, and she gained a false identity as a poor student. To compensate, she acted snobby so others wouldn't see her weakness. As a mother, Marianne couldn't let Libby show weakness, because then others would see them in Marianne too; after all, mother and daughter were one. So she wound up trying to look perfect and, as a result, seemed aloof.

In addition to warding off hurt with aloofness, Echo daughters ward off hurt with remoteness.

## *remote echo*

Echo daughters often put barriers around themselves to avoid feeling put off by their caregivers. Later on, their shields against hurt get in the way of relationships.

**Rosa:** Rosa, a twenty-seven-year-old woman whose family moved from Puerto Rico to the United States when she was ten, entered therapy because she felt that her distance from others prevented intimate relationships. Indeed, when she entered the room, I sensed a wall around her that she used to ward off hurt. After gazing at me intently one day early in treatment, Rosa spoke.

"I feel that I convince the world I'm cool, savvy, and relaxed, but underneath I feel scared and shaky with others, distant in a way I can't explain. I just feel out of place most of the time. I fake it well on the outside, but inside I'm a social mess. I get paralyzed when I'm in any scene beyond a one-to-one interaction. I don't understand any of it, except that it's been that way as far back as I can recall and my mother feels the same way a lot."

Rosa remembered often being in the same room with her mother, Nita, while feeling as if she were a canyon away. If Nita was reading the paper when Rosa came home from school, she wouldn't put down the paper to hear what Rosa had to say about her day. Instead, she'd alternate between looking at Rosa and reading an article while pretending to listen.

Rosa and Nita both had darker skin than that of many Latinas in their respective age groups, and this made mother and daughter feel inferior to their female peers. In contrast, Rosa's older sister, Serena, had the lighter skin tone that Nita coveted; as a result, Nita lived through Serena and rejected Rosa, whom she viewed as she did herself, as defective goods. "My mother would look at me and I could tell she wasn't looking at *me*. She was looking at her*self* in me." Because Nita couldn't see Rosa as an individual, Rosa took on her mother's self-image as inferior.

Nita and Rosa, like the other moms and daughters in this chapter, show us how the carnival-mirror self-image flows more smoothly from mother to daughter when the mother has trouble with her daughter's separation. Next, in the last section of the chapter we'll illustrate that idea through famous women and their mothers, whom I've placed in certain groupings to clarify themes.

# mothers and their famous Echo daughters

In the following passage, we will look at several famous daughters and their relationships with their mothers. I've placed these pairs in vignettes to help us categorize various types of relationships, in order to help us better understand our own interactions with our mothers and how they have affected our own self-images. Please keep in mind that I do not consider my theories about the celebrity daughters and their mothers to be conclusive. My ideas about the influence of the mothers on these daughters' lives are based on other authors' works and, in some cases, an autobiography or memoir, but they are simply ideas, not fact.

You may find that some of the pairs could be placed in a different category than the one I've placed them in. And the patterns shown in these examples don't represent the only mother-daughter interactions that exist. I've chosen these particular patterns and categories because I find them most visible in my work. As you read, you may find it useful to see which grouping you fit into with your mother, daughter, or both.

The first category includes a mother—*little-girl mother*—who lets her unmet childhood needs hang out for her daughter—*mini-mama daughter*—to see, and a daughter who responds by filling those needs. That role leads her to develop a distorted self-image in which her sense of worth rests on nurturing her mother.

## Little-Girl Mother and Mini-Mama Daughter

In this category, the mother views her daughter as her caregiver, furthering the distorted self-image that equates lovability with nurturing the mother. To illustrate, we'll explore the relationships of Margaret Mead both with her mother and daughter, Mary Catherine Bateson, and Judy Garland with her daughter, Liza Minnelli.

### *Margaret Mead and mother, Margaret Mead and daughter*

I view Margaret Mead as a "mini-mama" daughter with a little-girl mother. In *Margaret Mead: A Life*, Jane Howard (1989) writes, "By the time [Margaret] was four, she said she had become 'the pivotal family confidante'....Margaret sometimes had the confusing feeling that her parents were her children as much as she was theirs" (4).

We can see another possible effect of Mead's childhood mini-mama role in her three marriages that failed. Some of the problems (aside from those of her husbands) involved her inability to focus on her husbands' needs because her work took precedence over other roles. Her first husband, Luther Cressman, felt that Margaret spent much of her life studying others' families, in order to "[look] for new mothers, to pick her up when she fell…" (5).

In her autobiography, *Blackberry Winter: My Earlier Years,* Mead (1972) writes that her mother couldn't get into the playful side of mothering, and when she did plan games and parties, she did it in an obligatory manner: "By the time I was eight, I had taken over the preparations for festivities. I made the table decorations...and trimmed the Christmas tree, while Mother sat up half the night finishing a tie for Father's Christmas present. She could neither cook nor sew...what household skills she had were primarily managerial..." (28).

Mary Catherine Bateson (2001), Margaret's daughter, describes her experience with her mother in her book, *With a Daughter's Eye.* She writes about her own role as a compliant little girl who adapted to her mother's anthropological journeying: "All this moving around was made possible by the fact that I was usually a well-behaved child, laughing and contented....Now I believe that some of the goodness was my own solution to the comings and goings" (82–83).

Mary's caregiving of her mother came through subtly, by not upsetting her mother's applecart, while Margaret's appeared openly. Both mini-mama daughters seem to have shared a distorted self-image, based on the latent message from their little-girl mothers, that their worth was based on caring for the mother.

## *Judy Garland and daughter Liza Minnelli*

Judy Garland and Liza Minnelli make another little-girl mother–mini-mama daughter pair. In Gerald Clarke's (2000) *Get Happy,* the author writes that Judy's mother had her involved in a performance circuit from a young age. If Judy did something "wrong," such as let herself cry, her mother, Ethel, would angrily walk out and leave Judy alone in a hotel room. When Ethel did return after many hours, Judy would let her tears fall, calling her "the most wonderful mother in the world." To that Ethel would reply, "'Well, you're just lucky I came back at all this time...because the next time I won't'" (38).

Is it surprising that drugs and audience applause became substitutes for a mother's TLC in Judy Garland's adult life? Or that her eldest daughter, Liza, became a mimi-mama daughter for Judy, her little-girl mother? Clarke writes: "In a strange reversal of roles, Liza became almost a mother to her mother. She was the one who helped to manage the staff....She was the one who made sure that [her younger siblings] got off to school on time and that they were fed when they came home" (404).

Later, when Liza reached a level of stardom beyond Judy's, Judy rejected Liza and spiraled down into substance abuse. Liza's own spiraling came quick on the heels of her mother's. It is possible that Judy's self-image distortion arose from her mother's abuse, which conveyed the message that acceptance by her mother depended on her stage success, while the rest of her was inferior. And Liza's self-image distortion might have arisen from her mother's message that maternal acceptance depended on her not surpassing her mother in fame and glory.

With the next mother-daughter pair, the daughter's inaccurate self-image results from a catch-22. Her mother consciously wants her to do well. But when the daughter does achieve, the mother rejects her if the achievement doesn't reflect well on her. And if the daughter supersedes the mother, mother envies daughter.

## Jealous-Queen Mother and Snow White Daughter

Though *jealous-queen mother* is usually unaware of her rejecting and envious feelings, they lead to a self-image distortion in *Snow White daughter*. She either tries to prove she can succeed beyond her mother, or she holds herself back so she doesn't beat her mother in the competition and lose her love. Either way, a self-image distortion results, because worth gets mixed up with the rivalry, win or lose. Jackie O illustrates the "I can beat out Mother" pattern.

### *Jackie Kennedy Onassis and mother*

In *Mrs. Kennedy,* Barbara Leaming (2002) discusses how Jackie Kennedy Onassis's mother, Janet, competed with her daughter for Jackie's father's (another Jack, by the way) affections. Janet resented Jackie not only because he favored her but also because she physically resembled him. When Jack became an alcoholic who enraged Janet with his philandering, she directed her anger toward Jackie, calling her body too big, too masculine, and not attractive to the most desirable men: "It was as if, having been sexually rejected by Jack, Janet was sending him [and Jackie] a message that…he was as undesirable as the daughter who so strikingly resembled him" (7).

According to Leaming, when JFK asked for Jackie's hand in marriage, Jackie considered it a triumph over her mother. And when he cheated on her, having been "long told that no man would want her," Jackie blamed it on herself and focused on improving her looks. The author writes that Jackie's whispery, feminine voice was camouflage for her intelligence, worldliness, and love of books. The influence of her mother and the culture made her believe that men would be beyond her reach if they saw beneath the veneer of looks and charm. Though jealous-queen mother and Snow White daughter were rivals, they shared a self-image distortion greatly influenced by the culture: worth depends on getting the guy.

In my imagination, Jackie finds a truer self-image. She recognizes that her mother's view of her was shaped by the culture's emphasis on male validation and that her insecurity as a mistreated wife was not an inborn defect in herself. Then Jackie learns to value her innate qualities and see herself more accurately than her mother saw *her*self. In turn, that helps Jackie with later decisions about whom to partner with (her second marriage, to Ari Onassis, had its own problems).

The next mother-daughter pair involves a mother who unwittingly puts her daughter in the spotlight so the mother can share it or live through the daughter as the star. That situation distorts the daughter's self-image, because her giving her mother a chance to share the audience's applause becomes a measure of her worth. The *stage mother* sends her daughter messages from a young age saying that love equals performance. The stage mother is usually a woman who lacked affirmation as a child and lives through her *showgirl daughter* as a way to have the audience she didn't have in her parents. Below, first we'll discuss a classic stage mother–showgirl daughter pair, and then we'll see how the pattern appears in the daily life of an ordinary woman in treatment. (You may notice that this pattern overlaps that of little-girl mother–mini-mama daughter, because showgirl daughters mother their mothers by giving them vicarious celebrity status.)

## Stage Mother and Showgirl Daughter

The movie star Natalie Wood, who died at forty-three in 1981, had a stage mother in a literal sense.

## Natalie Wood and mother

In childhood Natalie's most famous role was as Susan Walker in the film *Miracle on 34th Street,* And she went on to appear in films such as *Rebel Without a Cause, Marjorie Morningstar, Splendor in the Grass, West Side Story,* and *Gypsy,* which told the story of the life of famed burlesque dancer Gypsy Rose Lee. As author Suzanne Finstad (2001) writes in *Natasha* (Russian for "Natalie"), "Natalie was driven by demons to play the stripper with the stage mother of all stage mothers" (278).

**Daughter embodies mother's fantasy.** Natalie's mother, Maria, had a traumatic childhood in Russia around the time of the Revolution. She viewed the idea of having a movie-star daughter as a way to live out a dream, after a fortune teller had prophesized that one of her daughters would have beauty and fame. After moving to America, Maria reportedly nursed her baby Natasha in movie theaters, hoping the infant might internalize celebrity power. As it turned out, Natasha-turned-Natalie, the adult, *was* a beauty and won fame. But her small stature made her feel inferior to the more statuesque actresses of her time. And she devalued her star identity, because she never viewed herself as the true artist she perceived other actresses to be.

**Showgirl daughter doesn't know her own needs.** Finstad shows how Natalie's focus on her mother's wishes blocked her from knowing what she wanted or who she was. She tells us that Natalie sought mother love in relationships with men and used alcohol to fill a void. Natalie died in a drowning accident. Ironically, she died in a way that she feared most—drowning—which was also her mother's terror. In a final hint at her mother's apparent need to live through Natalie, Finstad quotes Natalie's sister retelling Maria's comment after Natalie's death, "'God *made* her, but *I* invented her'" (45).

Maria and Natalie provide another picture of a mother's making her needs the same as her daughter's and furthering the carnival mirror's passage. We can tie Maria's distorted self-image, worth defined by elevated status, to her daughter's distorted self-image, worth defined by audience applause.

Let's now look at how the stage mother–showgirl daughter pattern might appear in everyday life.

## _Trudy and mother_

Trudy grew up feeling on display a lot. Her mother, Colleen, stressed that Trudy's hair, dress, and grooming be "just so" before Colleen would allow her to meet her friends. Trudy would feel her mother's eyes fixed on her before they entered a gathering, making sure she looked ready to "start the show." In her own childhood, Colleen had felt that she got "lost in the sauce" growing up with three siblings. Now, with Trudy in the spotlight and Colleen's peers acting as the audience, Colleen could get the attention that she didn't get as a child. The effect on Trudy's self-image was that she felt unworthy of her mother's love if she didn't act the celebrity role.

The next mother-daughter twosome involves a verbally hurtful mother and her emotionally wounded daughter, Eleanor Roosevelt, which led to Eleanor's distorted image of herself as inferior.

# Spirit-Dampening Mother and Spirit-Dampened Daughter

Eleanor's dampened spirit as a child contributed to her self-loathing as a wife, daughter-in-law, and mother.

## _Eleanor Roosevelt and mother_

Eleanor Roosevelt begins _The Autobiography of Eleanor Roosevelt_ (1992) writing, "My mother was one of the most beautiful women I have ever seen" (3). Later, she adds, "She looked so beautiful, I was grateful to be allowed to touch her dress or her jewels or anything that was part of the vision which I admired inordinately" (7).

Her mother, Anna, died when she was eight, which, according to Blanche Wiesen Cook (1993), author of _Eleanor Roosevelt, Volume 1_, probably furthered her existing idealization. Eleanor felt inferior to Anna, who put manners above feelings, and beauty over other traits. Anna rejected her daughter's looks and called her "Granny" from the time she was two, because she appeared "serious."

Thinking about Anna's era, we can imagine why she might have been so focused on externals. Being a woman of the upper class in the late 1800s would certainly lead her to place great value on outer appearances. But Eleanor as a child would have no way to know that and would, like all rejected children, blame herself for her mother's attitude. And since Anna seems to have viewed her daughter as a reflection of herself, her apparent self-image distortion—beauty equals worth—would have easily been transferred to Eleanor.

**How the Carnival Mirror Influences the Daughter as a Mother Herself:** Though Eleanor freed herself from some of the formal ways mandated by her mother in order to gain society's approval, she couldn't do it as a mother, particularly with her oldest child and only daughter, Anna, who was named after Eleanor's mother. We can glean from Cook's (1993) writing that while Eleanor's spirit was bashed by her mother's verbal harm, her daughter's spirit was bashed by Eleanor's rigidity.

"ER's own removal...from rituals she found suffocating, did not extend to her daughter. Badgered by her mother-in-law and her godmother, *with all the ghosts of her foremothers* [my italics] and all the pain of memory haunting her decision, ER was not free to share her liberation with her daughter..." (300). Further, "Eleanor behaved with her own daughter much as her own mother had with her: She became cold and distanced; she 'shut up like a clam' and refused to speak to Anna about any of the several issues that devastated her heart" (312).

Eleanor's mother equated classical beauty with worth and influenced her daughter to view herself using that value system. So Eleanor grew up with a distorted image of herself as less valuable than other women like her mother and mother-in-law. A truer self-image would have made her feel that other qualities counted too. Perhaps if she had viewed herself that way, she could have broken away from her mother's rigidity in raising her daughter; she might have loosened up if she had had more faith in her own mothering abilities.

The last category contains celebrity daughters with a self-image distortion influenced by the mother's absence, abuse, neglect, or a combination of all three due to death, illness, or mental health problems.

## Out-at-Sea Mother and Adrift Daughter

Jane Fonda, Marilyn Monroe, and Princess Diana were *adrift daughters*—insecure in their identities and searching for a way to feel valued. They had *out-at-sea mothers*—mothers who weren't there for their daughters in emotional and physical ways because of mental illness, death, or an inability to weather their own crises.

## *Jane Fonda and mother*

In *My Life So Far*, the actress Jane Fonda (2006), writes that her mother, Frances, was sexually abused at age eight, an event that "colored her life and mine." When Jane was thirteen, her emotionally fragile mother committed suicide at a mental hospital. Years later, Jane wrote, poignantly, "I can now understand...all that I had felt as a child—[mother was] a victim, a beautiful but damaged butterfly, unable to give me what I needed—to be loved, seen—because she could not give to herself" (29–30).

Jane found evidence in her mother's writing that she searched for a sense of worth through her sexuality, a self-image distortion that seems to have been passed on to Jane. Jane views her own pattern of taking the role of vamp in young adulthood, including early movies, as connected with her mother's view of herself. In Jane's exploration we see a great example of how we can forgive our childhood mothers for the harm they caused us and still explore how to separate our distorted self-images from theirs.

## *Marilyn Monroe and her mother*

Marilyn Monroe's mentally handicapped mother, Gladys, lived into her daughter's adulthood, but she was either physically absent or emotionally abusive when around. In *Marilyn Monroe*, Barbara Leaming (1998) writes that when Marilyn (born Norma Jean) was a baby, her mother was diagnosed as paranoid schizophrenic. Gladys rejected and verbally abused her daughter throughout her life. From family lore and comments Gladys made to her, Marilyn believed that Gladys had even attempted to kill her in infancy.

From Leaming's analysis we can glean that Gladys's severe mental illness caused her to see her daughter as a hated part of herself. "Gladys had somehow communicated the notion that, as an illegitimate child, Norma Jean was the embodiment of her own sins and had to be snuffed out" (56). And it seems that Gladys's hatred of Marilyn turned into Marilyn's self-loathing.

For example, Marilyn once insisted on wearing a costume (minus underwear) that she had been advised against, because it gave her a vulgar look rather than a sensual, seductive one. This story conveys that Marilyn may have viewed herself as Gladys viewed her, and as Gladys viewed her own self—as damaged goods.

With that self-image, Marilyn seems to have treated herself as she felt she deserved—with abuse—as shown in Leaming's writing about her in connection with one of her several miscarriages. In an apparent self-fulfilling prophecy, Marilyn had dismissed taboos about using alcohol and barbiturates during pregnancy and then took on the guilt. "For a long time, Marilyn had feared that one day she would become like her mother....Marilyn believed she had. Now, Marilyn had succeeded where [her mother] had failed. She was convinced she had killed her own daughter" (320).

In Gladys and Marilyn, we have another portrait of a mother with an inherited carnival-mirror self-image (Gladys was also abused by *her* mother, who died in a straitjacket). Gladys passed the heirloom on to her daughter, whom she viewed as an extension of her own rejected self.

## *Princess Diana and her mother*

As Tina Brown (2007) writes in *The Diana Chronicles*, the car that ushered Diana to her death in 1997 carried "the most famous woman in the world," "the icon of blondness." But with all her adult celebrity status and iconic beauty, in *Her True Story*, by Andrew Morton (1998), Diana presents her childhood as insecure, because she was caught between two parents in an ugly divorce. Diana's mother, Frances, who was pushed by her own mother to marry a guy with status and wealth, pushed Diana in similar ways. Her contentious divorce from Diana's father made her frequently absent, physically and emotionally. Diana describes her like herself, a pro at faking a happy face. Further on, Morton quotes Diana:

> "I knew I was going somewhere different but had no idea where. I said to my father when I was aged thirteen, 'I know I'm going to marry someone in the public eye'" (34).

When marriage to a prince didn't bring Diana inner worth, perhaps she tried to find it through marriage to the public and its camera. But the bottom line is that both Frances and Diana acted in ways that conformed to their respective mothers' needs, which formed a self-image based on who they *should* be, rather than on who they were. So in this mother-daughter pair, we have another illustration of the mother looking into the carnival mirror. And because she was apparently too burdened with problems to support her daughter's separation, she passed the mirror on to her daughter.

# let's recap

In this chapter we discussed healthy and unhealthy narcissism in the childhood mother. The healthy kind is shown when the mother, with a truer self-image, "has a life," can recognize her daughter's needs, and encourages her to have a life that's separate from the mother's. The daughter's healthy separation, paired with close attachment, occurs when the mother has healthy narcissism. A truer self-image is an outgrowth of this experience.

The unhealthy kind of narcissism is shown when the mother, with a distorted self-image, is too preoccupied with her own issues, just like the mythical Narcissus. She usually means well, but she can't recognize her daughter's needs, just as Narcissus can't recognize Echo's. And one of those needs is to become an individual. The daughter's tenuous separation leads to a skewed self-image.

Next, we looked at celebrity daughters and their self-absorbed mothers, and we explored how their relating patterns, similar to those of many mother-daughter pairs, allowed the carnival-mirror legacy to continue.

The following chapter presents a different aspect and effect of the early mother-daughter relationship: the experience with our mother during infancy when our body expresses our feelings, a process that reawakens when adult situations echo the early ones with our mothers.

## A Note for Mothers of Girls

You might now be thinking, "Oh, no, all those times I stayed home to rest when my daughter asked me to take her somewhere...I must be Madame Narcissus with my poor little Echo girl." If you're going there, change course and step into your own "Echo shoes" as a child with your mother, who might have acted preoccupied when you wanted her attention. Ask yourself how you felt then. Try to stay there as you read on, and keep the faith that you'll be able to cut yourself more of a break.

# Questions for Reflection

1. If you sense that your childhood mother was preoccupied, how did she show it?

2. If you think you grew up with any qualities of Echo, which trait do you feel you have most: loneliness, aloofness, or remoteness? Do you have another quality you can imagine Echo would have?

3. Can you place yourself and your mother in one or more of the categories we explored using famous daughters and their mothers as illustrations? Do a *free-write* exercise exploring a past interaction that relates to that category. Don't worry about the structure, grammar, or punctuation in your writing; just get the images and feelings down on paper as they come up for you. Here's an example:

   Jealous Queen Mother and Snow White Daughter: *summer 15th birthday met steve boardwalk night stars moon out made out big crush handsome first real boyfriend. came back rental house mom worried looking for me in the house i told her out that night. i'm happy with steve, guilty, hurts her?*

# Reading Touch Tool

*The Kitchen God's Wife,* by Amy Tan, tells a story of a complex mother-daughter bond. If you read the book, whether along with this one, later on your own, or in a book group, the following questions can help you identify aspects of thought link 1 that you can apply to your own relationship with your mother.

### The Kitchen God's Wife, by Amy Tan

- What aspects of Winnie Louie's past might have caused her to lack attunement to Pearl's needs?

- What aspect of Winnie Louie's distorted self-image passed on to Pearl?

- What parallels do you see between Pearl's relationship with her mother and its effect on her self-image, and your relationship with your mother and its effect on your self-image?

# CHAPTER 5

# the mind-body moments: echoes of the mother-daughter past

*I am not certain whether my earliest memories are truly mine, because when I bring them to mind, I feel my mother's breath on every word.*
— Anita Diamant, *The Red Tent*

*Yesterday, the aroma of my neighbor's sugar cookies baking wafted down the hall from her apartment, returning me to my grandpa's bakery, where my grandma babysat me from toddlerhood on. As a kid I'd scoop up the warm crumbs that fell off the sour-cream streusel cakes. When I got older she'd let me roll out dough for pies, which would emerge from the oven with their fruity insides oozing out through the little windows in the lattice crust. As a teen, after fights with my parents, I'd often go to the bakery to escape. My grandma never picked on me as my mom did about my cowlick or my weight. Whenever I think about that place, I get this warm feeling I can't describe. I go there in my head sometimes when I'm upset.*

*You know, it's funny. I was a binger from a young age, but I didn't binge in the bakery, with all those goodies around. Maybe that's because Grandma filled me up with hugs? Now I'm on*

*another one of those rigid diets I've been on since age fourteen. I
began with those liquid diets; that was after a diet of chips and
ice cream that my mom said would go from the spoon right onto
my hips.*

Jean wrote the above for an eating-disorder group that helped members
get in touch with what food meant to them from childhood on. After
she read it to me, she gave the details of her rigorous diet, saying that
she had to go to bed hungry every night. As we talked, we gradually
discovered her discomfort with my support, and we discussed why it
made her upset rather than soothed. Jean found the answer in tension
in her midriff, an echo of the same symptom she had in childhood. Our
conversations had sent her back to her youngest years, when she had
stomachaches and refused to "eat every bit of food on the plate." Even
though my words were meant as supportive and not aimed at getting her
to do anything, she viewed them as similar to the peas and carrots on
her plate during childhood: she felt she had to take in her mother's food
then, and she felt she had to take in my words now. Without being aware
of it, she saw me as a stand-in for her mother, who had a personal need
to get her daughter to go along with her, as opposed to a therapist trying
to empathize with her.

Jean had early experiences with caregivers that were both calming
and upsetting. During Jean's times with her grandmother before age
three, her emotions and body were soothed by her grandmother, during
calm *primal mind-body moments.* Those moments were awakened when
as a teen she would return to her grandmother to feel soothed after
upsets she'd felt at home; these were calm *revived mind-body moments.*

So how did all this come about? When Jean's mother, Helena, was a
young child and went to another family's house where the kids had extra
helpings of pancakes for breakfast, BLTs *and* soup for lunch, and piled-
high mashed potatoes for dinner, she assumed that the mother was ideal
and the kids were special. Because, in contrast, Helena's parents had
rationed food for various reasons, Helena had developed a distorted
image of herself as less valued than kids whose parents indulged them.
So, she wound up viewing the amounts Jean ate as defining her own
worth as a mother and Jean's worth as a child. The stress at meals very
likely led to Jean's uncomfortable mind-body moments.

Jean discovered from a cousin her mother's age that, during Jean's
mealtimes as a baby, Helena felt anxious about how much Jean ate, and
showed it through tight muscles and a serious manner. Because this type
of maternal input reaches physical channels in the early brain and forms
basic emotions later—which are differentiated into more complex, per-

sonal ones (Siegel 1999)—Helena's tense state could easily have formed tense primal emotion in Jean. And that could have created Jean's stomach symptoms, a product of stressful *mind-body moments.* (Of course, it's important to check out a physical symptom to see if there's a medical cause before ascribing it to an emotional source.) As an adult in therapy, Jean began to feel a connection between these early tense mind-body moments during mealtimes, and her present discomfort whenever she felt pushed to finish something, like a work project.

In this chapter, we'll first discuss how the early mind-body moments form. Next we'll explore what healthy mind-body moments are, how they lead to the freer sense of self, and what the qualities of a freer sense of self are. Following that, we'll consider what unhealthy mind-body moments are, how they lead to the thwarted sense of self, and how a symptom is one of its main qualities. We'll learn about a thought-link tool here also, pinpointing symptoms to use as clues to lead to growth. We'll end the chapter by discussing how three female stages of physical change create fertile ground for reviving early mind-body moments.

# how do mind-body moments form?

Neuroscientific researchers are finding early evidence that might shed light on the primal mind-body moments that form when we don't yet have the language to express feelings in words, so we express them through the body.

In *Attachment in Psychotherapy*, David Wallin (2007) highlights the body's role as main speaker for the mind during our earliest years: "[infants'] bodies keep the score rather than their minds....the body remembers as well as reveals" (293). We can see how our earliest emotions meld with our earliest physical reactions. And because these primal mind-body moments are *encoded*—set down in the forming of the brain's memory—they reawaken later in life when situations resemble the earliest ones we experienced with our caregivers. *Attachment theory* is based on the concept that the way the caregiver manages the infant's discomfort forms memory patterns that affect the child's relationships throughout life. The way of handling those emotions that leads to security is *affect regulation*, a process included in the hug cycle.

And in *The Neuroscience of Human Relationships*, Louis Cozolino (2006) discusses how "building the brain" occurs through many interactions with the caregiver's body, including hearing her heartbeat, seeing her face, and touching her physically: "reflexive smiling" builds the infant's brain; the baby's endorphin and dopamine (hormones and neurotransmitters related to pleasurable feeling) rise with the sight of the "mother's expressive face"; a mother's embrace increases her infant's body heat and supports the hypothalmus's regulation of temperature.

Let's now explore how mind-body moments of emotional and physical comfort, like Jean's experiences with her grandmother, form and boost the freer self.

# mind-body moments that liberate the self

When you have "pleasant all over" sensations that you can't explain, there's a good chance you're having a healthy mind-body moment echoing a primal one. If you suddenly go to a calm mental space when you smell cut grass, that may be the same smell you often inhaled as a toddler, sitting on your loving aunt's lap on the porch of her country house. If you can't pinpoint why you feel an inner warmth whenever your partner wears velour, it may echo the warmth you felt as an infant when your mother soothed you by wrapping you in a soft blanket. If you experience an indescribable serenity when you're in a wooded area with the smell of pine, your reaction may echo a similar one that you had as a child, when your mother took you to a pine grove to play and gained her own serenity there.

The healthy mind-body moments we've described allow the freer self to flourish.

## What Are Freer-Self Qualities?

Let's look at four of the freer-self qualities, mentioned in chapter 3—sensuality, playfulness, creativity, and desire. What's the tie between those qualities and healthy mind-body moments? When mind and body reactions calmly merge, they allow those outgrowths of the freer self to blossom.

## sensuality: offshoot of the freer self

The *American Heritage Dictionary, 4th edition* (2000) defines sensuality as "relating to or affecting any of the senses or a sense organ..." Women in love and in sexual relationships often describe sensual mind-body moments rooted in their earliest years with the childhood mother. Below are several comments I've heard from women in therapy, followed by my thoughts (in italics) based on their histories, drawing *imagined* connections between revived mind-body moments that reflect the primal ones.

Ingrid: "Why do I feel a warm tingling when Ray holds me?"

*When Mother held infant Ingrid closely, the emotional security heightened her circulation, her body warmth.*

Malvine: "I have a feeling of balance I can't explain when Mary returns after being away."

*Mother's presence brought Malvine a sense of emotional evenness.*

Alice: "When I have sex with a guy I'm close to, I'm able to feel free."

*Mother gave Alice a freedom to explore her own body and her mother's. Alice's current ability to let go of control with someone she trusts during lovemaking harks back to those primal mind-body moments.*

Though sensuality often goes along with sexuality, that's not always the case. In *Under the Tuscan Sun*, by Frances Mayes (1996), we feel the author's sensuality through the visual, auditory, and tactile images she uses in describing food. We can see her childhood mother's influence in her words:

> I [would listen] for the *whoosh* of the seal I heard as Mother's green tomato pickles cooled. I remember my mother tapping the tops to make sure the lid had sucked down...I drop the peaches into boiling water for a moment, watching the rosy colors intensify, then spoon them out and slide the skins off as easily as taking off a silk slip...I remember my mother putting in a kernel from inside the peach pit, an almond-scented secret nut...I have five lovely jars of jam, peachy but not too sweet (72–74).

Part of the reason we get a sensual picture of food from Mayes is that she writes about it in a creative way—she uses evocative images to bring out our senses. Creativity, like sensuality, often has roots in our earliest years. And, although those roots include an innate ability combined with modeling after caregivers, our focus here is on another aspect of creativity: healthy mind-body moments that let our innate self go its own way.

## *creativity: offshoot of the freer self*

When we call something "creative," we usually refer to a unique or original product. But creativity as I discuss it here is not about the final product. I'm talking about immersing yourself in an experience and enjoying it—like Frances Mayes seems to do through writing the piece of hers previously quoted.

**The Transformative Power of Creativity.** Creativity becomes part of you when you're engaged in a process that transforms you; it changes you physically and emotionally in a positive way. The transformation I mean is the kind you achieve by releasing your freer self. And the earliest mind-body moments that give a sense of "all's right with the world" allow that release.

- **The "transformative experience".** Transformation is described by Christopher Bollas (1987) in *The Shadow of the Object*. He calls a positive dramatic change in infants a *transformative experience*: when a frustrated infant is soothed by the mother, let's say, through the hug cycle. The infant then finds herself feeling more contented than she did before the hug. Bollas writes that this early experience is part of later creativity.

  I use a phrase that tells how you know you're transformed through a creative process—*finding yourself lost* in a pleasurable experience that engages you. This is the kind of "lost" that gives you the control to return to your regular state—as opposed to "getting carried away" with something, a process that is connected with loss of control. For example, Daryl gets into putting flowers together in a way she never did before, and she enjoys it even when the tulips overshadow the lilacs and throw the whole bouquet out of whack. Fay plans on following a familiar carrot-cake recipe to play it safe for the company coming that night, but instead she gets lost in baking a German chocolate cake she'd always wanted to try. When it falls apart as it comes out of the pan, she decides to call it a "crumb cake" party.

Besides the transformative experience, another ingredient for adult creativity includes an infant's freeness in relating to her mother's body.

- **Free mother-infant body language.** Gilbert Rose (1992), in *The Power of Form,* discusses how the physical dance of mother and infant influences adult creativity. He writes that imagination emerges from the time when mother and infant's boundaries are blurred, before the infant knows she's separate. She moves in the space around her mother's body and touches it freely or not. Creative adult outgrowths of unbounded physical relating between mother and infant might include artful hair styling; a doctor's sensitivity to body language that permits her to diagnose a patient's problem early on; a delicate touch when working with flour that results in a light and flaky lattice crust; and freedom in a sculptor's hands that allows the fingers to go where the clay goes.

## *playfulness: offshoot of the freer self*

In *The Maturational Processes and the Facilitating Environment,* Donald Winnicott (1994), pediatrician and analyst, tells us how creativity springs from the time when babies don't yet feel fully separate from their mothers but are able to hold something in their hands, such as a security blanket. When infants feel secure, they use the blanket in their own "creative" way. Many drag it along, some rub it against their noses, and others twirl it in their fingers. Winnicott calls the security blanket a *transitional object,* because it's the first object that the baby makes her own without her mother's direct input but with the feeling of security in her presence.

Play with the blanket leads to other kinds of play, which eventually spawns adult creativity, including the playful mind: imagination. Seeing how Jackie's unplayful mind works helps us understand this concept: "When a group art therapist I went to once put clay and figurines on a table and asked us to put the stuff together in any way we liked, I couldn't get started. I just sat there for what seemed like forever and watched others to get ideas." As a tot in the sandbox Jackie would often sit for a while watching other kids using shovels and pails. Perhaps her uncertainty in the toddler's sandbox was echoed in some way by her uncertainty in the "adult sandbox" of art therapy.

We use many phrases that reflect how playfulness happens in adults, such as "play with ideas," "play it by ear," "play it up," "play it out," "play with fire," "play with someone's mind," and "play with time." There's playfulness in trying new sexual positions, cooking with flair, and using humor—as we know, telling a joke often means playing with the absurd, and our audience plays with us in return when we make a self-effacing joke.

Besides sensuality, creativity, and playfulness, there's a fourth outgrowth of the freer self that we'll explore: desire.

## desire: offshoot of the freer self

In order to really ache for a massage tonight or want to go to bed with that guy or crave that corned-beef sandwich, you need a freer self that allows you to have desire. Part of that entitlement comes from modeling yourself after the childhood mother who herself felt entitled to experience desire. Let's look at that influence in the light of our culture.

In *The Bonds of Love*, Jessica Benjamin (1988) writes about how our culture has influenced women to deny themselves the right to desire. And in *Hunger Strike*, Susie Orbach (1986) zeroes in on how society's demand for repression of female desire carries over to constraints on eating and the body. The self-denial leads to frustration, often soothed by extreme behavior with food or eating disorders. When mothers absorb these cultural messages, they gain a distorted view of themselves as lacking entitlement, which they unwittingly hand to their daughters.

In classic novels, few heroines can gratify full-blown desire without full-blown punishment. When Anna Karenina engages in passionate adultery, for example, her need for penance is over the top, and she throws herself in front of a moving train. Madame Bovary also meets her demise after living out her romantic fantasies.

After the women's movement in the 1970s, we did begin to see some female characters who experience desire without paying a great price. A prime example is found in Erica Jong's (1973) *Fear of Flying*, with the "zipless fuck" (an anonymous, guilt-free, motiveless sexual encounter) experienced by the main character, Isadora Wing. She can have her cake and eat it too, with fantasized and realized erotic relationships with husbands and lovers. *Fear of Flying* sold like hotcakes when it came out, and Western society ostensibly proclaimed that women have a right to desire. But many mothers don't allow that permission into their own daily lives or their daughters', any more than *their* mothers and grand-mothers did. For example, I've noticed that often women won't order dessert but will heartily participate in eating a chocolate soufflé offered by someone else. Desire, like sensuality, creativity, and playfulness, arises from comforting mind-body moments in the earliest life stage, releasing the inborn self (coupled with cultural permission given to women to have that desire). In contrast are symptoms (those not caused by medical problems) that are rooted in upsetting mind-body moments during that same time, squelching the inborn self.

# symptoms: mind-body moments that detour the self

Eloise twirls her hair and purses her lips. She's annoyed with me for asking her to look at a possible connection between her physical language and a stressful moment. Expressing negative feelings through words was not accepted during her childhood, so she's expressing them to me instead through her body, through a *symptom*, as I'm defining it. (Of course, be sure to have any worrisome physical symptoms checked out by your health care provider before assuming they are rooted in an emotional issue.)

A current mind-body symptom often echoes an experience early in life, when an interaction with your caregiver led to an upsetting mind-body moment. And the present event that stirs the mind-body moment—the *trigger event*—in some way echoes that primal interaction. For example, Eloise's twirling her hair and pursing her lips, a red face due to shame, an acne breakout from tension, difficulty sleeping set off by anxiety, excessive talking due to insecurity, and pacing back and forth when you're silently fuming might very well be echoes of earlier experiences.

## Betsy's Life Cycle

Let's look at Betsy's life cycle to see how stressful mind-body moments in one's earliest years can emerge as adult mind-body symptoms. Then we'll introduce the concept of pinpointing, which helps us ward off symptoms (we will discuss this more fully in chapters 11 and 12).

## *toddler*

Betsy's early years were topsy-turvy, because her parents moved often and her mother, who didn't adjust well to the changes, was unpredictable.

As a two-year-old, Betsy got more of the boomerang than the hug and, after each move, had tantrums (more than the average number for a child of her age). This was very likely anger expressed through the body.

## *"tween"*

An echo of that mind-body process played out again when, at age eleven, Betsy showed anger by running away. This was a reaction to her parents' rigidity in not allowing her to date (her girlfriends were permitted to go out with boys). And she also began getting frequent stress-related headaches.

## *menopause*

In menopause, Betsy once again expressed upset through her body. When her oldest child went away to college, she re-experienced tension-caused headaches.

Betsy got help through *pinpointing*: tuning in to your symptom and connecting it with your trigger event and mother image. I think of pinpointing as similar to making lemonade out of lemons, because an unpleasant symptom is used as a step toward positive change.

# Pinpointing

The process is introduced here from Betsy's viewpoint to give you an idea of how it works. If you are feeling confused now, have patience. I believe this concept will get clearer to you by the end of the book. (If you want more of a feel for pinpointing now, see chapter 11.)

1.  **Tune in.** Identify the symptom that reflects a tense mind-body moment. "I've been having more headaches lately. A

physician checked me out as fine and said they're probably from stress," says Betsy.

2.  **Connect to trigger event.** Tie the symptom to the trigger event that set it off. "My oldest child, Lila, recently left for college. I've had a short fuse with my other kids at home. Could it be that I'm sad because I miss her?"

3.  **Connect to mother image.** Tie the symptom to your mother image that keeps alive your self-image distortion and reaction to the trigger event. "I can't view myself as sad, because sad means 'weak.' Growing up I had to show my mother I was strong in order to win her love, just as she did for my grandmother. I guess because I still see her saying I have to show strength I didn't feel, it's safer for me to show anger than sadness. So it's easier to fly off the handle with my kids rather than admit that I'm sad because my daughter's away."

4.  **Reflect on how the symptom thwarts you.** Be mindful of how the symptom harms you. When Betsy reflects, she realizes, "I'm not enjoying my kids at home, it does them no good either, and these headaches hold me back from living life more."

Next we'll shift from Betsy's pinpointing to my own, while I wrote this book.

## *a personal illustration*

This book made me return to my mother's dying and my feelings about letting her down by not being the rescuing daughter when she was still conscious. One night, after a day of writing about that issue, I had a couple of mind-body symptoms: I had trouble sleeping, and I found that I couldn't write anything productive for a few days (writing is physical, in that the body is involved in typing the words, and it is also emotional, in the sense that one must be inspired in order to generate something creative). I *tuned in* to the symptoms but couldn't pinpoint the trigger event or mother image for another week. The sleeping issue continued while I faltered with the writing.

It wasn't until a week later, when I experienced an unexpected, pleasurable sense of flow in my writing, that I was able to *connect* to what might have triggered the symptoms. While "finding myself lost" in the writing, I thought, "How can I enjoy myself this way while recalling my mother's death?" I stayed with my uncomfortable feelings and looked at them.

From that experience of being in the moment—mindfulness— I gained insight and *connected* to my mother image. I realized I was letting my mother image affect my enjoyment of my writing; I sensed that image saying that I could have rescued my mother one more time. Then I began to contrast the reality of what doctors had said about my mother's dying process with my fantasy that I could have saved her. I *reflected* on how my symptom of guilt had thwarted my rest and creativity. My insights led to an improved flow in my sleeping and writing.

In the next section we'll return to the mother-daughter pair Sonya and Jenny, and take another look at how the carnival mirror affects them. In chapter 1 we learned about the influence of grandma Nadia's distorted self-image on daughter Sonya's self-image, and the influence of Sonya's distorted self-image on daughter Jenny's self-image. Earlier we focused on Jenny's experience while growing up. Now we'll focus more on Sonya's growing up and explore the carnival mirror's effect on her female watershed events. But first, let's take note of a couple of important points:

- Let's assume that there are no medical causes for the watershed experiences we'll discuss below.

- Though the revived mind-body moments appear to directly connect with the primal ones in these examples, that's not the reality of the situation. In life the connections are complex, occur over time, and aren't linear. The interpretations here are given for clarity and are not in any way meant to be conclusive statements.

# the female watersheds

The body's physical changes during the watershed events of puberty, pregnancy, and menopause trigger responses in a woman that echo the earliest mind-body moments with her primary caregiver.

## The Puberty Watershed

Puberty, with its dramatic physical changes, is fertile territory for primal mind-body moments to awaken. Old self-image issues get aggravated or new ones emerge because of the body's transformations: breasts too flat or full too early, pimples that emerge without notice, hips that suddenly proclaim their bulky presence, pounds in unwanted places. And menstruation, with its bleeding, staining, odor, and messiness, awakens unsettling mind-body moments from early in life. Let's look at Sonya's primal mind-body moments that set the stage for revived ones at puberty.

### *primal mind-body moments*

Throughout Sonya's third year, she began wetting the bed frequently, after a long period of having full bladder control. Her doctor ruled out a medical cause. He felt that the bedwetting had an emotional root, because Nadia confided in him that it made her feel like a defective mother, so she scrutinized the bed looking for urine, and tensed up when Sonya lost control. Sonya would tense up in turn and say things like "Sonya bad."

### *revived mind-body moments*

When Sonya was fourteen, her period began, and the smell and messy feeling disgusted her. She had bad menstrual cramps from the start and hated the bleeding. She came to realize that the dread of staining her clothes under an observant schoolmate's eye echoed her earlier dread of bedwetting under her observant mother's eye. A doctor thought the severity of Sonya's cramps—which we can call revived mind-body moments as symptoms—was related to tension.

Next, we'll look at pregnancy as a watershed event, and then we'll relate it to Sonya's situation.

## The Pregnancy Watershed

Let's say that you are trying to conceive. (We'll assume that there aren't medical causes for any of the experiences described here.) Perhaps anxiety-filled mind-body moments play a part in your lack of success in conceiving, and that makes you decide to give up trying (I'll interject here that you can use "pinpointing" to gain a calmer state. First you tune into the symptom: tension. Next, connect it to your trigger event: trying to conceive. Then connect it to your mother image: a feeling, absorbed from your childhood mother, that having a child is no piece of cake. Finally, reflect on how the symptom thwarts you; obviously, it is interfering with conception.

A merging of mind and body occurs with conception and pregnancy. Calm or tense feelings about these physical experiences echo calm or tense feelings about the body in our earliest experiences of relating with our primary caregiver. Conception has parallels with other creative acts, when a free feeling moves the process along.

In *Mother-Daughter Wisdom,* Christiane Northrup (2005) discusses how stress during pregnancy leads to a release of "hormones such as cortisol, epinephrine, and vasopressin, that help regulate placental blood flow and thus affect the amount of nutrients and oxygen the child is receiving" (66). The pregnant woman is less likely to have early bleeding, miscarriage, or cramping if mind and body are relaxed. And the length of labor is affected by how relaxed the muscles are, which is largely based on how relaxed the mind is.

### *revived mind-body moments*

Doctors said Sonya's inability to conceive was probably related to anxiety. She noted that she tensed up when her ovulation kit told her it was time to try. Sonya's stressful mind-body moments in the present and the related symptom—difficulty with conception—could very well have echoed her earlier symptoms at different stages (bedwetting and menstrual cramps). When she got to an emotional place where she could relax more, she eventually did conceive.

In the following piece from Sonya's diary, which she wrote while in therapy after Jenny had become an adult, we can see her mind-body moments as an anxiety symptom again, and we can also see how her carnival-mirror self-image would easily flow over to her daughter. "During my pregnancy with Jenny, I was anxious that I'd have a baby

94

with a defect. Since mom had made me so aware of my imperfections, I expected a daughter of mine to have them too. So when Jenny was born with cute little features, I prayed they would stay that way. When she became a teen and she grew, so did her nose. I couldn't stop thinking the way my mother did with me, and I think I made Jenny too aware of a problem that was really mine. Mom had focused her 'microscope' on my breasts, and I focused mine on Jenny's nose."

We've discussed how the puberty and pregnancy watersheds can trigger powerful mind-body moments. Similarly, the menopause watershed, particularly with its themes of loss, sets off mind-body moments that strongly affect a woman's quality of life.

## The Menopause Watershed

At menopause, mind-body moments are expressed in symptoms common to many women. Depression and mood swings occur, partly because of hormonal shifts and partly because of the sense of loss sparked by the body's changes.

### *fluid hormones, fluid memories*

When wrinkles, sagging skin, hair loss, lowered energy, vaginal dryness, loss of fertility, and hot flashes enter the picture, mind-body moments related to self-love or self-loathing revive primal ones. In *The Wisdom of Menopause,* Christiane Northrup (2001) writes that the brain areas that are most receptive to the fluctuating hormones at this time are also pivotal in bringing back memories.

It follows that if a woman experienced more of the hug cycle than the boomerang cycle early on, and continued to have soothing mind-body experiences while growing up, she's more primed to be resilient in the face of menopause's assault on the body. She's more likely to feel a calmer acceptance of her body, because her earliest mind-body memories which are now being revived, contain the mother's tenderness. Similarly, if the boomerang cycle defined her early relating experiences and patterns, it will also define the mind-body moments (such as menopause symptoms) that revive it. In that case, signs of aging will just reinforce the discomfort with her body that the woman has had all along.

So, in addition to hormonal changes that contribute to a menopausal funk, distress is also stored in early mind-body memory.

Because breasts are the most overt bodily sign of femininity, menopausal effects on them can set off some of women's most charged emotions. Tension in mind and body, connected with a lack of comforting in early childhood, is revived around the time of menopause, and sometimes earlier, when breasts sag, show dents after lumpectomies, or become distorted from cancer surgery.

In *Dr. Susan Love's Breast Book,* Love (1995) asks older women facing breast-cancer surgery about their feelings regarding their breasts in the past. We can see from her quotes that these women had positive or negative emotions toward their breasts long before the surgeon's knife played a role in altering their appearance.

One woman describes the first day she wore a bra: "'I was so proud: I was the second girl in the sixth grade to have one'" (Love 1995, 13–14). Another woman thought as a teen, "'Oh, shit, now I'm supposed to be a girl!'" (14). Yet another felt shame about her breasts and thought about how to "'cut them off with my grandmother's long, thin embroidery scissors'" (14).

While anxious mind-body moments often aggravate menopausal symptoms, calm mind-body moments play an important part in a woman's ability to adapt to bodily losses experienced during that watershed. Since we've discussed the negative mother image in a previous section, let's now explore its opposite.

## *more-positive mother image, more-positive menopause*

In an article, "Female Passion and the Matrix of Mother, Daughter, and Body," Barbara Marcus (2004) discusses a middle-aged patient who reveals aspects of her positive mother image, sustained through life. The patient says about her mother, "'She'd put her large, square hands in mine and say mine were lovely, so artistic, so soft and white. She'd worked in factories all her life…I still love my hands, in spite of arthritis and age spots. When I bit my nails, I knew they'd grow again. Isn't it odd that mother's appreciation in the end is still what makes them lovely to me?'" (688).

# let's recap

In the first part of the chapter, we explored how mind-body moments form. In the second part we considered how calm mind-body moments allow the freer self to bear fruit. We discussed four offshoots of the freer self: sensuality, creativity (including two of its sources, the transformative experience and free mother-infant body language), playfulness, and desire. In the third part of the chapter we explored the symptoms formed from stressful mind-body moments. In that section we were introduced to a thought-link phase, pinpointing symptoms. And the last part discussed the three female watersheds, when dramatic physical change sparks a revival of primal mind-body moments.

## A Note to Daughters

You might be wondering whether your aches and pains mean that your mother didn't hold you properly when you were two months old. You might blame her, then feel bad, and finally withdraw from thinking about the "mind-body moments" concept. My advice? Reread the mother mantras at the beginning of this book. Remember that if your mom had an unconscious distorted self-image that prevented her from giving you optimal TLC as a baby, she most likely *couldn't help it*; the issue was probably passed on to her by her own mother. Besides, many physical symptoms are purely biochemical, and many others are aggravated by stress but rooted in bodily causes. If you have patience, you'll see how the five thought links can help you control the emotional aspect of physical symptoms.

# Questions for Reflection

1. How might you describe an outgrowth of your freer self—sensuality, creativity, playfulness, desire—as it appears in daily life?

2. If you've ever "found yourself lost" in a creative experience, how would you describe it?

3. Tune in to a symptom and see if you can connect it to its trigger event and the related mother image.

4. Try to freewrite about your most upsetting female watershed and how mind-body symptoms thwarted you. Then describe how that experience continues to affect you now.

## *Reading Touch Tool*

*The Red Tent,* by Anita Diamant, touches on many women's feelings about puberty and how the relationship with their mothers plays a role at that stage. If you try to answer these questions in conjunction with reading *My Mother, My Mirror,* you can gain insight into your own feelings and experience.

### *The Red Tent,* by Anita Diamant

- Do you see anything in Dinah's puberty watershed experience and her relationship with her mother that resembles your relationship with your mother at that time in your life?

- What mind-body moments do you recall having then?

- How would you describe the influence of her mother on Dinah's sense of her body? Can you find a parallel with your mother and your sense of your body?

# self-image to self: how I see myself is how I sense myself

*Her mother had accused her of being a slut; tonight,*
*Marilyn seemed intent on...behaving like one...*
*she appeared hell-bent on self-destruction.*

— Barbara Leaming, *Marilyn Monroe*

As always during autumn and spring, the afternoon sun's angled rays performed a shadow-and-light ballet on the plaid couch in my consulting room, while dust particles, indifferent to finding a landing place, aimlessly parachuted down. I noticed these details in the space between Beryl and myself, because being with her meant sharply tuning in to my mind-body moments, since so much of what she communicated came through hers. She squinted a bit, moved awkwardly to avoid the light, and daintily dabbed each eye to blot her mascara. I squelched a desire to give her a tissue, knowing that, for Beryl, taking something from someone meant too much self-indulgence; showing her need for me at this stage in treatment would make her look weak, vulnerable. However, the yearning in her eyes belied the self-sufficiency she showed the world. (Note: Parts of the following case are drawn from a chapter in *Mind-Body Problems* [Fuerstein 1997].)

Beryl had entered therapy at twenty-two with lots of anxiety and "a [periodic] sense of a punching at her heart and...an expansion of her chest," all with no medical cause. These symptoms would happen often after she'd had a good sexual experience. The night before this particular session, she'd gone out with a guy and felt good about her body in bed, but when she came home, her symptom appeared. She then reported a dream she'd had that same night: "'I'm undressing my baby niece, and there's a gaping wound on her chest, with all the cartilage and muscle showing'" (Fuerstein 1997, 166). Beryl thought that her niece in the dream must represent herself being punished for freely enjoying her sexuality. That thought brought her back to her memories of puberty, when her mother would act judgmental and put a damper on a good time after Beryl had gone out and had fun.

## mother's—and daughter's—carnival-mirror self-image

Beryl's mother apparently had a skewed self-image. Though she was a bright woman with a college degree, she never used her intelligence and education, because she did not feel entitled to do so; she saw herself instead as her husband's servant. He ruled the roost, often letting his wife know that he favored his daughter over her.

In therapy, Beryl concluded that maybe in puberty she'd kept herself back socially and sexually, in order to protect her mother. "'I think [my mom] gave me a message that if I was free, she'd be threatened. Maybe I thought she would literally break apart or go crazy if I left her'" (165). Her heart symptom began during puberty after making out with a guy she'd flirted with at sleepaway camp. She interpreted the jabbing at her chest as a penance for leaving her mother behind to enjoy her burgeoning sexuality.

Beryl was handed her mother's carnival-mirror self-image (which told her she was undeserving in general), and that image was manifested in Beryl's skewed view of herself (which told her she was undeserving of sex). That perception led her to punish herself through a mind-body symptom after sex. Further, it thwarted her sexual sense of self by making her feel fragile during intercourse: she'd freeze up, because she feared she'd "break apart" during orgasm.

Beryl wondered with me how that anxiety came about. After discussing it for a while, she recalled a memory: at age thirteen, just one day after she'd begun menstruating, she overheard her mother tell a friend that she was "going to fall apart," and a few days later her mother began hemorrhaging because of a gynecological problem. Beryl began to have dreams in which her own body was breaking up along with her mother's.

Her mother's bleeding and her own got joined into one image. So maybe, as a teen, Beryl kept herself back with her mother by feeling she'd "fall apart" at the onset of each period. And now, the fear was being reflected in her feeling fragile during orgasm.

Her situation leads us to the main theme of this chapter: how the distorted self-image thwarts the sense of self. First we'll discuss what the self is. Next we'll explore three of its parts and how each looks when it is either free or thwarted.

# what is "me"?

In the West, neuroscientists and therapists write that one of the main things that separates our minds from those of animals is that we know we exist. As Mark Solms and Oliver Turnbull (2002) state in *The Brain and the Inner World*, our brain is the unique, enigmatic organ that gives us that sense: "The brain...is the seat of the mind, somehow producing our feeling of *being* ourselves in the world *right now*" (45).

And pediatrician and analyst Donald Winnicott (1986) writes in *Playing and Reality* that we must have that experience of "just being" before we can act, create, explore, relate, or do. Winnicott's "false self"—rigid and inauthentic—will emerge if an infant has to adapt to her caregiver's needs. The false self covers over the true self—which is fluid and authentic—if that's what's needed in order for the child to keep her mother's love.

Buddhist thoughts about the self contrast with Western ones, as described above. As Mark Epstein (1995) tells us in *Thoughts Without a Thinker*, Buddhist scholars write that it is only when we stop trying to find a true self that we experience life in a real way: "In the Buddhist view, a realized being has realized her own *lack* of a true self" (72).

In the following section, I include ideas about the self described above and blend them with those given in chapter 3, to form my own definition of *self*: our experience of being, which can be free or thwarted depending on how we experienced our primary caregiver's traits. Her flowing traits would allow for a truer self-image and freer self. Her imposing traits would encourage a distorted self-image and thwarted self.

We'll explore three major "selfs": physical, relating, and working. I place the sexual self at times with the physical self, and at other times with the relating self; it's an experience of the self that easily crosses both boundaries.

Let's now turn to the physical sense of self: how we experience our body's appearance, frame, motion, sensuality, sexuality, and connection to our mind.

## Physical Self

With a sheepish look, her eyes averted, Gerri, a menopausal woman, hesitated and stroked her hair a few times before telling me about making love with her husband the night before: "I had a good time... but...and..." When I said I sensed her difficulty with telling me that she had enjoyed her sexual experience, I asked if she thought I'd disapprove. She replied, "Well wouldn't you? My mother, Carolyn, always gave me the sense when I was a teen that if I had any sexual pleasure I was bad. She let me know that through silence rather than direct messages."

We explored that time in Gerri's life, which led us to look at her mother's teen self-image. Carolyn was taller and lankier than her older sister, Melanie, and viewed her body as second-rate next to Melanie's. This was a distorted self-image; Carolyn had a fine body, just one that was different from Melanie's. Carolyn's mother, Pearl, favored Melanie's neatly proportioned, petite body and rejected Carolyn's, because it resembled Pearl's own tall and lanky one. One day after Pearl and her two teenage daughters came back from a run with their dog, Pearl whispered to Melanie something that Carolyn overheard from the other room: "When you run, you have that graceful way about you that's all neatly stowed in that cute little shape of yours. I wish I could look like that. Your poor sister. She got stuck with the same ostrich legs I have."

### *carnival-mirror roadblocks*

Carolyn once told Gerri that at puberty she'd felt she had to be seductive with boys in order to be desired. And she expressed guilt about getting the guys that way.

But when Gerri entered puberty, instead of helping her daughter to celebrate her blossoming, she reacted with anxiety. She'd often bite her lip and furrow her brow when Gerri talked about going out on dates. Sensing her mother's discomfort with her sexuality, Gerri echoed her mother's teen social situation. She developed a negative view of her body—a distorted self-image, since she had a fine body also—and wound up seducing the boys to win their favor and then felt guilty. The carnival-mirror legacy had been passed to yet another female generation.

Now, as an adult in menopause, even though she was in a loving relationship with her husband, Gerri's guilt about her past "assertiveness" with boys carried over to her present sex life. When talking with me, she felt she had to hide the fact that she enjoyed herself or that she had desire, because she assumed I would be like her mother and disapprove of the experience.

We can more fully understand Gerri's situation with her mother if we compare a freer physical self with her thwarted one.

## *the open road*

A freer physical self can appear in a ballerina's leaps across the stage, a basketball player's awesome jumps, or a mother's game of hide-and-seek with her child. But the freer physical self isn't always shown so dramatically. Sometimes it's just about an inner openness of motion, feeling free within while hardly moving at all.

When a mother's flowing traits—pleasure in her daughter—come through, the daughter not only gives back to her mother what's been given to her but sees herself as a beauty, the way her mother has portrayed her. She gives of herself freely to her mother. In *Beyond the Reflection*, Paulina Kernberg (2006) illustrates this concept. She writes about a secure two-year-old (let's call her Hannah) looking in a mirror with her mother, who asks, "Who is that beautiful girl in the mirror?" And the girl answers with a smile, "Two beautiful girls" (18), meaning her mother and herself. If we picture Hannah moving toward the mirror, we might also imagine a freedom of motion.

Like the physical sense of self, the relating sense of self—the part of us that interacts with others—can be freer or thwarted.

## It's About the Relationship

Zoe would often giggle, even when she talked about something upsetting. Each time, I sensed neediness below the surface when she gazed at me for a few minutes afterward with imploring eyes. As a "change of life" baby, she'd grown up with a feeling that she was a pain for both parents to raise. The only way she could hope to have her needs met was by making believe nothing bothered her much, even when she felt hurt by her parents, who had little patience with her: "Go with your sister to the store; I need a rest," or "Can't you ask your brother to help you with the homework? I'm too busy." Zoe would often put on a smile after each of these interactions and walk away.

So, in my consulting room, she was showing me that same easy-going exterior while her deeper hunger to have her needs met, which would make her feel more valued, was revealed in her look. Her self-image was skewed, because she felt she wasn't worth her parents' time, which carried over to others, like me. Her fear of rejection caused her to give confusing messages that said she was content when she was far from it. As a result, she didn't get what she wanted. Zoe's relating self was guided by her distorted self-image. If she viewed herself as more valued, she would have given clearer messages and gotten more of what she desired from others.

Let's discuss how a restricted relating sense of self like Zoe's leads to a restricted choice of relationships—and usually not the best relationships.

Many of us are familiar with the idea that a woman "marries her father." Fewer realize how frequently a woman is unconsciously drawn to a man who reminds her of her mother. By partnering with him or marrying him, on some level the daughter holds on to her mother and to the relating patterns she had with her as a child.

## _couples in the carnival mirror_

I've found three types of partnership patterns that most clearly show how the carnival mirror is at the root of many relationship problems. The first involves women who didn't get the nurturing they needed from their mothers. The daughters grow up to unwittingly look for the nurturing in their male mates.

**Needy daughters seek mothering partners.** Esther's childhood mother, Mary, had a distorted image of herself as needy. She actually was a competent woman, but she had grown up being viewed by _her_ mother as the baby in the family; they called her "Kitten." So Mary took on the role of relying on others in an over-the-top way. And when she raised Esther, she still felt dependent, and she unknowingly gave Esther cues that she should not have needs of her own, because Mary's needs were greater. Many times her neediness came through in daily requests made to her daughter, such as, "Esther, I know you have to meet your friends after school, but I need you to come home early to go food shopping," or "Please clean the house for me before the guests come. I have to nap in order to be at my best for them." Esther would comply and Mary would give her strokes. "That's my girl. Only you can take care of me this way." So Esther grew up thinking that she would be unworthy of love if she showed her own needs, and that she would be most valued if she didn't.

Because of her caregiver role, she had many unmet feelings of longing from childhood and chose a mate, Len, who *appeared* to meet her needs. He seemed so ready to take care of her—by helping her cook, mowing her lawn, walking her dog, and buying her a warmer coat during a very cold winter—that she married him. But Len's tangible mothering behavior was only on the surface. Soon after marrying, Esther discovered his neediness, which was similar to her mother's. After some time, she learned that he had used his TLC to seduce women before. In addition, once he was in the relationship, he allowed his hypochondria to emerge; if Esther asked for care from him, Len couldn't give it, because his joints were achy, his muscles were tight, he had heartburn, or he was coming down with a cold.

Next, we'll look at daughters who grow up feeling guilty and select mates who they sense, on some level, will punish them for their past "misdemeanors."

**Guilt-filled daughters choose abusive partners.** Frannie's childhood mother, Marion, had an inaccurate image of herself as responsible for "crimes" that she didn't commit. When Marion was twelve, her younger sister almost drowned after Marion had fought with her. So Marion felt as if her anger had made it happen. When Marion grew up to be a mother, she passed on her distorted guiltful self-image to Frannie by saying things that were guilt provoking, like, "If you hadn't done that..." and "I felt okay until you..." As an adult, Frannie chose a partner who verbally abused her and made her feel that just about everything that went wrong was her fault. On some level she felt she deserved to be punished for all her wrongs. Frannie's distorted self-image led her to choose a mate who abused her by making her feel to blame for anything that went wrong, in the same way her mother had.

The next type of relationship involves daughters who grow up with a skewed image of themselves as undeserving, just like their mothers, and select mates who seem beneath them because that's all they're entitled to.

**Daughters who feel second rate choose second-rate partners.**
Rebecca's childhood mother, Olivia, saw herself as undeserving of fulfillment. Olivia, who had grown up feeling deprived, made Rebecca feel
that if she got what she wanted in life, it would take something away
from Olivia. The family was financially well off; however, when Rebecca
asked for something like an extra piece of cake, her mother might give
it to her but with a sigh of resentment. So, when Rebecca grew up, she
married a man who wasn't her intellectual equal, because she didn't feel
that she deserved to look for someone better. They had little to share,
and the marriage was troubled.

As you can see, the self-image can have a profound effect on the
kinds of partners we choose, and those choices can further influence
our self-image. Now, let's turn our attention to the *working self,* the part
of us that works, whether in a career, in school, or during sports practice
session, for example.

## Free Labor?

If your sense of your working self is freer, you can feel creative, let
yourself go, try new approaches, see things in new ways, show belief in
yourself, have determination, or really immerse yourself in a project. If
your working self is constrained, you may feel fuzzy when making decisions about what track you want to be on, you may have trouble getting
things off the ground, or you might move from one job to another
searching for something outside yourself to fill you up.

The freer and more-restricted sides of the working self play out in
the stories of two famous women. In her writing, Ruth Reichl (former
*New York Times* food editor and, more recently, the editor in chief of
*Gourmet* magazine) shows how sometimes, despite a mother's skewed
self-image, a daughter can take the best of what is offered and put it to
good use in a career. Sylvia Plath's life demonstrates how extraordinary
creativity and success don't always fully counter the influence of the carnival mirror.

### *Ruth Reichl: from mom's wacky stew to a fulfilling career*

In her memoir *Tender at the Bone,* when Ruth Reichl (1998)
describes her childhood mother, she infuses her writing with a steady
flow of humor about her mother's bizarre cooking (which at times actu-

ally made guests sick). Though Reichl's writing gives the impression that her mother had a mental imbalance, we can still use her inflated sense of herself as a superb cook as a clear illustration of a distorted self-image: "'I can make a meal out of anything,' Mom told her friends proudly.... She liked to brag about 'Everything Stew'..." (5).

With positive input from her father and the help of a nurturing female relative, Ruth unknowingly groomed herself for her future work as a food writer and editor: "Like a hearing child born to deaf parents, I was shaped by my mother's handicap, discovering that food could be a way of making sense of the world" (6). It appears that Ruth's own creativity, the steadiness of other caregivers, and perhaps a touch of her unstable mother's imagination allowed her to succeed in her career despite her mother's skewed self-image.

## Sylvia Plath: poetic perfection

In *Rough Magic*, Paul Alexander (2003) tells us that Sylvia Plath's husband, Ted Hughes, is reported to have been emotionally abusive throughout the couple's marriage and also to have conducted an affair with another woman. As a result, Alexander writes that Hughes may be seen as the main cause of her suicide at age thirty. The event occurred a few months after they had separated, leaving her to raise their two children alone.

Her father, who reportedly didn't spend much time with her while alive, died when Sylvia was eight through his own neglect of an illness. And her mother, thrown into a tailspin, became more self-absorbed than she was before and sought perfection in her daughter. We can guess that her mother had some distortion in her self-image, shown by her need for her daughter to be an ideal version of herself. Sylvia frequently put herself down throughout her life for not reaching that level of perfection.

In *The Compulsion to Create*, Susan Kavaler-Adler (1993) discusses how Sylvia tried to be a perfect daughter. "In letters to her mother, she herself is false, grandiosely being on top of everything" (101). One way to view Sylvia's self-loathing is to say that she grew up viewing herself as lacking worth for not being "perfect," and she married a man whose traits fed right into her need to keep putting herself down.

Sylvia Plath's life story demonstrates that while her freer self's creativity brought her professional success, her self-image distortion weighed too heavily on her, and her thwarted self won out.

## *Touch Tool:* Freewriting————————————————

Find photos of yourself at different stages of life that reflect various aspects of your freer or thwarted self: physical, relating, working. Label each photo according to these three aspects, and separate them into groups. Then, in a notebook or journal, try freewriting about your self-image and sense of self in connection with each group. Here's a brief example of freewriting (you may choose to write more): "Me toddler blocks knock down tower doubt self image can't do it."

# let's recap

In this chapter, we first discussed what the self is, followed by a look at how a truer self-image allows the self the freest rein, and how the carnival-mirror self-image gets in its way. We ended by exploring how the self appears when free or thwarted in physical, relating, and working areas.

The next chapter will present the first thought link, which involves getting in touch with feelings about your mother's self-image at the time she raised you, and with how distortions in her view of herself have affected your own self-image.

## A Note to Mothers of Girls

You might now be blaming yourself, thinking about how your skewed self-image might have caused your daughter to see herself inaccurately and therefore not live up to her potential. But hold on: you weren't aware you were doing anything to her! The following chapters, which take you through the thought links, should help you gradually move away from guilt and toward self-acceptance.

# Questions for Reflection

1. What aspect of your physical self might be freer or more thwarted?

2. What aspect of your relating self might be freer or more thwarted?

3. What aspect of your working self might be freer or more thwarted?

## *Reading Touch Tool*

Linda Carroll's book reveals how the self-image and sense of self in a mother who was an adopted child can affect her daughter's self-image and sense of self.

### *Her Mother's Daughter: A Memoir of the Mother I Never Knew and of My Daughter, Courtney Love,* by Linda Carroll

- How did Linda's view of herself as an adopted daughter influence her view of Courtney? How might that view have influenced Courtney's sense of self?

- What dreams for her yet-unborn child did Linda have that might have shown a distorted self-image in her?

- Can you imagine any fantasies your mother might have had about you before you were born that influenced your sense of self?

# thought links that deepen feeling

# CHAPTER 7

# thought link 1:
# mommy, how did you see you?
# how do I see me?

*Finally, I understood the nature of one of the shadows I inherited from [Mother] that has incubated in my body for so long—the shadow of guilt that an abused girl like Mother carries.*

— Jane Fonda, *My Life So Far*

Years before my mother's death, in therapy I'd painted a colorful, textured, full description of my mother image, with its bits and pieces of reality and fantasy. In the process, I homed in more on who my mother may have actually been during my childhood and what made her tick. Many times I had to step into her shoes to see how her own issues might have shaped mine.

Specifically, I felt that if I could better understand her self-image when she raised me, I could better understand its influence on mine. One day, I found myself looking at a sepia-toned photo of her in the second grade. She died before I could ask her which of those poised-looking girls in the picture—with hands folded on broad wooden desks—was my mother. I figure she's the girl in the first row, second from left, with the straight bangs and eyelet-trimmed blouse, because when I peer into that kid's eyes, I think I see a bit of me.

Gazing at the photo made me think about something she'd told me a number of times during my childhood: Immigrant kids were crowded into classes in lower Manhattan, where she grew up in the early twentieth century. So the elementary schools adhered to a system of half-year terms, and academically capable students would skip a term here or there to make room for others. My mother often mentioned that she was in that group. I had the sense that she'd been strongly affected by the experience, but I didn't recognize its lingering influence on her adult view of herself.

Then I considered how singing for an audience enlivened her. I recalled her radiance as she modeled her vocal tone after Ella Fitzgerald's, trying on a sultry voice from high to low with the family as her audience, while my uncle accompanied her at the piano. I realized that getting special attention from her mother when she sang for her must have gone a long way to help her feel validated, in the face of being shuffled about at school.

As I mentioned in chapter 1, my mother must have grown up viewing herself as someone who is most valued when she is seen as special. That need revealed a distortion in her self-image, since she had plenty of innate qualities that could have made her feel equally valued. And she passed the carnival mirror to me. Even though she gave me strokes in lots of ways, I gained the perception that a bit too much of my worth was tied up with feeling special too—by making things better for her when she felt stress.

My musings led me to write this chapter, which explores thought link 1, reflection aspects of my own process just described. The first section will introduce the phases of thought link 1. The second section will discuss the mental tools that can help you gain deeper insights through thought link 1 and the thought links that follow it.

# the first thought link

This thought link has three phases: *exploring, stepping into Mother's shoes,* and *sifting out.*

## Exploring

In this phase, you note any distortions in your self-image so that you can later separate your own from your mother's.

A self-image distortion is a view of your qualities, skills, and worth that greatly differs from your innate self if it were allowed to grow freely, without your mother's self-image issues weighing it down. Having a distorted self-image can mean not only that you see yourself inaccurately, but that you make one trait define your whole sense of worth.

When exploring, start by asking yourself some key questions. You can often find a clue to a distortion by pinpointing a belief about yourself that has kept you from experiencing a fuller life. Below are a few examples of questions you might ask yourself:

- Do I keep myself from going to the beach because I really should be ashamed of my body? Or is it because I make an issue of my extra weight, because Mom made an issue of hers and let me know that we could be close as long as we were in the same boat?

- Do I frequently question my mothering even though my kids are doing fine socially, physically, and academically, and even though others scratch their heads when I mention my anxious feelings about them?

- Do I keep myself back from new activities because I'm actually not capable of doing them or because I fear others will see me as a fool, as I see myself?

- Do I have a hard time accepting compliments or gifts because I truly don't deserve them or because I don't view myself as deserving of them?

- Do I hold myself back in bed for legitimate reason or because Mom felt afraid of sex and she passed that feeling on to me through her warnings about getting involved with "sexed-up" men?

- Do I sabotage myself after a sports achievement because I actually don't deserve to have the satisfaction or because I feel guilty for excelling when my little sister was so uncoordinated?

The next phase will help you try to sense what your mother felt about herself when she was raising you; this process will increase your understanding of why she affected you the way she did. If your mother is alive, it's natural for you to think that you might be able to get valuable information from her, and it's true that getting some of the facts can

**115**

be useful. However, this is not at all essential, because a lot of what you need to learn about her actually comes from you.

## Stepping into Mother's Shoes

It might seem strange to think that you could learn what was in your mother's mind in the past. Obviously you won't be able to fully achieve that, but getting as close as possible to this level of understanding will help you separate your self-image from hers.

First, let's review an important point: stepping into your mother's shoes means that you can also step out of them. The idea here is not to remain stuck with her self-image issues. And in suggesting that you try to feel what she felt, I don't mean that you should engage in a forced process or one that makes you guilt ridden. I'm pointing toward something that may take a while, particularly if you're in touch with anger toward her that's been simmering—or overflowing—for a long time.

The idea behind stepping into her shoes is to try to see how her problems helped skew your self-image in childhood. The aim is to let her have the responsibility but not to put energy into blaming her for what happened when you were a dependent child. If you feel immensely hurt by your mother and extremely angry at her for things that happened in the past, stepping into her shoes might seem impossible. If you can't accomplish this feat, don't get down on yourself or give up the whole process, because your self-image changes occur through other influences. And besides, over time you may come to understand that unexamined impulses, not conscious intent, probably made her act the way she did.

### _anger before empathy?_

One of the reasons I use the phrase "step into Mother's shoes" rather than "try to feel empathy" toward her, is that in situations with punitive, abusive, neglectful, or cold mothers, empathy, which often implies forgiveness, may not be realistic or even healthy. Sometimes extremely negative feelings toward the mother can cause a woman to try, without being aware of it, to force empathy prematurely. As Kim Chernin (1998) writes in _The Woman Who Gave Birth to Her Mother,_ many women "rush into forgiveness before they have discovered anger" (29).

When we try too quickly to gain understanding of our mothers, we often wind up turning anger against ourselves. It's really important to allow yourself resentment, hostility, annoyance, or irritation toward your childhood mother without judging yourself. The more able you are to do that, the more likely it is that you'll find empathy for yourself and, in turn, empathy for your mother.

## Samantha steps into Mother's shoes and faces anger

Samantha's story illustrates how, by stepping into your childhood mother's shoes, you can deal with your anger toward her.

Samantha entered treatment saying, "I've written off my mother, who never was one of those motherly types in the old movies with the gingham curtains surrounding her in the cozy kitchen where she baked apple pies every other day. She never gave me much and I'm still bitter about it. Meanwhile, I've also felt guilty because she seemed to need a lot that I couldn't give her. So now I think I punish myself by not feeling entitled to much."

While stepping into Mother's shoes, Samantha learned that her grandmother had died when her mother, Dorothea, was twelve years old. At that point her grandfather gave housekeeping responsibilities over to Dorothea. She became a premature adult and didn't get many of her own needs met. Samantha saw that Dorothea's background had left her with needs that she unwittingly felt she had a right to gratify before Samantha's. She realized that Dorothea had a distorted image of herself as deserving more than others did, but this was because she had felt cheated in the past.

Samantha recognized that when Dorothea hadn't come to one of Samantha's school events because of a card game or other adult distraction, she might have been behaving, unknowingly, as the child whose needs come before anyone else's. She could also see that it was her mother's problems that unconsciously had driven her behavior, not Samantha's unworthiness. So she could now put some of the responsibility on her mother without clinging to a burdensome bitterness that made her see herself as undeserving. Samantha began to accept and enjoy gifts from friends, take compliments more easily, and recognize when others' giving came from the heart.

Like Samantha, you may find it challenging to see where the responsibility for your childhood experiences lies. Why? If you and your mother were not just joined at the hip but were glued together with Elmer's, your self-images probably got pretty well stuck together. Once you can see each self-image separately, on its own, you'll be better able to sift yours out of the mother-daughter mix.

## Sifting Out

"Sift" is defined by the *American Heritage Dictionary* (4th ed., s.v. "Sift") as follows: "To put (flour, for example) through a sieve or other straining device in order to separate the fine from the coarse particles." Your task is to separate your self-image from the blended mother-daughter self-image. The steps of *sifting out* include the following (a list on paper simplifies learning, but in real life the steps don't always occur in order and sometimes they overlap):

* Describe the issue that thwarts you most.

* Describe your self-image distortion that keeps the issue going.

* Identify your mother's self-image distortion during your childhood that might have helped create the issue for you.

* Separate "pictures" of your self-image from "pictures" of hers.

Let's look at the sifting process that Krysta, Carmen, and Adrienne undertook to separate their self-images from those of their mothers.

### *Krysta's stuck-in-molasses dieting efforts*

**The issue that thwarts Krysta.** "I'm stuck in molasses with trying and failing to lose weight. It's always been that way."

**Daughter's distortion and mother's distortion that influenced it.** "Mom would often say to me when I was a kid that she felt stuck in molasses with the same problem. When in my teens I gained about the same amount of excess weight, she'd say, 'Well, honey, I think we both have the family stuck-in-molasses gene.' I've viewed myself as my mother views herself, as if I have an inborn defect that would make working at a healthy diet a wasted effort."

118

**Separate pictures: Daughter's self-image and mother's.** "Stuck-in-molasses gene? No way. I'm totally capable of staying with a diet and losing weight, even if Mom couldn't."

## Carmen's over-the-top caregiving

**The issue that thwarts Carmen.** "As a teen I'd be racing out to a party and Mom would say something like, 'Just one thing, Carmen. Could you please fold that load of laundry before you go?' I'd do it, because I felt that if I didn't I'd be leaving her flat, even if she didn't give back. I think I'm still stuck in that pattern of over-the-top caregiving."

**Daughter's distortion and mother's distortion that influenced it.** "I always needed to give up my own needs for Mom's in order to feel accepted. Now I do the same with friends. I don't feel free to express my own desires for fear they'll leave me, and I don't feel free to leave them even though they've been crummy to me. I discovered that Mom didn't see herself as accepted by Grandma. She was told she was a change-of-life baby. I think that she needed me to cater to her in order to bolster her self-esteem."

**Separate pictures: Daughter's self-image and mother's.** "I don't have to doubt that I pass the 'okay' test just because Mom doubted that she'd pass the 'okay' test. She did it in a very different way from me, but deep down I think she felt she never made the grade. I can learn how to let someone know I have needs too, without fearing they'll dump me."

## Adrienne's lack of connection

**The issue that thwarts Adrienne.** "When I was a kid, Mom was super involved with what I did but wasn't really tuned in to me. I think Bruce is like her. Maybe that's why I married him. Being together but not close was familiar territory. One time, I came home from school upset about a quarrel with my friend. When I still looked teary eyed after dinner, Mom said several times, 'You're fine now, right? Everything's fine? Right?' Was there any way for me to tell the truth?"

**Daughter's distortion and mother's distortion that influenced it.** "When I considered how Mom acted close but didn't understand me, I thought she probably had the same feeling about Grandma with *her*. She told me about a campout she was invited to as a kid, and Grandma discouraged her because she really wanted Mom to stay with her at home while Grandpa was away. She told Mom the bugs would bite, the bears would come, and the tent would collapse. I think we both share the view of ourselves as unable to have real closeness, and that if you have even a veneer of closeness, you have to let the other person control you. But we won't let him or her really know us."

**Separate pictures: Daughter's self-image and mother's.** "I don't have to keep the same self-image Mom had when she raised me. I can feel close to Bruce or anyone else I want to feel close to without applying the barter system in which you yield control in order to maintain the relationship."

Whether you explore, step into Mother's shoes, or sift out your self-image from your mother's, using your sense of your mother's self-image during your earliest years will deepen the process. The touch tools below will help you do that. In earlier chapters, we've used the reading touch tools to stir the senses and gain insight. Here, we'll delve into those and a variety of other touch tools more fully. And, though we see them illustrated here in this chapter on thought link 1, they can be used for any of the thought links.

# the touch tools

Touch tools are objects, writings, and processes that help you get in touch with your feelings and inner thoughts. For clarity, I've organized the sources for these tools into two groups: sources found outside you and those that come from within. As you use them in your life, the two sources will intertwine with one another. Gardening serves as a great example of how that interweaving works. You can be doing something creative, planting flowers in a style your childhood mother liked (inner source), and smelling and touching the flowers (outer source) at the same time. You can also use the same touch tool to evoke feelings about any female forebear; your great-grandmother, grandmother, or mother, for example.

# Outer Sources

The touch tools below can stir emotions that lead to insight about your grandmother's life experience before motherhood and after, and about your mother's during the same periods in her life. Each touch tool is followed by the sources for it.

> **Words:** Stories told by grandmother, mother, or others who knew them then; diaries; books about their eras; books they read or writing they generated.
>
> **Sensory stirrers:** These evoke memories of your grandmother or mother, or of how you experienced her during childhood. Some ideas:
>
> > **See:** Yarn, wildflowers, paints, birds, embroidery thread, snow, photos, movies, scrapbooks
> >
> > **Smell:** Cantering horses, cooking aromas, new leather, rotting apples
> >
> > **Touch:** Fresh soil, supple suede, crumbly pie dough, wiry puppy's coat
> >
> > **Hear:** Howling wind, moving jazz music, hard rain, electrifying concert

Here are suggestions for how you might use the outer-source touch tools.

## *words*

Stories can show how your grandmother's early experiences influenced your mother's childhood or how your mother's influenced yours. For example, my mother told me that my grandmother, a Russian immigrant who arrived as a teen at Ellis Island with a younger sister, had to wait for months for her parents to arrive. She was the second of ten children and was viewed by her siblings as the advice giver. I also know she worked in a sweatshop type of sewing factory before having children, and that her housework was strenuous.

Your grandmother's or mother's writing can fill you in on how she experienced childhood or about how she felt rearing her daughter. To illustrate, Maureen found postcards sent by her mother each summer when she was a child at sleepaway camp, revealing closeness between her mother and grandmother. Besides comments showing affection, the writing showed that the grandmother knew her daughter well enough to mention that her favorite color was yellow and her favorite sport was waterskiing.

Books on your grandmother's or mother's era reveal influences on her early life. Reading David Von Drehle's (2004) *Triangle*, which focuses on the famous Triangle Shirt Factory fire in lower Manhattan in the early twentieth century, helped me understand the working experience of young female immigrants like my grandmother. Other personal accounts such as *In My Mother's House*, by Kim Chernin (1994), about her grandmother, her immigrant mother, and herself, were also useful.

## *sensory stirrers (see)*

Photos, movies, or scrapbooks can reveal something of your grandmother's, mother's, or your own childhood experience. I discussed how I studied my mother's second-grade class photo, which stirred my ability to identify with her as a child. With those experiences in mind, I've imagined how my mother's own needs might easily have been overlooked in her younger years.

Gerri found photos of her mother before she was born, showing her aglow, dancing in a swirling ruffled dress. In contrast, a few photos taken when Gerri was two—after her father began drinking—reveal her mother's worn look as she stands next to Gerri, arms at her sides. A faint smile seems placed to hide sadness.

## *sensory stirrers (smell, see, touch)*

Melissa was spending her late-fall vacation at a farmhouse converted into an inn. The smell of rotting crab apples that had fallen to the ground from the trees dotting the surrounding pasture evoked memories of her loving grandmother, who had a hotel in the country when Melissa was a child. She touched the exposed, gnarled branches on the trees, which reminded Melissa of how, as a little girl, she thought they resembled her grandmother's hands.

# Inner Sources

Many inner-source touch tools are centered on the arts, which include writing, creating visual art, gazing at or experiencing art, and listening to or making music. Of course, having nature around you while using the touch tools furthers your experience.

Below are some of those with inner sources:

**Writing.** Your own journal writings, stories, memoirs, poetry, random thoughts

**Hands-on art.** Cooking, baking, cake decorating, painting, sculpture, crafts, ceramics, drawing, knitting, crocheting, quilting, sewing, embroidering, crewelwork, hooking rugs, weaving, gardening, and any other form of art you engage in

**Gazing at art.** Gardens, photography, paintings, drawings, quilts, tapestries, or any of the products of hands-on art described above

**Music.** Listening, composing, playing an instrument, singing

Because the inner sources come from within you and the creative aspects of you, they evoke some of your deepest feelings. In addition, as Daniel J. Levitin (2007, 244) states in *This Is Your Brain on Music*, art's power comes from its way of linking us to each other, "and to larger truths about what it means to be alive and what it means to be human." The emphasis here is on the process—your unique creative process that may or may not lead to a tangible product. We all have a means of personal expression within us to be mined.

In that vein, Julia Cameron (1992) writes in *The Artist's Way*, "...all the stories, painting, music, performances in the world live just under the surface of our normal consciousness. Like an underground river, they flow through us as a stream of ideas that we can tap down into" (118). Your creative process is there to be found, although perhaps it is not yet known to you. When engaged in any of the arts, you can experience a sense of transformation.

In *On Not Being Able to Paint*, Marion Milner (1990) writes that if we try not to watch ourselves while drawing or painting, we can put something new on the paper. And "the process always [seems] to be accompanied by a feeling that the ordinary sense of self [has] temporarily disappeared" (154). In that open state of mind, we're more likely to find a way back to our childhood mother's feelings, thoughts, and actions, and to our own experience of her. We can apply the idea of transformation to other art forms. As mentioned in chapter 5, in *The Shadow of the Object*, Christopher Bollas (1987) writes that the arts afford us a transformative experience that returns us to our earliest times with our mothers, when the experience of being soothed created a dramatic change in our internal state.

Below, let's view a sampling of women's experiences using three of the arts: writing, hands-on art, and music touch tools.

## *writing*

*one day a week grandma and aunt sarah took me to grand
street for yarn, bell yarns their favorite store. the old country
women knitted gorgeous sweaters you could taste delicious,
hats, gloves you know, it was cold, damp because of the east
river, especially in winter in those days there were certain colors
yarn girls had purple, red, pink and boys brown green rust but
wool was so warm really warm not like now with the synthetics.
And grandma and aunt sarah made such even stitches, knit-
purl straight lines, every popcorn stitch like little blossoms, shell
stitches all the same like macaroni and the cables crossed over
one another like planned little roads. two yarn carriers stood
on legs you know the kind that I have now with that cloth like
a sling between two bars always stood on the floor with piles of
skeins flowing over in every color. wanted her to show me how to
knit when we got home but busy.*

*Freewriting* is automatic, free-flowing writing, absent of correct structure, grammar, or punctuation, like the one above, which I wrote in my mother's voice about an experience I imagined she might have had as a child.

**How Freewriting Frees You:** If you've never written the way I did in the sample above, you might try writing about anything that strikes you at any moment. You can use this kind of writing to capture a time, place, scene, or memory involving your mother during her or your childhood. No need to worry about order or logic.

Think of this process, and others that use other aspects of your creativity, as starting a jigsaw puzzle with pieces scattered on a table, gradually forming separate areas that lead to a clearer picture. You might gain from ideas offered to any writer who wishes to open herself up, like those in *Bird by Bird,* by Anne Lamott (1995, 6):

> You train your unconscious to kick in for you creatively, by sitting down...and then you stare at [the computer or pad] for an hour or so....You look at the ceiling, and over at the clock, yawn, and stare at the paper again. Then...you squint at an image that is forming in your mind—a scene, a locale, a character, whatever—and you try to quiet your mind so you can hear what that landscape or character has to say above the other voices in your mind.

Some more ideas for freewriting come from Natalie Goldberg (1986, 8) in *Writing Down the Bones*:

> You may time yourself for ten minutes, twenty minutes, or an hour...and for that full period:
> 1. Keep your hand moving...
> 2. Don't cross out...
> 3. Don't worry about spelling, punctuation, grammar...
> 4. Lose control...
> 5. Don't think. Don't get logical...
> 6. Go for the jugular. (If something comes up in your writing that is scary or naked, dive right into it. It probably has lots of energy).

**Memoirs:** We'll use June Cross's memoir *Secret Daughter* (2006) as another model for how you might use writing to explore, step into your mother's shoes, and sift your self-image from your mother's. The author is the child of a mixed-race single mother (Norma) and a black comedian who didn't stick around. When Norma's shame grew too much about having a child with kinky hair whose skin had darkened with time, she gave June away to be raised by a black family.

- June explores. June describes her mother as "born, literally, on the wrong side of the tracks," (80) a glamorous, bright perfectionist who saw acting as a way of escaping from the past that shamed her. "She refused to let children stand in the way of her dreams," (81) but always felt conflict about giving June away.

In exploring her mother's self-image—inferior because her background was inferior—June comes to understand her own self-image—inferior because her mother saw her as inferior (of course the father's absence had to play a role too).

- June steps into her mother's shoes. While angry that she couldn't get her mother to fully come clean about giving her away, June sees that her mother had spent most of her life seeking a way to deny her background and that "the blueprint for the decisions she would make about her own children seemed, somehow, predetermined" (261). June steps into her mother's shoes by seeing that her mother probably couldn't control her actions, because they came from some deep place within her.

- June sifts out. Her awareness of the relationship between her own self-image distortion and Norma's allows June to see Norma's rejection of her as based on her distorted picture of reality. June writes that her hairdresser's feelings sum up her problem well: "He thought I was trying to downplay my light skin...because [I was] afraid to be beautiful" (300). She thinks he is right. She realizes she was holding onto a self-image distortion similar to her mother's. Though each is rooted in something different, the common thread is shame.

## *hands-on art*

Another tool to stir feeling when journeying through the phases of thought link 1 is hands-on art. Self-transformation is possible while you're engaged with this touch tool. Let's look at how Melinda used art to work through her self-image distortion.

*I'm in a mess about whether to have a baby or not. I'm afraid that my womb won't be a healthy home for a fetus, even though doctors say there's nothing wrong with it. Where did this come from? I don't know, but I've been having dreams lately about butterflies. That's probably because I went back to watercolors a few weeks ago and kept working over a painting with three butterflies emerging from one another. Though each was spectacularly gorgeous, it also had something that was wrong: a jagged wing, a harsh color, an incomplete part. Like a baby of mine?*

**Painting:** After talking about her painting, Melinda recalled a memory of herself as an eight-year-old visiting a butterfly conservatory with her mother. She heard her mother say to a friend that she wished she could have felt the same way a caterpillar must feel about giving birth, knowing that a beautiful butterfly would emerge from its body.

* Melinda explored. Melinda and I began to discuss the idea that maybe the painted butterflies represented her mother, her, and a future baby and that perhaps her mother's own inaccurate self-image regarding motherhood had influenced Melinda's. She later discovered from an aunt that her mother had long feared that she would give birth to an abnormal child, because she'd grown up with a handicapped first cousin.

* Melinda stepped into her mother's shoes. Melinda sensed her mother's fears while picturing her as a young woman before Melinda was born, anxious about having a baby with her cousin's problem.

* Melinda sifted out her own self-image from her mother's in the mother-daughter mix. She realized that her self-image had distortions because she was essentially gazing into the carnival mirror, just as her mother had done.

## *music*

Music is another form of art that leads to feeling transformed and evokes powerful emotions. In *This Is Your Brain on Music,* neuroscientist Daniel J. Levitin (2007) writes that music stirs up strong, deep feelings because it touches the primal areas of the brain related to emotion. And if we had musical experiences early in life, the sound and rhythm get encoded in our early memory, to be awakened later. According to research, Levitin says, a one-year-old baby will reveal a preference for music that she heard within the womb. "When we love a piece of music, it reminds us of other music we have heard, and it activates memory traces of emotional times in our lives" (192).

**Playing Piano:**

> *I'm in such a rut. I won't try new things because I'm afraid I'll
> fail at them. My mother would often say to me, "Oh, come on,
> Annette, you can do anything." Somewhere deep down, I knew
> that was impossible, but I had to act as if I believed it to please
> her. Of course, I also liked hearing it and wanted to believe
> it. When I was seven and joined a tap-dance class two weeks
> after it had started, my friend Janice was literally always a
> step ahead of me, and I felt embarrassed when I had to copy
> her steps in order to stay in sync with the music's beats. But I
> couldn't tell my mother that, because I felt that if I let her know
> I was failing at the class, I'd fail her too.*

One of Annette's challenges was to recognize that her mother's
message, "You can do anything," could've been driven by her wish to
counter her own sense of falling short. As an adult, Annette decided
to take up piano, something she'd left behind as a child because she
would get too frustrated over her mistakes while practicing, especially if
her mother was near enough to hear it. One day when she began *Claire
de Lune,* the melody went through her. She suddenly recalled that her
mother used to play that piece too but always stopped somewhere in the
middle, seeming frustrated.

- Annette explored her memories by picturing her mother
  going over the same difficult spot in the piece many times
  and then walking away from the piano with heavy measured
  steps, a downturned mouth, and a look of resignation. As if
  in a ritual, her mother would often then mechanically put
  on her apron and go back to household chores.

- Annette stepped into her mother's shoes when she recalled,
  while playing the piece to the end, that her mother, Regina,
  had said that *her* mother had favored Regina's older sister
  Peggy and paid for lessons for her but not for Regina, despite
  the fact that teachers told Regina that she had a good ear for
  music. Annette figured that her mother must have felt frustrated as a result. More than that, she'd told Annette once
  that as a kid she felt second rate next to "Perfect Peggy"
  because of Peggy's better looks.

- Annette began to sift out and view her mother's self-image
  as distorted. She wasn't actually second rate next to a perfect
  sister; she had strengths she'd never tapped into, probably

because of her childhood view of herself as inferior. By separating her mother's self-image from her own, Annette could start to see herself in a truer way. She realized that she couldn't possibly be "perfect" in the way her mother needed her to be to make up for her own past problem, and this inability to reach perfection did not mean that she was defective. Annette had talents she could enjoy, one of which was playing piano. Though she'd gained empathy for her mother, she didn't have to blend her mother's self-image into her own.

## let's recap

We began by looking at the three phases in thought link 1: exploring, stepping into Mother's shoes, and sifting out. Next we discussed the touch tools that help you move through those steps and those in the other thought links: writing, hands-on art or art gazing, and listening to or making music.

In the next chapter we'll explore thought link 2, showing why and how women bury anger toward the childhood mother, hindering them in adulthood. And we'll discuss how to face that anger in order to change your self-image and free yourself.

### A Note to Daughters

All of this looking at your mother's past, trying to feel what she felt as a kid, and then separating your own self-image from hers might seem too complicated. Besides, you might open a door into a part of your mother's history that you'd rather not know about. But keep going. As you move through the five thought links, the steps should become more familiar, and your anxieties will very likely fade into the background.

# Questions for Reflection

1. If you step into your childhood mother's shoes, what experience of hers makes you feel the most empathy toward her, and what about her is hardest to understand?

2. After sifting out, how would you compare your self-image with your mother's?

3. If you note distortions in hers and see distortions in yours, what are they?

## *Reading Touch Tool*

*The Kitchen God's Wife*, by Amy Tan, tells a story of a complex mother-daughter bond. If you read the book, either along with *My Mother, My Mirror*, separately, or in a book group, you may find that the following questions help you identify aspects of thought link 1 to apply to your own relationship with your mother.

### *The Kitchen God's Wife*, by Amy Tan

+ What in Winnie Louie's past might have caused her to be unattuned to Pearl's needs?

+ What aspect of Winnie Louie's distorted self-image was passed on to Pearl?

+ What parallels do you see between Pearl's relationship with her mother and its effect on her self-image, and your relationship with your mother and its effect on your self-image?

+ Freewrite when answering the last question: for example, "self-doubt Winnie louie self-doubt pearl mom felt dump wasn't I feel dumpy not really."

# thought link 2: mommy, I was afraid I'd hurt you

*Suddenly I had never loved anyone so or hated anyone so. But to say hate—what did I mean by that?...I couldn't wish my mother dead. If my mother died, what would become of me?*

— Jamaica Kincaid, *Annie John*

When a woman in therapy speaks, I try to put myself into her shoes. When I manage to achieve this, I often feel something powerful within me, so that our emotions, our reveries, even our fantasies at times intertwine. My senses are primed, my thoughts sparked, to tune in to what she's feeling. Sometimes she speaks through the action of holding her keys, stroking a pillow, folding her hands, straightening her posture, cracking a knuckle, smoothing her hair, turning a button. Other times there's one exquisite moment when her words lead me to draw meaning out of memory, life out of emptiness, and direction out of searching, all at once. That experience brings me to a place I haven't been—a mental space I haven't known or a past I haven't recalled.

Corinne began one such session by saying that her mother, Trudy, had put herself down and had seen her grandmother as existing on some lofty plane. "Whenever she spoke about Grandma Irene, my mother's eyes seemed to focus on some distant point, as if her relationship with her were in some private place. She'd say, 'Oh, when Grandma did something, she did it right. She was the perfect craftswoman. I never had the patience or the talent to do what she did. She'd take shells from the beach and arrange them in evenly distributed patterns, sizes, shadings, and shapes to make beautiful lamp bases admired by anyone who saw them. And she was the perfect gardener. Her flowers' colors created a perfect palette, her plantings around them were just the right height to serve as backdrops, and her vegetables grew big enough to win a prize at the country fair.'"

# how did your mother, as a child, view your grandmother?

After the session I began thinking about what Corinne had said. It brought up thoughts of my mother's view of my grandmother, and of how she often put her on a pedestal, just as it seemed that Corinne's mother had done with *her* own mother. For me, my grandmother was real and someone I could touch. But I think that, for my mother, she inhabited a more ethereal space.

When my mother talked about my grandmother, she often had that same far-off look that Corinne saw in her mother's eyes when she talked about *her* mother—as if what she was saying came from some kingdom of truth. My grandmother's knitting, cooking, intelligence—most things about her—seemed as good as they could possibly be. But my mother also would say, with compassion in her voice and a slight shake of her head, "Grandma worked so hard."

Those words made me curious about how my mother might have felt as a younger child living in a tenement in lower Manhattan. Though she moved away later on in her childhood, many of the threads of that experience emerged in the texture of our relationship. I visited the Tenement Museum in lower Manhattan and later wrote a narrative in my mother's voice, based on some real details she'd provided me with, along with elements from my own imagination. It's as if she were filling me in about my grandmother's "hard work" from her child's perspective.

*I think I was about five, waiting for a bath, when I first noticed how your grandma looked, hauling that heavy metal tub she'd fill with water to give me a bath. Her face was scrunched up and she'd groan—achh—making the same sound I guess I make sometimes when I'm tired. The basin's corners would hit the walls as she took it from the back room to the kitchen.*

*Grandma would always twist her hands together after setting down her load. I could see how the tub's rim had made red lines in her palms.*

*Then she lifted the heavy kettle to heat the water on the stove. The steam rose up as it filled the basin. When I got in, the water sloshed heavily from one side to the other and some of it spilled over the sides, making tiny puddles on the cracked checkerboard tile floor. The black and white of the tiles had blended into a shade of gray in the most worn parts. As she bent down, a few strands of hair would loosen from her bun held together with hair pins and form a soft frame for the sides of her face. I recall the message of strain her gray eyes conveyed— although I wouldn't have had a name for it then. But I knew she loved me by the way she looked at me and tried to keep the shampoo out of my eyes.*

*And I remember what shopping days on Saturdays were like for her. She'd start out the morning doing the laundry with the washboard, in the same tub she bathed me in. After she'd hung the clothes outside to dry on the line connected to the wall of the neighboring apartment house, she'd take me with her to shop at the pushcarts in the crowded streets—Delancey, Grand, Hester, Rivington. So many peddlers yelling at once, you couldn't hear what any one of them was calling out. Fabric, yarn, thread, tools, nails, kitchen stuff piled high, fruit, nuts, vegetables, and cheeses sat in colorful neat rows. Men were selling half-sour pickles from barrels on Essex Street, one for a penny. When we came home, sometimes I'd pick out the spices for her to put in our dinner that night. At the end of those days, while reading the newspaper she'd fall asleep with her glasses sliding down her nose, always stopping at the same point above the bridge.*

My writing made me realize how my mother's role as the entertainer, livening things up on a Sunday after a long week, would have made her feel valued by my grandmother. But she also might have had some hidden resentment that other things she was good at weren't noticed enough—like her ability to draw, pointed out by her teachers. If she felt any irritation with my grandmother, I would never know it. Maybe she countered her anger by feeling sorry for her sometimes, and idealizing her at others. But when she became a mother and still had some lingering need for special attention, who else but her only daughter would provide it?

# self-sacrificing or idealized mother

That idea brought me back to Corinne, whose mother, Trudy, idealized *her* mother, Irene, and it made me ponder how the carnival-mirror heirloom was passed on to Corinne. Trudy, Corinne's mother, had enrolled her in many enriching after-school activities as a kid—extracurricular this, intramural that—in an effort to make her into the perfect all-around girl. Trudy unwittingly wanted Corinne to be more like Irene. However, Corinne had lots of trouble feeling resentment toward Trudy over this. Instead, she put her mother on a pedestal, just as Trudy had done with Irene—except that in Corinne's case, the idealizing involved seeing her mother as a self-sacrificer who had tried her best to be a good mother, despite her own childhood difficulties.

Through the years, Corinne had gained a distorted view of herself as "bad" if she showed resentment toward Trudy. And, since Corinne could never show defiance, when she grew up to be a mother of two girls, she lived through their defiant behavior with others. Unknowingly, she gave them a covert message that they could—and, at times, should—act rebellious toward authority figures, since she could never do anything of the sort without feeling her childhood mother's rejection.

If one of her daughters talked back to a teacher in class, Corinne would take her daughter's side, saying the schoolwork was too easy and therefore her daughter was bored. At the same time, just as Trudy had done with Corinne, Corinne would get upset when her daughters showed defiance toward *her.* With Corinne's daughters, the carnival-mirror legacy extended into the fourth female generation. With each new mother-daughter pair, the daughter had to hold back negative feelings toward her mother, which kept the boomerang cycle going, while they were thwarted in outside relationships where they acted out the anger.

Below, we'll first discuss what makes it so difficult for women to allow themselves negative feelings toward their mothers, and what shields they build to avoid those feelings. The section following that shows how to use thought link 2 to face and work through those emotions—anger, resentment, ambivalence, hostility, annoyance, rage, animosity, frustration, or irritation—so they don't fester and control you. And in the last section we will look at a work of fiction to illustrate how this thought link can help you deal with those kinds of feelings toward your mother.

Note: Not all daughters hold back their negative emotions toward their mothers. Some show those emotions, but they do so in the wrong way and then have a hard time dealing with them constructively. Also, the degree of negativity varies greatly with each daughter, and often she feels a lot of love for her mother. The focus here is on the difficult feelings that lie hidden within her, however intense or mild: when we don't own and face discomforting emotions toward our childhood mothers, they fester and appear in some way that impedes us.

# mommy, I was afraid I'd hurt you

*Just get over it.* That's been Western culture's timeless remedy for uncomfortable feelings. As Bruno Bettleheim (1976) writes in *The Uses of Enchantment*, many modern fairy tales encourage children to deny their deepest fears about and most frightening wishes toward their parents. In contrast, the old Grimms' tales help them face those bad feelings. The witch represents the side of the mother that makes the daughter angry or scared. She casts spells from which the main character eventually frees herself (sometimes with help from others). By connecting with Cinderella, Snow White, or Sleeping Beauty, little girls can deal with bad feelings toward their mothers and see that they and their mothers can survive. And when the witch's negative influences are countered by a fairy godmother's positive ones, little girls feel that their mothers will live on too—even if they do have anger toward them. But sometimes one tiny window that opens onto anger toward the mother can create the fear that we'll go full steam into dangerous, perhaps destructive, territory.

As adults we need to experience what Grimms' fairy tales taught us as children: that we can own resentment toward our childhood mothers and also preserve the best parts of our relationship with them. Further, if we don't feel the anger, it's hard for many of us to feel the love also. Let's now look at those issues as they're influenced by our culture.

## Our Culture Denies Women's Anger

When the idea of anger toward the mother comes up during treatment, many women say, "Me, peeved at my mother? What do you mean?" They might just try to change the subject or defend their mothers, whether they're living or have died, as if I'm blaming them for something. These daughters will go on, saying things like this: "How can I blame her for anything? What could beating up on myself have to do with *her*?" "My mom was a good mom. She tried her best when my dad was drinking to keep the family together." They also think of their present relationships with their mothers and say, "No way. We don't fight. We have a great relationship. We're best friends."

Where does all this denial of anger come from? First, there's Western society's general view, which is quietly, but pervasively, imprinted on each of us: anger in a woman is unacceptable. It makes her too aggressive, assertive, destructive, and bitchy. And anger at our mother is particularly frowned upon.

But the fact is, that because our mothers have the confusing, complex job of caring for us and guiding us as we go from children to young adults, they're bound to make mistakes along the way, which usually creates resentment within us without our knowing it. Yet our need to ensure our survival may cause us to deny our negative feelings toward them.

## Another Reason We May Bury Anger: Survival

Since we feel overly powerful as small children because we think in magical ways, we fear we might harm our mothers with our anger. So, as we discussed regarding the boomerang cycle, we turn that anger against ourselves as a kind of self-sacrifice in order to keep our mothers whole and able to function for us. Further, we bury those feelings, and unbeknownst to us, they percolate within us into adulthood.

Some daughters squelch these negative emotions by putting their childhood mothers on pedestals; we'll call them "pedestal mothers." And others might pity their mothers, whom they see as too fragile to withstand the daughters' anger, possibly because the mothers have been treated as fragile by other family members. As a result, the mothers' view of themselves as vulnerable gets strengthened; let's call them "sad-sack mothers."

## Pedestal Mother or Sad-Sack Mother?

The following women's narratives show varied versions of the pedestal mother or sad-sack mother. But regardless of which perception these women had of their mothers when they entered therapy, the common thread among them was fear of hurting them with their hidden hostility.

*I weighed nine pounds at birth. My mother had hoped for a
petite baby because she hated her big-boned body. (Actually,
I was told by my aunt and uncle that she was attractive as a
young woman, but it seems as if she just couldn't see herself
that way.) My sister, who felt like being mean to me one day,
told me that my mother compared me to smaller infants in the
maternity ward whom she felt must have been chosen for bath
demonstrations because they were cute.*

## Lilly's pedestal mother

During Lilly's growing up, her mother picked on her a lot instead of
picking on herself. She'd say things like "That extra scoop of ice cream
will go straight from the spoon to your waist," and "Why are you wearing
a belt when it exaggerates your hips?" Lilly couldn't show anger at her
mother, because she feared her mother would be damaged. So, to ward
off harming her mother with her feelings, she unconsciously put her on
a pedestal. Her mother's cool manner increased Lilly's idealization of
her.

Lilly was in a boomerang cycle. She unconsciously turned resentment toward her mother against herself. Like her mother, she viewed
her body as unattractive (although she really was attractive). And she'd
date guys who would emotionally abuse her as her mother had done. She
couldn't tell them to get lost, because of another self-image distortion:
she didn't view herself as worthy of better treatment.

Her self-image issues shackled her in various ways. During a sexual
crisis in her marriage, Lilly couldn't tell her husband about her frustration with his diminished desire. Instead she assumed he was turned off
sexually because of her physical defects, and she widened the distance
between them. And, without knowing it, Lilly often viewed other adults
who irritated her as if they were her mother—she couldn't express negative feelings toward them for fear they'd reject her.

In contrast with Lilly, Candace had a view of her mother at the
opposite end of the spectrum.

*My mother always gave me a weird message about success. On
the surface, I think she wanted me to surpass her by achieving
in areas where she couldn't go as a young woman. She'd say to
me when I doubted myself as a child, "Oh, come on, you can do*

137

*it." But when I did achieve a goal, like making the honor roll or getting on the soccer team, and I'd come home all excited with the news, she'd act blasé or even down at times.*

## Candace's sad-sack mother

We discovered in therapy that, although Candace's mother, Maureen, consciously wanted her to succeed, on a deeper level her daughter's successes threatened her because she'd never had them herself. Candace had picked up the unconscious cues through Maureen's nonverbal language. She came to therapy because whenever she gained entry to a high-level job position, she couldn't act assertively with certain women she supervised. We discovered that those "certain women" reminded her of her mother, and her distorted view of herself as harmful put the brakes on her forward motion.

*I felt ashamed of my boozing mother as a kid and kept a distance from her in my teens. When I got married, I moved far away from her, so I didn't have to feel sorry for her and guilty about my feelings. When I became pregnant, I felt tense a lot, and that's when I thought I needed therapy.*

## Cecille's sad-sack mother

Cecille discovered that she viewed herself as bad and believed she didn't deserve to enjoy motherhood because of her angry feelings toward what she called her "pathetic" mother. Though Cecille had moved far away geographically, she hadn't moved anywhere emotionally. She had to deal with her negative emotions toward her mother and forgive herself in order to enjoy her pregnancy.

In the next section we'll see how thought link 2 can help you face the fear of negative feelings toward your childhood mother, so you can begin to shift from the carnival mirror to the truer mirror.

# facing fear of anger through thought link 2

*My mother went hot and cold all the time. One moment she'd be in an up mood, and at another she'd have this face that went with that phrase, "If looks could kill." I always assumed it was*

*about me, something I did, something I said. I spent half my*
*childhood trying to figure out what to do to make her happy.*

It was snowing one day when Lindsay said the above words in her session. Because ice had settled on the path to my consulting room. I'd thrown sand on it earlier and thought that that would make it safe enough to walk on. I hadn't gone out to check on the path, because I'd been working steadily all morning. Lindsey sat in the waiting room with her coat on, and she then entered the consulting room looking at me shyly, muttering short sentences interrupted by long silences. She seemed to have built a barricade around herself.

When I asked if she felt uncomfortable about something, she said it was hard for her to talk about it because she didn't want to upset me. When I encouraged her to express her feelings, she blurted out that I must not care about her, because if I did I would've made the path safer. I told her I was glad she had told me about the path, and I then asked her what had made telling me about her anger seem so calamitous. She responded that that's how things were with her mother and that she'd expected me to react as her mother had done whenever she blew off steam.

## But Don't Negative Feelings Hurt Mom?

From there she talked about how, as a child, she had often been afraid of hurting her mother by upsetting her with anything unpleasant. She recalled a memory, emblazoned in her mind, of her two pet parakeets, which her parents had given her. Some months after she'd received them, she came home from school to find them gone. Her mother said they had both gotten sick and had to be taken away. Even at the age of eight, she had a sense that her mother had made up the story. She felt angry that she hadn't even had a chance to say good-bye to her pets. When she started to cry, her mother began crying in turn, saying "What do you want from me?" Lindsey felt bad about hurting her, an echo of her emotions in past interactions with her mother.

## Uncover Anger, Let It Be, and Plumb Its Depths

By noting when she got upset in a session and didn't know why, Lindsey began exploring her feelings. She embarked on the three phases

**139**

of thought link 2: uncovering the anger, letting it be, and plumbing its depths. She first *uncovered* fear of resentment toward me that she later connected to a fear of having the same feeling toward her childhood mother. With this new awareness, she learned to *let the anger be* by using mindfulness in not judging herself for having it, and not acting on it. Finally, she began to *plumb the anger*, making connections between childhood moments and the present time, and seeing how they appeared in her relationship with me. The more in touch she got with those feelings, the more she could see her distorted view of herself as bad for just having anger. As we dealt with this issue over time, Lindsey's self-image began to shift to a truer one: she could see herself as able to express negative feelings toward others and still feel likable to them.

In the next section we'll look at a novel to help us imagine how it might be difficult for a daughter in her teens to deal with resentment toward her mother, and how she might use thought link 2 later on to reshape the relationship with her.

# thought link 2 in fiction

In Betty Smith's (1943) *A Tree Grows in Brooklyn,* set in the early 1900s, the mother, Katie, experiences hardship as the financially deprived wife of an alcoholic. Her problems make what she asks of her daughter, Francie, seem more appropriate than they might be considered otherwise. And the palpable love between mother and daughter adds to that sense.

As the story continues, Katie is expecting a third child after her husband has died. In reading her comments to her daughter, we should note that the culture of the time accepted a double standard for men and women, which is obvious in the following section (254).

> 'Francie, I expect the baby any day now and I'd feel better if you were never very far away from me...I can't count on Neeley, because a boy's no use at a time like this.'
>
> 'I won't ever go away from you, Mama,' [Francie] said.
>
> Maybe, thought Francie, she doesn't love me as much as she loves Neeley. But she needs me more than she needs him, and I guess being needed is almost as good as being loved. Maybe better.

Later, Katie tells Francie that because of the family's strained finances, Neeley, who is younger than Francie, will be the only child to enter high school in the fall—even though Francie's the one who is excited to go and Neeley is highly resistant to attending. Katie overlooks both children's feelings and says that, if Neeley is to become a doctor, Francie's earnings will have to be used for his schooling, and Francie will have to wait to go back to school.

'Why do you make him go when he doesn't want to,' cried Francie, 'and keep me out of school when I want to go so much?'

'Because if I don't make him, he'll never go back,' said Mama, 'where you, Francie, will fight and manage to get back somehow' (293).

Further on, Francie notices her mother's hand tremble while picking up the new baby.

'I shouldn't be so mean to her,' she thought.

'Don't be mad at me, Mama, because I fought you. You, yourself, taught me to fight for what I thought was right....'

'I know....You're like me that way....'

'And that's where the whole trouble is,' thought Francie. *'We're too much alike to understand each other, because we don't understand our own selves....*[my italics]'

'Then everything's all right now between us?' Katie asked with a smile.

'Of course.' Francie smiled back and kissed her mother's cheek.

But in their secret hearts, each knew that it wasn't all right and would never be...again (295).

If Francie were able to use thought link 2 to face her concealed anger toward Katie, she might be able to disprove that last statement in the quoted passage above. Once she were able to face her anger, she might better understand her mother and reshape the relationship.

# let's recap

In this chapter, we've explored what makes it so difficult for most women to allow themselves to have negative feelings toward their mothers. And we've looked at how women either idealize their mothers or keep them preserved as pathetic figures, in order to avoid anger or resentment toward them. We also discussed the three phases of thought link 2, which you can use to help you face your buried anger: *uncover the anger, let the anger be,* and *plumb the anger's depths.*

In the next chapter we'll explore the flip side: fear of facing love for them. Women may avoid owning love for their childhood mothers because expressing it might have made them feel too vulnerable while growing up.

## A Note to Daughters

I'm guessing that this chapter might've made you think, "Me, angry at Mom and blaming her? That's a scary thought. Besides, it's not true. I loved her, and she tried her best."

As you continue reading, keep in mind that we're not blaming your mother at all. It's likely that she meant well and did her best, but she still played a part in your inaccurate view of yourself. That's because *she* had a carnival-mirror self-image herself, inherited from her mother. So it's not about your living mother now. It's about the image of her in your mind. To heal and change the pattern, you must first just *have* the resentment without judging it or taking action on it. From there, you have more control over it and can decide whether you want to express it in some way or not at all. It's helpful to think of the anger as a ghost that haunts us until we look it straight in the eye. Then we see that it's not so scary.

# Questions for Reflection

1. Do you think that fear of hurting your childhood mother has made you hold yourself at a distance from your negative feelings toward her? Can you think of ways in which that thwarts you?

2. Can you think of ways your childhood mother gave you messages that made your resentment or irritation difficult to express?

3. Do you put her on a pedestal or make her a sad sack in order to ward off anger toward her?

## *Reading Touch Tool*

This chapter used *A Tree Grows in Brooklyn* to depict a daughter's struggle with anger toward the mother she deeply loves. If you read the book now or at another time, the following questions can help you see the influence of Katie on Francie, and the influence of your mother on you.

### *A Tree Grows in Brooklyn,* by Betty Smith

- What part shows that Francie struggled with her anger at Katie?

- In what ways did the anger work against her because she didn't face it openly?

- How would you imagine Francie using thought link 2 to help her face her anger at Katie and not let it weigh her down?

- Does Francie's experience remind you of your own negative feelings toward your mother that you haven't faced? How would you describe those feelings?

# CHAPTER 9

# thought link 3: mommy, I was afraid to love you

*In working through, from a Buddhist perspective the first step...is to learn to be with threatening emotions in a nonjudgmental way.*
— Mark Epstein, *Thoughts Without a Thinker*

Let's now look at how fear of anger and love can affect mother-daughter relationships in powerful ways.

## alternating between anger and love

Like many women, Kerry, Elana, Gloria, and Adele alternated between anger and love for their childhood mothers.

### Kerry

*It just seemed that so often you spoke to me through a screen that wouldn't let your real feelings through. I was afraid to love you, Mom. Remember the time you began writing a letter to Willie saying you couldn't attend his graduation, and I found it in a drawer of yours? You went anyway, but you arrived after the family photos. I figured it out much later on. You were ashamed of your body being seen in front of so many people. But instead of telling me how hard it was for you, you kept it to yourself. Why couldn't you have told me? I wanted to put my arms around you and dry your tears, but you were in the nursing home by the time I figured it out, and at that point you couldn't fully realize what I felt.*

## Elana

*When I looked in your nightstand after you died, Mom, I found all the letters I'd sent you from Amsterdam during my college semester abroad. All those years, and you never told me you'd saved them? I would have felt closer to you if you had. I guess, because Grandma couldn't show she cared, you did the same with me.*

## Gloria

*Mom, you were always on a diet, and you talked as if you and I had the same "ugly" problem. You'd always say that Donna had inherited her body from Dad's side of the family—slim, long legs, you know. I was afraid to let you know more about me because you'd always go back to our issue. I've been angry at you for so long because you did this to me. It wasn't until you were close to death that I discovered that you always played second fiddle to your younger sister, whom all the guys—a lot of them your peers—asked out before you. I felt so bad for you. But it was too late for me to get closer to you when I learned this; Aunt Bonnie only told me after you'd had the stroke. What a waste. All those years, I kept a distance for fear you'd get at me with our issue.*

## Adele

*I have to act as if I'm good at everything I do, because my mother put me on a pedestal. I could never let her know about my weaknesses, my self-doubts, my feeling at times that I was a fraud. If only she had told me the reason for putting a*

145

*halo on me:* she *had so many self-doubts because her parents had put her down so much. So she needed to live through my "perfection." She didn't let me love her, because I never felt I could be open with her. So I carried resentment with me.*

What appeared as anger in these women covered a deeper love for their mothers, and at times, vice versa. Some of us consistently use one emotion to hide the other. The neighbor who sounds sugary when describing her mother might be keeping a deeper anger under wraps; that's why she may get judgmental if you say something negative about your mother: it sparks her own ire that she's afraid to face. And your friend who seems forever in a battle with her mother may be keeping a deeper love stored away, because she felt rejected when she openly showed it as a child. That's why she may change the subject when you get a little gushy about your mother. She longs for those warm feelings herself, or she avoids close relationships with women for fear she'll get hurt, as she did at times with her mother.

In the section below, we'll explore why many of us have trouble feeling love for our childhood mothers. Next, we'll discuss how we avoid the emotion. And in the last part of the chapter we'll illustrate how to use thought link 3 to uncover the love that we've buried and how to experience its depths. That process frees us because when we no longer have to camouflage our primal love for our mothers, we can use it as part of a healthy expression of ourselves.

# mommy, I was afraid to love you

I picked up the phone and heard Meryl's voice message: "I can't come in today, because I can't get a sitter." Perhaps she couldn't get a sitter for her children, but she began calling for one at the last minute. We learned at the next session that part of the reason for her canceling the previous one was my recent summer vacation: she felt I had abandoned her. Just before I left, Meryl was beginning to break down the barrier that kept her from getting close to me because closeness meant vulnerability. As she put it, she had a shield in front of her when she started treatment, and now she was putting chiffon curtains in its place.

In one session before I left for my trip, she was showing that closeness in subtle ways. She said that, after being angry at her kids and feeling guilty about it one day, she had recalled my saying that she could forgive herself when she made a mistake. Because her background hadn't given her enough emotional tools for handling her three children when they were demanding, thinking about having compassion for herself made her feel relieved. She also said that she thought she would miss our sessions. That was a big leap for Meryl, who for six months couldn't say that the therapy or I mattered much.

I guessed that my taking a nearly two-month break would send her back to retreating at least partially behind the shield. My hunch seemed right when she canceled her session on the day we were to meet after I returned. Meryl's relationship with her childhood mother had set the foundation for her to experience my vacation as a painful rejection.

## Distance Leads to Daughter's Fear of Love

When Meryl was eight, her younger brother was injured by a biker speeding along a sidewalk. Her mother, Lou, felt guilty for not paying more attention to him; the accident had happened when she'd turned her head to respond to something Meryl had said. Secretly, Lou also blamed her daughter for what had happened. From that point on, Lou withdrew from her daughter, who didn't understand the change. Before the accident, Lou had seemed patient and cheerful while helping her comb her hair or get ready for bed, and after it she had a brusque and moody way about her. Before, Lou had cooked Meryl's favorite meals, but afterward, dinners didn't seem special.

When daughters like Meryl experience their childhood mothers as distant, withdrawing, or rejecting, showing them love makes them feel vulnerable. So they construct a bulwark of anger and defiance, they engage in rebel modeling (as discussed in chapter 1), or they distance themselves from their mothers in turn. All of these responses lead them to use the same bulwark with others in adulthood, which obviously creates intimacy problems.

So, like Meryl, daughters afraid to face love for their childhood mothers will create a shield of anger against it.

## The Shield of Anger Helps Deny Love for Mother

As an adult in therapy, Meryl looked back at this time in her childhood and recognized the effect that Lou's change had had on her. Deep inside, Meryl felt she'd lost the mother she'd had before the accident, the mother who had tended to her needs easily, comforted her naturally, and enjoyed her presence consistently.

Once Meryl began constructing the shield to protect herself from her mother's distancing, she would balk when Lou tried to guide her, such as when helping her select clothes, teaching her skiing, or suggesting sources for homework research. And she developed an angry edge as she grew older. By her teens she was acting defiant and cold with Lou. In therapy, Meryl noted that her self-image distortion came from viewing herself as rotten inside because she'd acted this way with Lou in the past.

## Shield of Anger Causes Skewed Self-Image

After I returned from vacation, it took months for Meryl to get back to the hurt little girl inside, the little girl who viewed herself as bad, and the little girl who once had an open love for her mother. I stayed with Meryl and didn't withdraw when she tried to distance me with sarcasm in her tone, lateness, or cancellations (it took a lot of believing in myself to see her ways as protection against hurt). Eventually, she changed her self-image from rotten to basically good, but she remained a bit self-protective. Gradually her fear of getting hurt abated. She could say things with a flavor of appreciation: "You know, I like that stuff you said last week. It really worked with my supervisor at work," and "I can feel myself changing here. I don't know what you're doing, but I think it's working."

Many women like Meryl, who once knew their childhood mothers' love and lost it, bury the yearning for it in their unconscious while acting angry and pretending to themselves that they don't need it. These are women who often appear self-sufficient. But their self-image suffers from distortions. They view themselves as bad, bad because they were once rejected and bad because of their negative feelings toward their mothers. In turn, they might direct the anger inward, or soothe themselves through overeating, drinking, or other addictions.

When women build an angry exterior because of fear of rejection by their childhood mothers, they often recognize in therapy how the pattern started when the carnival mirror was passed on to them. Lou's guilt about her son's accident made her blame Meryl for what happened and withdraw from her, which in turn made Meryl view herself as rotten. We can see how, unwittingly, a mother passes her distorted self-image on to her daughter, which leads to her daughter's fear of love.

In Meryl's case the change in her mother was marked, which created in Meryl a sense of grieving over the loss of the way things used to be. In other situations, the issue might be the daughter's lack of a warm response from her mother earlier on. In either case, the main focus here is that in the earliest time of life, we all are primed to embrace our mothers with open arms, a wide smile, and an innocent exuberance. It is this primal layer of love that we need to touch if we're to become able to love others in an open way. And thought link 3 can help you get there.

# facing fear of love through thought link 3

In *O* Magazine, P. Hunter (May, 2007) writes about her young-adult experience with her mother, who intruded in her dating life, flirted with her potential suitors, and acted inappropriately with her female friends. Later, as a married woman and mother herself, the author went through two phases with her mother. First, she let her get to her, and second, she tried to distance herself geographically in order to distance herself emotionally.

However, she realized that neither extreme worked, because she found herself acting with her young daughter as her mother had acted with *her*: having a low tolerance for crying, and snapping and "screaming like a madwoman" when her daughter was defiant. She said, "I saw that separating myself from my mother wasn't enough. I needed to try to understand her. Her own mother, I recalled, had been an alcoholic...I saw that she must suffer from the same shaky sense of self I had" (286). From that place of realization, the author could find a balance between intensity and distance with her mother. As an added perk, her daughter gained a relationship with her grandmother.

The author was able to find a tie between herself and her mother, and gain tolerance of her difficult ways. She accomplished this by exploring her mother's self-image and seeing how it resembled her own, and by essentially following the first phase of thought link 3 (obviously without knowing it): she *uncovered her fear of love* by looking beneath the surface of her relationship with her mother. If she were to use the other phases of thought link 3, she might take that growth further and use mindfulness—*letting the love be*—to look at it nonjudgmentally, without taking action. And, later she could *plumb the depths of love*. She could perhaps get in touch with some earlier warmth in the relationship that had gotten lost along the way.

## Sometimes "Connection" Is More Apt Than Love

It's easy to see why P. Hunter's open show of love to her mother would have made her feel vulnerable. For women like her, sometimes the word "connection" is a better description than "love." As Christine Ann Lawson (2000) writes in *Understanding the Borderline Mother*, when a mother is too disturbed, too unpredictable, too self-absorbed, or too neglectful, the daughter's defense against hurt might be healthy. These daughters need to find ways to connect with their mothers without acting as their salvation, without rewarding their frightening ways, without being under their control, and without becoming their victims.

Regardless of how hurt a daughter might feel by her childhood mother's treatment of her, it's important that she face the fear of love in adulthood, so that the armor she constructed against vulnerability doesn't deny her a free sense of self.

# let's recap

In this chapter we discussed why many of us have trouble feeling a deeper love for our childhood mothers because anger covers over it, how we avoid feeling it, and how to use thought link 3 to find and touch the love that anger conceals.

The next chapter will explore women's difficulty in facing buried sadness regarding their childhood mothers. We'll discuss what makes the sadness hard to confront, what women use to avoid it, and how to apply thought link 4 to deal with it. In the process, you can begin to view yourself more accurately and loosen the shackles that deny you fulfillment.

## A Note to Daughters

If you're thinking that you'll never be able to rid yourself of anger toward your mother to find more love for her, give yourself a chance to journey further through the five thought links. It's a one-step-at-a-time process, and getting to that buried love takes time.

# Questions for Reflection

1. If you think that you've feared facing love for your child-hood mother and you've built a shield of anger, how do you show it? Through nitpicking, biting humor, defiance, indifference, intolerance, or something else?

2. Can you think of ways your childhood mother made you stop trying to get close to her?

3. What touch tools could you use to uncover love for your childhood mother? Could you read letters or journals she wrote, or look at photos of her as a child?

4. What touch tools could you use to plumb that feeling of love? Could you listen to music she loved, look at memorabilia of yours that she saved from your childhood, or write in your journal?

## *Reading Touch Tool*

In *Annie John* and *Lucy*, Jamaica Kincaid reveals how love and anger intertwine in the relationships that the main characters have with their mothers. If you read the books, you can use the following questions to spark thoughts about those issues between you and your own mother.

### *Annie John,* by Jamaica Kincaid

- What are some ways that Annie describes her little-girl love for her mother?

- What separation issues at puberty shaped her struggle with love for her mother?

### *Lucy,* by Jamaica Kincaid

- What quotes show Lucy's use of anger to block out love for her mother?

- How does Lucy describe her awareness that part of her *is* her mother and geographical distance doesn't deny that?

# thought link 4: mommy, I was afraid to face what you never were

*The refusal to mourn the disappointments and losses of childhood, to bury them once and for all, condemns us to live in their shadows.*

— Sheldon B. Kopp, *The Refusal to Mourn*

*I had two dreams about my mother and me last night. In the first I'm a little girl, and it's all in this surreal, golden kind of light. We're at the kitchen table after school. I'm ten, having my snack of milk and a sugar doughnut, pressing my fingers onto the sugar that falls on the table and then licking it off, one finger at a time. She's dipping a cruller into her coffee and then eating it soaked at one end, as she used to do. Next, she's sitting at her dressing table with the pink fleur-de-lis painted on, getting ready for bed. She's taking out her barrettes, letting her hair dangle on her shoulders. But it's wavy, golden hair, like the princesses have in fairy tales, not brown as hers was. Then I'm opening a lacquered box and unfolding tissue paper inside to find the braids I had asked her to cut off when I turned ten. They're neatly tied with shiny red ribbons.*

*I woke up for a moment, a little scared. I don't know—I had the feeling in the dream that they were not really braids, but some other part of me I'd lose for good. Then I went back to sleep and had another dream. This one starts out with my getting ready for my friend's sweet-sixteen party. There's a gloomy light and it's weird. Trees are inside the house, with rustling leaves and creaking branches, like before a thunderstorm. I'm alone, running from room to room, searching for my mom, and can't find her. Suddenly she comes out of the attic with wild hair, sort of like Mr. Rochester's wife in* Jane Eyre *(I just finished it the other night), and I woke up yelling "Ma,"* my husband said.

## loving mother or rejecting mother?

When Rachel entered treatment as a thirty-two-year-old, she was lonely and didn't realize that a lot of her problems stemmed from her carnival-mirror self-image. When friends let her down, she didn't realize she'd pushed them away: when they didn't offer unconditional love she'd get sulky and uptight with them.

During therapy Rachel discovered that she had glorified her life before age sixteen, just as her dreams above show. However, her mother, Sasha, had been there for her, to a large extent, in those early years, which was unlike her behavior after Rachel turned sixteen.

## lovable daughter or rejectable daughter?

During Rachel's earlier childhood, despite Sasha's sudden outbursts and anxiety, she could be loving and enjoyed being with her daughter when she was calmer. So, as a little girl, Rachel formed a split self-image—one side lovable and the other rejectable, based on her mother's moods. She said she had "rejectable DNA" that must have set her mother off at those times. Sasha's mother, Emelia, had also influenced the same split self-image: lovable when she cheered her mother up and rejectable when she didn't. So mother and daughter viewed themselves in a distorted way. In contrast, a truer self-image lets a daughter see her lovability, whether she can cheer her mother up or not.

Around the time that Rachel turned sixteen, her older sister went off to college and Sasha went into menopause. Sasha got more anxious than before, and her anxiety veiled a depression: what used to be swings from uptightness to calmness became swings from uptightness to gloominess. Rachel felt put off but also sensed even more pressure to cheer her mother up. She began to distance herself from her to avoid guilt feelings. Unknowingly she sought out girlfriends who she felt would make up for her loss by acting like the better mother of her childhood; she hoped that they would not make her feel that she had to play the role of the booster club to win their affection. On a deeper level she held onto the fantasy of an ideal mother who would give her the no-holds-barred love that her actual mother never could provide.

Let's read a narrative that Rachel wrote in Sasha's voice, a piece that she used as a touch tool to understand why Sasha related differently to her after she turned sixteen.

> When Rachel was born, I was thrilled. She was so cute. I still have the ribbon the nurse put in her hair and the tiny pink and white bracelet she put on her wrist. When she got older, I loved taking her to a show in the city during summer and having lunch together in the park. But I think I asked too much of her, because I made her the one to ease my nerves. How could I have done that? That's what my mother did to me, and I hated it. When she turned sixteen and I went downhill, I put even more pressure on her to make me happy, and we got distant. My older daughter, Marion, went to college and I began menopause, with hot flashes and mood swings. I felt wired and down at the same time, and I think Rachel got the brunt of it. I have a lot of regrets about that. I wish I could do her teens over.

The writing helped Rachel get into Sasha's shoes and realize that her change toward Rachel had more to do with her own past relationship with Emelia than it did with Rachel.

## Sadness Often Lies Buried Beneath Anger and Love

In order to avoid feeling the sadness about losing the connection with her mother, Rachel buried it. In the previous chapters we discussed two other emotions that women avoid facing: anger toward their mothers and love for their mothers, built up from years past. We also discussed the fact that at times the daughter's negativity conceals love for her mother and at other times her display of love conceals anger. And, in my experience, as hard as it is for women to face the anger or love toward their mothers, sadness about what they lost or never got from the mother is often even more difficult to face. So this kind of sadness is often more deeply buried than the other two emotions.

I believe that one of the reasons sadness about loss is so difficult to express comes from our culture's pooh-poohing of weakness; America's early history put a high value on rugged individualism. The familiar phrase, "Cry and you cry alone," is ingrained in our society, as is the women's movement credo: "I am woman; I am strong." "Toughness" lends a sense of control we usually don't have, not just over others but also over ourselves.

This chapter begins by exploring what makes it so hard for women to face sadness over what they never had with their childhood mothers. Next, we'll discuss how either putting your mother on a pedestal or seeing her as a sad-sack mother is one way that helps you to avoid feeling sadness about that loss. Then we'll consider children's mourning for a mother who has died, the difference between actual and emotional loss of the mother, and how immigration often represents a fusion of actual and emotional loss. Finally, we'll explore how to use thought link 4 to face sadness related to your childhood mother, in order to shift your view from the carnival mirror to the truer mirror.

# mommy, I was afraid to face what you never were

Early in treatment Rachel explored how to face her sadness about the change in her mother when she turned sixteen. Not confronting it was causing her to hold onto the hope for a perfect mother and view friends in unrealistic ways that could only lead to disappointment. One day, during a session, she was working on important issues and suddenly felt upset. Unfortunately, it was time to end the session, and I gently told her we had to stop. Ordinarily I would have given her a few more moments, but that day I had an urgent appointment to get to, so instead I offered her an extra session the next day. She walked out of the room with plodding steps and a blank look on her face. It didn't surprise me that my way of stopping had probably hurt Rachel's feelings, because to her it meant that she wasn't as important as my next appointment.

## Rachel's Shift to a Truer Self-Image

When she came to the next session, she said that if I really cared for her, I would've made time for her right then at the end of the last session, regardless of what I had to do afterward. She didn't believe I had an appointment that was so urgent. She felt I must've seen her as rejectable, a sign of her inaccurate self-image. I said that I didn't feel that way at all, but I knew I couldn't make her believe that just by saying it. I thought we should look at what made her seem to suddenly latch on to that idea, when just days before she had felt that I cared about her in a way that no one else in her life had.

Looking at her many similar interactions with other women allowed Rachel to see how she often tried to gain an ideal mother in them and then pushed them away when they didn't live up to her expectations. After struggling in therapy with many moments of anger toward, and love for, her childhood mother, Rachel began to cry tears of sadness and have dreams of loss. And through her exploration of Sasha's self-image as it was when she raised her, Rachel recognized that Sasha had passed on the carnival mirror just as it had been passed on by Emelia to *her*. With that awareness, Rachel could then see herself more accurately; she could free herself from the need to have other people's approval in order to feel valued.

In turn, her expectations of friends became more balanced. No longer holding on to the fantasy of an all-good mother, Rachel slowly realized that Sasha loved her as best she could, which was *never* "perfectly." And she realized that, since Sasha had passed the carnival mirror on to Rachel, she gained the same self-image distortion: both mother and daughter felt lovable when they could bring their mothers happiness, and unlovable when they couldn't. When Rachel took note of her unconscious desire for *me* to be the ideal mother for her, even though I couldn't be, she began to feel sadness over how she'd been let down by Sasha.

Just as many women who fear facing anger or love toward their childhood mothers use the pedestal mother image or sad-sack mother image to avoid the anger or love, many who fear facing sadness about what they didn't have in childhood use similar images to avoid that emotion.

## Pedestal Mother or Sad-Sack Mother

*When I joined a support group for women with breast cancer, a woman, Jane, who'd had the same type as I had, said, "You're*

*lucky your mother died, so you don't have to go through telling*
*her about your illness. It was so hard to tell my mother and see*
*the fear in her eyes. But she was able to hug me and say she'd*
*be with me through whatever I'd have to endure." I felt envious*
*of Jane. I was embarrassed to tell her that when my mother*
*was alive, I couldn't have told her anything about my ordeal,*
*because it would've become her ordeal. I was actually relieved*
*that she'd died, because I would've had to hide the truth from*
*her if she were alive.*

## pedestal mother counters sadness

Ellie, a fifty-two-year-old woman speaking above, was told that her cancer had been detected at a very early stage. Of course, the time leading up to the surgery was scary for her. Ellie's mother, who'd died shortly before her daughter got her initial diagnosis, had never been able to nurture her daughter well in times of stress. She saw herself as fragile and felt she needed soothing from her daughter when her daughter needed soothing from *her.*

Ellie didn't consciously feel the loss of her actual mother in the way that Jane did, because her mother had too many problems to show her love freely. In therapy, Ellie came to see that she'd clung to an image of an all-good mother. And, like the women we've discussed who avoid anger or love through holding on to perfect-mother images, Ellie never had to feel the depth of her sadness regarding what she wished for from her actual mother, because the pedestal mother image is powerful and doesn't allow feelings about the actual mother to intrude—unless we face it head on through use of thought link 4, described in this chapter. Ellie unwittingly pinned her hopes on receiving that ideal-mother type of love from her husband. Indeed, after marriage she never gave up the hope that her husband would make her life better, rather than seeing the strength within herself to do that. Not surprisingly, that tendency caused ongoing marital problems.

## sad-sack mother image counters sadness

As happens with the fear of facing anger toward or love for our mother, when we fear facing sadness related to her, we often set up the opposite of an ideal image of her: a pathetic mother. If in our minds we make her a "sad sack," then we can't feel upset about our own loss, because on some level, we're caring about hers.

### sad-sack mother helps deny anger related to sadness

Also, the guilt that goes along with a sad-sack mother image keeps us from feeling angry toward our mothers. So our sad-sack mother creation provides a way to keep two unpleasant emotions buried: (1) sadness about loss and (2) anger toward our childhood mothers for contributing to it.

Emily's story helps illustrate this concept. Her mother had been orphaned at a young age and lived in foster homes through her teens. Though she was stronger than she appeared and met challenges outside the home, she learned how to make family members feel sorry for her by suddenly slumping and pouting a bit whenever they confronted her in any way. The combination of her troubled background and sympathy-seeking ways made Emily feel guilty when she felt sad for herself about the strong, capable mother she didn't have. By creating an image of her mother as pitiable, Emily never had to face grief about her losses. Her mother image's voice said, "Feel sorry for Mommy before you feel sorry for yourself."

Let's now look at what happens when a mother dies during her daughter's childhood: usually, it's the image of the pedestal mother that emerges, because children need to preserve a sense of a strong parental figure that the pedestal mother provides, even if the actual mother wasn't a strong positive force while alive.

# real loss or emotional loss?

Author Peter Shabad (1990) writes about how, when a loving mother-child relationship existed while the mother lived, a phase of idealization after her death allows constructive grieving. It lets the child retain the positive feeling about the mother as a role model and source of support throughout life.

Death is difficult to grasp for all of us, but for a young child it's even harder, especially when the deceased is a parent, for two main reasons:

(1) the child's survival is at stake, and (2) it takes a while for a child's abstract thinking to develop. So children can use denial in ways adults can't, to ward off the horrible realization that a parent will never return. And a child's idealized vision of her loving mother after her death is a good thing, because it allows her to further internalize the support she gave. Other times, the ideal mother image is a saving grace when adorned with stellar traits, because they overshadow the actual mother's gaps in nurturing and let the child feel less responsible for her death.

## Survival Instincts Lead to Pedestal Mother Image After Mother's Death

Miriam's mother, Helga, died when she was eight. Although Helga loved Miriam, she had a temper that created some imbalance in their relationship. Helga's carnival-mirror self-image was the cause of her temper: whenever she felt needful at home she viewed herself as weak, and that had been seen as bad in *her* mother's eyes. And instead of feeling angry at herself for her dependency, she let out the anger on Miriam.

Through early modeling, Miriam had gained Helga's carnival-mirror self-image that caused her to see herself as weak when needful. So, after Helga died, Miriam had to bury her sadness, because in her mind it was equated with dependency. And her image of her mother contained an always-soothing presence with only a soft tone and a gentle touch, which kept the grief deep underground. Miriam then didn't have to experience feelings about what she didn't have, as long as the ideal-mother image filled her mind.

But when she allowed herself a more realistic picture of Helga, temper and all, she could touch the parts of her she loved when she died. She then explored Helga's distorted self-image, which told her she was valued only when self-sufficient. Now, with a more accurate picture of her mother, she saw that she'd inherited the carnival-mirror self-image, and she shifted to a more accurate picture of herself. And because she no longer had to feign strength when she felt dependent, others felt closer to her and she gained healthier relationships than she'd had before the change.

Like Helga, whose mother image may make the mother appear perfect, the child can, with the help of loving caregivers, gradually shift to a more realistic picture of her.

## From Pedestal Mother to Healthy Mourning

As just mentioned, it's common for a child whose mother has died to place her mother on a pedestal for a time. When the child is ready, her rosy-cheeked, agile, and perfectly attuned mother image transforms over time into a more realistic one that includes the actual mother's wrinkled brow, sallow complexion, occasional clumsiness, or out-of-step responses. In that way she goes from the pedestal to a firmer middle ground. That transformation helps the daughter see other relationships in a healthy way; she doesn't need to seek substitutes for a mother who exists on a higher plane and would crash to the ground if she were to act human.

## Face Sadness About Emotional Loss When Mother Dies, and Face Rejection

Abandonment and rejection are frequent emotions that children feel when their mother dies. However, one thing that diminishes a child's sense of abandonment when a parent dies from illness or accident is that the dying is beyond her control. The child can think, "Mommy loved me and didn't want to leave me, but she couldn't help it." So, while sadness is a natural part of the experience, feeling rejected *because* of the loss is not.

On the other hand, when a mother doesn't connect with her child, or emotionally leaves her—regardless of the cause, such as mental illness—the child's facing her sadness about the abandonment becomes equated with her facing the rejection. All this goes on beneath the child's awareness, and that makes grieving doubly difficult—the child can't describe what she's going through, and caregivers usually can't see it and can't help her with it. So, while often a child has an open mourning process for her mother's death, she rarely has such grieving about the emotional loss of her. The child feels alone with her sadness and has no recourse but to bury it, as Betsy did.

Betsy and her mother had classic pre-puberty battles for about a year before her mother died of cancer. Betsy blamed herself, thinking that aggravating her mother had caused the cancer. Her buried guilt made her view herself as unworthy of love, which revealed itself in her marriage to a man who flaunted two affairs, one of which Betsy knew about during her engagement. She allowed her husband to degrade her until she realized that she was using his ill treatment of her as a way to atone for "causing" her mother's death.

## Deny Sadness, and Deny Emotional Loss of Mother

We see the symbol of the ideal mother when the fairy godmother, a protector against emotional loss, emerges to rescue Cinderella in Disney's version of the tale. (Of course, fairy tales tend to magnify issues; the stepmother's not just emotionally absent—she's abusive.) Many women grow up to realize that their mothers, like Cinderella's stepmother, have left them with hurt or gaps in nurturing. In therapy the daughters become aware of how thinking of their mothers as fairy godmothers has stayed with them. Keeping that portrait lets them avoid sadness about the nurturing they missed. Joyce is one woman with that experience.

### _Joyce_

Her mother let her know early on that she always expected more of her, no matter what she achieved. To counter the feeling of such conditional love, as a young child Joyce would sing "When You Wish Upon a Star" and believed that a lovely princess would appear in her life, become her mother, and love her freely. She believed she could make this fantasy come true by being good, which meant being less expressive of her own needs, more compliant, and higher achieving. In adulthood, in order to gain an ideal mother, she acted "good" with anyone she defined as an authority figure: a domineering friend, a grocery manager, a PTA president.

Another way daughters grow up denying sadness about a void in their nurturing is through trying to please their mothers by being different for them, better for them, more worthy of their love. They carry those traits into adulthood and relate to others with them. One particular case (McWilliams 2004) described in _Psychoanalytic Psychotherapy_ shows how a daughter's attempt to comply, as a way of bartering for love, plays out with other women.

## _Molly_

McWilliams's patient, Molly, let her mother down from birth on, because she wasn't the calm, huggable baby she wished for, but a squirmy one with colic. The mother criticized and rejected Molly throughout childhood. The author tells us that sadness and anger were particularly difficult emotions for Molly to feel. So I think it's possible that her lack of expression of those feelings was part of why "she had never given up the wish to win her mother's love [and] she acted out her efforts to gain that love with virtually everyone" (McWilliams 2004, 200). Perhaps clinging to the fantasy of a different mother kept her from facing her buried anger and sadness. Even as an adult, she'd go along with others' needs instead of her own. She'd also fabricate stories about herself in order to tell 'people what they want to hear' (200).

Women like Joyce and Molly avoid sadness about emotional loss through varied means, including an image that they maintain or a way of behaving that they mechanically repeat. So far, when we've discussed loss, we've mostly referred to the loss of something or someone we once had, or both. But when I pondered Joyce's and Molly's situations, I noted that they didn't actually _lose_ something (we can't lose something we've never had, after all). So I want to call their kind of sadness something else. The experience I'm referring to is harder to touch and harder to put into words. It's what I call _not-loss._

## Not-Loss or Loss?

Not-loss is similar to the idea behind the Mad Hatter's "un-birthday" party in Lewis Carroll's _Through the Looking Glass_. Instead of something positive being there and then being taken away, it's an emotional void created from the beginning, while parents are alive; it may involve a lack of attention, or just the wrong kind of attention.

### _daughters don't identify their "not-loss," and mothers don't see how they create it_

Children who experience not-loss are usually clothed well, kept warm, and fed adequately, and aren't physically abused. But their feelings are overlooked; they're alone a lot in their rooms; or the home lacks the warmth or spirit that comes from lively talks at dinner, visitors on holidays, or family involvement in the community. Children can't realize they've had not-loss until they're old enough to recognize the contrast between their lives and movie or book characters, or the lives of other children whose life at home seems more whole.

Most parents who create a not-loss experience for their children usually have no idea they're doing it. They just can't see beyond their own issues; they may be overly burdened with daily problems, emotionally disturbed or handicapped, or overly self-focused. Whatever the reason, not-loss becomes part of a buried sadness that many women uncover in therapy after they've dealt with buried anger and love; it's a sadness about what never was.

That feeling is hard for us to reach, because we can't identify it as young children, and we fill the void with fantasy. So as adults we must first spell out what we think we've missed and then begin to get in touch with those unmet needs. But whether we've had a not-loss beyond words or a loss we can describe, we need to deal with the sadness related to either experience so that it doesn't hinder our freer self.

We've explored real loss of the childhood mother through death, psychic loss of the childhood mother when she's too troubled to tend to her daughter's needs, and not-loss, which relates to psychic loss. There's a fourth kind of childhood loss that's more specific than the others and combines real with emotional aspects of the experience: the loss of the daughter of an immigrant mother.

Of course, there are other, more dramatic, life-change situations besides immigration that represent a fusion of actual loss and feelings of loss, such as sudden maternal physical impairment. But I'm focusing on immigration, because the relationships of so many mothers and daughters in the United States are greatly influenced by it. And the immigration experience can be applied to other major life-changing experiences.

## immigration: from real loss to emotional loss

The tangible losses experienced by the immigrant woman—culture, relationships, identity, a shared language—often lead to her feelings of loss. The latter can accentuate self-image distortions in her that already existed, or it can bring out those that may have been hidden. In turn, these distortions get passed on to the daughter.

## New Land, New Loss

In the beginning of the twentieth century, when my grandmother, then eighteen years old, came to Ellis Island, she left behind family members whom she would never see again, and she brought with her a language and culture that must have seemed strange to most Americans born here. Although her parents eventually joined her, she must have experienced plenty of loss that she never talked about. I'll never know which of those feelings might have related to my grandmother's self-image, to the carnival mirror she passed on to my mother, or to the one my mother passed on to me, because she and other relatives who knew her are long gone.

But many other women's immigrant experiences that are similar to my grandmother's have been recorded. In *Psychotherapy with Women*, Marsha Pravder Mirkin (Llerena-Quinn and Mirkin 2005) illustrates how a daughter inherits her mother's carnival-mirror self-image, a process furthered by the real losses resulting from immigration. The author writes about her grandmother, who arrived in the United States from Poland in 1921 with her young daughter, Marsha's future mother. The grandmother came here already feeling a great loss: the Polish government had required that she leave her adolescent son in the Old Country for the army, "and she never saw him again" (90).

Further on, she writes, "My grandmother's losses carried over to my own mother, leaving her feeling both depressed and responsible, waiting always for the 'other shoe to fall.' Her witnessing of [my grandmother's] loss of authority made her claim unyielding and total household authority....As her daughter I was...the witness of the depression, anger, and fear that my mother carried as part of her Jewish immigrant experience—an experience I would have to understand...in order to [avoid] taking on the depressive, angry, scared parts of the legacy" (91).

Because of real events in her home country, the grandmother *was* helpless, but it appears that she maintained a view of herself as needful long after she emigrated. That distortion seems to have influenced her daughter to lean the other way and view herself as overly responsible— also a distortion, since children shouldn't feel responsible for their parents' well-being, nor should they feel totally responsible for their own well-being. In turn, *her* daughter, the author, had to be vigilant to avoid internalizing her grandmother's and mother's views of themselves and of their lives. It seems that she was able to achieve that goal in some way, through gaining insight about her grandmother's and mother's influence on her self-image.

# Immigrant Mothers and Teen Daughters' Storms

The book *Ethnicity and Family Therapy* (McGoldrick, McGoldrick, and McGoldrick 2005) contains numerous descriptions of how immigrant women's losses affect their self-perceptions, which get reflected in their daughters' self-perceptions. The book reveals that it's often in the teen years, when separation crises are in full swing, that the daughter begins to feel shame about the differences between her mother and other girls' mothers, who were born here. (This comes as no surprise, because teens are generally very aware of likeness and difference, and they're more apt to feel embarrassment about the way their mothers differ from their peers' mothers. But for obvious reasons the issue is often magnified with immigrant mothers.)

If the mother had a fairly accurate self-image before she arrived in this country and before she raised her daughter, it's more likely that she'll retain that view and weather her daughter's adolescent storms. If not, the distortion in her self-image often becomes stronger when her teen daughter tests her, as Mary tested her mother.

## *Mary*

Mary's mother arrived in America from Russia with her husband, and Mary was born two years later. When Mary turned fourteen, her social life began to take off, but she wouldn't invite friends to her home because she didn't want them to see her mother, who dressed in "peasant outfits" and spoke with an accent. If they noticed her mother's different appearance, Mary worried that maybe they'd think she was different too.

Her mother had viewed herself as out of the norm, even in the Old Country. So when she arrived here, that distortion just got magnified. When Mary rubbed in the fact that her mother *was* out of the norm, her mother believed her daughter's views and began to isolate herself to hide her shame. At the same time, Mary unknowingly modeled herself more and more after her mother, and began seeing herself in a distorted way, as her mother had. She gained an inaccurate self-image like that of her mother—feeling that she had been born out of sync—which led her to feel ashamed, also like her mother. And she began to isolate herself from her peers. As an adult in therapy, she uncovered sadness about what she'd missed. Through plenty of work, she learned to let that sadness be, without judging or taking action, and she plumbed its depths, discovering her mother's inability to bolster Mary's separateness from her.

In the next section we'll see how difficult it is for a woman like Mary to feel grief about the nurturing she missed, and we'll explore how that avoidance affects her self-image. Her experience will serve as a model for how you can use the touch tools to face the sadness and thereby open the way to a truer self-image and freer self—the essence of thought link 4. At the same time, we'll see how therapy furthers the process.

# thought link 4

*My mother would never know how many tears fell on my rag doll's head—enough to turn her string hair a deeper yellow than it already was. Little did I know that when I turned twelve and my mother's sister, Aunt Delia, died, I would lose my mother too. She got depressed. I wasn't like my friends, who went into their teens with mothers who guided them about whether to choose pink or mauve lipstick and had girls' shopping days with dessert breaks at Buxton's, where the petit fours' icing was heaven and the malteds were thick enough to make the chocolate flavor meld with your taste buds. I only knew about these things because my friends' mothers took me there.*

Natalie developed a fantasy during her teens that she'd make up for what she wasn't getting from her mother through her own daughter, once she was a mother herself. She pictured herself in many situations with her make-believe daughter at age twelve. She fantasized about having "makeup and manicure days" with her, taking her to cafes for dessert, going on skiing trips, and buying her a puppy like the one Natalie's mother talked about but never got her.

When she did have a daughter, Sharon, Natalie was thrilled. But because she and her husband had raised her to be independent, by the time Sharon turned twelve, she had very set ideas about what she'd let Natalie teach her, where she would shop, and how she'd spend her time. Sharon giggled about the way Natalie wore her hair and said she thought a lot of her mother's clothes were boring, so why should Sharon shop with her? Also, dessert wasn't her thing, because she was always aware of calories, and she didn't like skiing because she inevitably wound up shivering on the mountain.

Natalie was very let down, because she'd held on so tightly to her fantasy of a specific, ideal mother-daughter relationship to make up for what she didn't have with her mother. On some level she felt anger toward Sharon for depriving her of fulfilling her long-held wishes. And since she had a distorted self-image, she viewed herself as defective because she hadn't created the ideal relationship with her daughter that she'd envisioned, especially since her friends somehow got their daughters to do what Natalie couldn't get Sharon to do. But as she *uncovered the sadness* about what she'd missed with her mother, which was now reinforced in her relationship with Sharon, and learned to use mindfulness (*letting the sadness be*, by not judging it or taking action on it), she could begin to *plumb the depths of her sadness.* That allowed Natalie to see that she had held onto the perfect mother-daughter fantasy relationship in order to avoid facing buried sadness about her relationship with her mother. At this point she entered therapy in order to more fully explore the insight she'd gained from use of thought link 4.

After several years of helpful treatment, Natalie terminated. Several months later she began feeling another type of loss when Sharon was leaving for college. So she returned to the three steps of thought link 4 by using touch tools, such as books about loss, like *Necessary Losses* by Judith Viorst. One day she sat down at the piano and began playing pop music her mother had liked. The music led her to look at family photo albums with pictures of herself growing up. She noted a pattern: photos taken before Natalie turned twelve included her mother and herself looking vibrant and smiling openly. After her mother's sister died, they usually showed Natalie alone or with her father or siblings; if her mother was in the photo, she often looked posed, without expression. She guessed that the change in her and her mother's body language must reveal something about her mother's connection to her before Natalie's aunt died, and her distance later.

After a few years, Natalie returned to therapy to enhance her process of uncovering her sadness, not judging it, and exploring its depths. Sharon was engaged to be married and some of Natalie's past issues with her did arise occasionally, but now Natalie was also facing the idea that Sharon would leave her again, by becoming a married woman. She knew she needed to let go of more of the fantasy of repairing her childhood through her daughter; in doing so, she gained a better relationship with Sharon: she now saw her as more of an individual, and not as a means of making up for her own past losses. And because she was feeling better as a mother, she also began to view herself in a truer way, as less defective.

# let's recap

We've discussed the difference between the physical lack or loss of the childhood mother and the emotional lack or loss of her. And we also talked about the fact that when the mother dies and there has been a basically healthy mother-daughter relationship before her death, though the daughter usually idealizes the mother, she can gradually mourn the loss. But if the childhood mother physically or emotionally abandons the daughter while alive, the daughter often creates an unbending fantasy of having an ideal daughter and being an ideal mother, to compensate for her childhood loss. Holding onto that fantasy into adulthood prevents a woman from feeling sadness about what she never got from her mother, and it keeps her self-image distortions alive. When she can uncover the sadness, use mindfulness to let the sadness be, without judging it or taking action on it, and plumb its depths, it becomes less formidable. She then has a better chance of reducing the fantasy and viewing herself and others more realistically.

The next chapter will discuss how to use thought link 5, which integrates all the phases of the previous thought links. Jenny's therapy stages will serve as a model for how to apply the five thought links to your daily life.

## A Note to Daughters

This chapter might have been the hardest to read, because facing loss is one of the most difficult human experiences. You may want to just run away from the whole approach, for fear you'll have to keep feeling these awful emotions. But if you let yourself continue through all of the chapters, I believe that you'll gradually get better at it and see that dealing with these discomforting emotions pays off in the end.

# Questions for Reflection

1. Can you note a time during your childhood when your mother's behavior toward you changed in a way that made you feel a loss?

2. When did it occur, and how would you describe the change in her nurturing?

3. What mother fantasy might have helped you counter sadness about the loss, for example, a pedestal mother or a sad-sack mother?

4. How do you think that fantasy affects your relationships now? Do you ask too much of your friends or partner? Do you deny your own wants because you make your husband a sad sack (as you made your mother)?

## *Reading Touch Tool*

Jackie Lyden, author of the memoir, *Daughter of the Queen of Sheba*, shows us her sadness about loss mixed with love in her complex relationship with her mother, diagnosed as manic depressive (a condition now called *bipolar disorder*). Consider the following questions related to her book.

### *Daughter of the Queen of Sheba*

- How did Jackie's love for her mother show through the negative mother image?

- Jackie's mother's mental illness caused her daughter to have negative feelings that she turned against herself at times. In what way did she do this?

- Even if your mother is not disturbed, as Lyden's mother was, can you find parallel feelings of love and loss related to her while you were growing up?

**169**

# carnival mirrors and
# truer mirrors

# CHAPTER 11

# thought link 5:
# from the carnival mirror
# to the truer mirror

*"We are not stuck with the brain we were born with but have the capacity to willfully direct which functions will flower and which will wither...which emotions flourish and which are stilled."*

— Sharon Begley, *Train Your Mind, Change Your Brain*

"I give up. I'll never make it with men. I went out again last night with Bill. We had the best dinner and wine at Cyrano's. He bought me white gardenias. Can you believe it? He once heard me say I love them. But when we got to my place, I couldn't let him stay. I kept imagining him staring at my nose instead of gazing at my eyes when we're in bed. I put on that make-believe tough facade and asked him to leave. I said I thought I was coming down with something. He'll probably never call again."

"What makes you think that?"

"Because he knows. He knows I'm a loser. What date would treat him like that after he wined and dined her?"

"I'm not so sure he'll never call again. He seems really interested in you, from what you say. But where do you get this feeling that you're a loser?"

"I'm a loser because I have a loser nose."

"How so?"

"I can't get it out of my mind that it makes me less than other women. I heard this most of my life from my mother: 'You got the man's nose from Dad's side of the family.' It's so deeply ingrained."

"Okay. I'm going to say this, knowing you won't believe it: I think you're an attractive woman and your nose fits with the rest of you really nicely."

"You're right. I don't believe it."

"So you feel that men will focus so much on your nose that they won't see anything else? And the rest of you doesn't count?"

"Yeah, that's the way I feel."

Jenny gingerly drew a tissue from the box. She patted her eyes to avoid smearing mascara already watered down by tears, and daintily folded the tissue into squares to have a clean side; taking another one might have been too indulgent. As I pushed the box closer to her, I noticed how her smooth, luminous skin contrasted sharply with the dull, coarse fabrics she was wearing.

I wondered why her usually exuberant curly hair seemed tamped down that day and why, instead of her vibrant patterned skirts and tops, she wore this matched outfit drained of life. I sensed that today Jenny was letting me see the sad girl within her who needed her tears wiped. She awakened me to her deep need to be held.

"You seem a bit tense. Usually when you talk about your shame here, you're able to let go in a way you say you can't anywhere else. But today you seem more held in. I wonder what's changed since our last session."

"I saw you yesterday. I was across the street and you didn't see me, but I noticed you with a woman, I assume a friend, with those perfect looks that haunt me. It made me think that you and I wouldn't be friends if you weren't my therapist. I wouldn't make the grade."

"So you feel inferior next to the woman I was walking with and assume that I must also find you inferior to her and wouldn't want you for my friend if you weren't in treatment with me? Wow. You've taken quite a few leaps. Do I ever act as if I think you're inferior?"

"No, not at all. In fact I feel that you like me. I guess I just go into autopilot when I see a woman my mother would have put on a pedestal. I had a dream that I think tells the whole story. After Bill left my apartment last night, I dreamed about this doll I called Lucy that my mother bought me when I turned seven. In the dream Lucy lay next to Bill in bed, and then she came alive as me, now. So there I was with Bill, looking perfect like Lucy. She had the model's figure that my mother idealized, and the tiny button nose that I lack."

"In the dream, as Lucy come-to-life, my nose had the perfect upturn. My flowing hair barely touched my blue Victoria's Secret pajamas. Bill's hazel eyes opened wide, and he couldn't take them off mine. Then his face morphed into my mother's, and he disappeared. Suddenly my mom and I were in a closed-in space like the dormer in the house I lived in as a kid."

During this session about a year into Jenny's treatment, we talked about how the dream revealed her shame about her nose, which kept her distant from men. We explored how since childhood, just as Jenny stayed tied to Sonya, her self-image stayed tied to Sonya's self-image. She mentioned her mother's frequent comment, "We're two peas in a pod," which she'd chant when Jenny complained she didn't match up to cuter girls. Because Sonya was overfocused on a flaw in her own looks, she was also overfocused on a flaw in Jenny's looks. She didn't include Jenny's lovely body, smooth skin, generosity, expressive green eyes, and sense of humor in her view of her; nor did she acknowledge her artistic talent and social adeptness. So she couldn't help Jenny appreciate the whole being that she was, with many special qualities beyond her nose.

Jenny considered how staying in that pea pod with Sonya hindered her, because she never had a chance to see herself in a way that was different from the way Sonya saw herself. Their mother-daughter car-nival-mirror self-image defined overall worth as equal to ideal beauty—the kind Jenny's maternal grandmother, Nadia, had (this is discussed further on). Jenny then mentioned how Sonya had once knitted a lus-cious red-and-black popcorn-stitch coat for Lucy the doll, but nothing of the kind for Jenny. Similarly to Natalie in the previous chapter, as a child, Jenny would frequently daydream about herself as a future mother with a perfect daughter. Jenny would call her daughter Madeline, and Madeleine would look like Lucy, in a red and black outfit. She pictured herself holding Madeleine's hand: the model mother and daughter, viewing the Christmas tree at Rockefeller Center and the Fifth Avenue store windows. She realized that Madeleine, her own creation, was the ideal daughter that Jenny wasn't.

This chapter will use Jenny's expedition through five stages of therapy to model your own journey through the five thought links. Keep in mind that Jenny's treatment occurred over years, while the time you'll take to read this chapter probably won't come close to that amount of time (strong hunch)!

Before we explore further, let's describe certain issues from the backgrounds of Nadia, Sonya, and Jenny that would have made them prime candidates for the thought-links strategy.

# the carnival-mirror dolls

The body images that Nadia, Sonya, and Jenny had weren't problems in and of themselves. In fact, each had a fairly accurate view of her physical being. Nadia had an ideal hourglass body and saw it that way. Sonya had a relatively small bust and saw it that way. Jenny had a wider nose than a classically beautiful one and saw it that way. The problem with each woman's self-image was what she did with it rather than what it was: grandmother, mother, and daughter made looks a measuring stick for worth. A truer self-image would base self-worth on the whole person.

I learned about Jenny's body image and self-image through her feelings about her doll, Lucy, whom Jenny thought of as an ideal version of herself in a future daughter. In fact, most girls playing with dolls reveal something about the person they wish to be or who they are. When six-year-old Hanna hugs her doll a lot, we can be pretty sure that some important figure hugs Hanna a lot. And when five-year-old Vicki tosses her doll around, she might be showing that she's not treated with the greatest tenderness (although, of course, not all doll tossing is a sign of something negative; it could mean just having fun!).

Nadia, Sonya, and Jenny each conveyed an image that led me to think of a particular doll. I saw Nadia as a china doll, valued for her delicate features and perfect figure but also fragile; Sonya as a rag doll, lacking a backbone and conviction because she views her body as inferior to her

176

mother's and that of other women; and Jenny as a straw doll, warding off attempts at closeness with a brittle front that easily breaks.

The following passages about Nadia's background came from her comments to Sonya a short time before Nadia died. Nadia felt a need to reveal to Sonya previously hidden information about her past, in an effort to connect with her before she died. Some facts shocked Sonya.

## China Doll Grandmother

Nadia was born into privilege in Hungary. She married a man who was later killed in World War I, leaving her in dire straits with two young children, Sonya and her older brother, to support. As a teen before marriage, Nadia had been known for her delicate features, regal presence, and hourglass figure revealed by clinging dresses that showed off her narrow waist. She once told Sonya that she could've had any suitor she wanted when she married Sonya's father.

When life came apart after his death, Nadia groveled for money to meet the family's needs. Out of desperation she engaged in promiscuity for a time, using her looks to attract wealthy men who helped pay her expenses.

During Nadia's childhood, her mother played up the magic of the hourglass figure: "If you have that, you have it all." However, despite her appearance, Nadia grew up feeling inferior to two older brothers who outshone her in school. As a teen, when she'd tell her mother she felt stupid next to them, her mother would take her to a mirror. "Look at your perfect proportions. Don't worry, you'll see; you'll get a wealthy husband, and schoolwork won't matter." She had an aptitude for science that she could've developed, but her parents, going along with the male-dominated culture, discouraged her from pursuing her interest. So Nadia clung to her looks in order to feel valued, despite her deeply buried view of herself as damaged goods. But she couldn't let anyone know that she felt that way, including herself, until right before her death. When she had a daughter, she wound up unconsciously living through her to regain that superficial sense of worth she'd felt before promiscuity and aging shattered it.

## Rag Doll Mother

Sonya recalls Nadia's pushing her into ballet lessons at a very young age because that was "the foundation for a great body," not because of its health and self-esteem benefits. When Sonya reached puberty, Nadia got her to wear padded bras even before her breasts were fully developed. When the teen party scene began, Nadia often asked how Sonya was doing with the boys. Before Sonya had a chance to respond, Nadia would begin boasting of her own popularity at Sonya's age: "The boys ran after me. My figure counted for a lot." Sonya got the covert message that she didn't match up to her mother or other women who resembled her. Sonya's negative feeling about her appearance spread to include her whole self, including her thoughts and ideas: if *she* didn't count for much, then her opinions didn't either.

While growing up, Sonya lacked a model in Nadia for healthy separation between mother and daughter, and didn't receive the understanding that a healthy separation can actually make for a more secure connection. So, when Sonya had Jenny, she was so fixated on her own shape that it was only a matter of time before she was fixated on Jenny's. And since Sonya viewed *her* body as inferior to Nadia's, she viewed *Jenny's* body as inferior to Nadia's too.

## Straw Doll Daughter

When Jenny's nose grew at puberty, Sonya said, "You're stuck with your father's nose. It comes from a long line of males in his family." The distorted mother-to-daughter message, now in its third generation, essentially said, "The less ideal the body, the less worth a woman has." So, since mother and daughter both lacked Nadia's classic good looks, both questioned their worth overall. In Sonya that led to a lack of conviction. In Jenny it led to self-created taboos; she'd built a brittle barrier between herself and others—and, like straw, it could snap.

We'll now follow Jenny's treatment to see how, as her self-image changed, the protective barrier with which she shielded herself softened; this began to allow for closer relationships. We'll also see how each of the five thought links relates to each of Jenny's treatment stages.

# five treatment stages and five thought links

This last thought link is a key to creating change in your daily life, because it brings all of the previous thought links together to use in a practical form. Before you begin to journey through this final thought link, imagine the entire approach as a sculpture of permanently soft clay. You can alter details of the basic creation at any time. Life changes, crises, and emotional-growth phases may motivate you to return to the five thought links later on and apply them to new or different issues.

Unique definitions for the terms *sowing* and *reaping* are introduced in this chapter. When you sow, you think and write in a peaceful place where you can concentrate and build inner knowledge, or insight. When you reap, you use your stored insight to change your responses to trigger events at any given moment. The beginning phases of the approach highlight sowing; the later phases gradually focus more on reaping.

Note: The terms for concepts previously discussed are in italics.

## Stage 1: I Hate My Nose!

Jenny's first treatment stage focused on her shame about her nose and how that shame hindered her social and sex life. She explored how Sonya's tendency to put her own self-image issues onto Jenny was the main source of the problem.

### *thought link 1—sowing*

In this thought link, the task is to parse the mother-daughter self-image, and this is done in three phases: *exploring, stepping into Mother's shoes,* and *sifting out.*

It's important to first discover what your mother's self-image was when she raised you. If you find that she had a skewed view of herself and you can understand the roots of her problem, you can then separate your own self-image from hers.

**Exploring: Learn About Mother's Self-Image, and Compare It with Yours.** Some time in the first year of treatment, Jenny discovered her mother's diary, left in a drawer after her death years before, and read it; using this *touch tool* helped her to define the distorted self-image that she and Sonya shared. Sonya's writing went back to the time of Jenny's early years, and it was filled with derogatory synonyms for her "small breasts": "puny boobs," "munchkin boobs," and the like. "Whoa, it seems my mom had a looks obsession even then," Jenny noted. "Like mine?" She found a common thread in Sonya's self-image and hers: both women viewed a perceived body flaw as a flaw in their whole selves.

At thirteen, Sonya had written about herself and her mother in her diary. It helped Jenny understand more about her grandmother's influence on her mother's self-image: "Greg asked me to dance with him last Friday night and took me out for a shake at Smitty's. The girls were jealous, I think. He's so cute. This weekend I'll probably see him at Mary Jo's party. So yesterday I asked Mom to take me shopping for new clothes. I wanted something sexy. I fell in love with the green cashmere sweater that I pictured clinging to me as Greg looked me over. Mom goes, 'I don't think you're ready for that unless you wear a different bra with padding.' So we bought the bra. What is she, afraid my boobs aren't good enough for that sweater?"

**Stepping into Mother's Shoes: What Did She Feel About Herself When She Raised you?** Jenny studied photos of Sonya as a child (*touch tool*) to try to feel what would've made her grow up to be so focused on one body flaw. Nadia always appeared perfectly dressed and statuesque; Sonya seemed to be a tagalong in the aura of her mother. These pictures clued Jenny in to one reason why Sonya might have put Jenny into the same "pea pod" with her. It created a sense of closeness, however forced, with her daughter that she'd never had with her mother. And her negative focus on Jenny's body probably came from her negative focus on herself when compared to Nadia.

**Sifting Out: Parse Your Self-Image and Your Mother's.** Jenny brought in a piece she had written about her mother (*touch tool*) in her process of separating her self-image from the mother-daughter mix:

"No wonder my mom focused so much on our bodies when she raised me. My grandmother focused on her shape and on my mom's, big time. And that's probably why my mom couldn't help me when I said I felt less attractive than those cute little girls in my class with the perfect noses. She did tell me she had the same feelings when she was a teen. That calmed me a bit, because I didn't feel so alone with my problem. But then she'd say we were two peas in a pod, which made me feel I could never crawl out of the pea pod without abandoning her. Was Grandma Nadia's influence on my mom the same as my mom's on me?"

"Whenever I use eye makeup to distract from my nose, I think of my mom. Recently I studied a photo of her at high-school graduation and thought about how into her appearance she must have always been, and the way that carried over to me. Her hair looks sculpted, probably into some copy of Elizabeth Taylor's hair—her idol, I think, because she had that busty figure that my mom lacked. I see a satiny sheen on her jacket. It's slightly opened, probably just the right amount to show the neatly tied bow of her polka-dot blouse. There's the perfect little high-school girl who grew up to be my mother—whose mantra was, 'Jenny, do whatever you can to distract people's eyes from your nose.'"

The more Jenny realized that she could see herself as separate from her mother, the more open she became. She got better at appreciating her own positive qualities, and she realized that Sonya couldn't help Jenny see those positive traits, because Sonya needed her to stay close by and share her problems.

After working through these three phases, Jenny found that her insights were stored in her memory, and she began to open up socially.

## Stage 2: Flawed Nose, Flawed Sex

Jenny made two new friends and began biking with them on weekends. Her love for the sport led her to join a biking club, where she got to know Bill, on whom she developed a secret crush. At first she thought he would never give her the time of day. Then she realized that he actually liked her, and they started dating.

When sex entered the picture, so did her anxiety. In bed she returned to feeling self-conscious about her nose, because she knew that Bill would see her up close. She had an awful vision of his first studying her eyes—in her mind, her best feature—and then changing his smile into a tight line as his gaze fixed on her nose. By trying to discover why shame weighed on her sex life, Jenny began to see that her mother's negative body image had become hers during childhood. With that awareness, she got in touch with her anger toward Sonya for letting that happen.

## *thought link 2—sowing*

In this thought link, you face the buried anger toward your child-hood mother. The anger serves to tie you to her in unhealthy ways you didn't realize. The three phases of this thought link are *uncovering the anger*, *letting the anger be*, and *plumbing the depths of anger*.

When you look at that anger toward your childhood mother, you'll likely see that you've kept it buried through the years because of the fear that you'd hurt her. Then you'll be able to simply look at it without judging yourself. Have courage! From there, you can more fully explore it.

**Uncovering the Anger: Touch Your Hidden Anger Toward Your Childhood Mother.** Jenny began to peel away layers of denial of her anger, which appeared at times as sugary compliments. "She's so great; she's so beautiful; she's so smart." One of the hardest things for Jenny to accept was that she was allowed to resent her mother for what had happened in the past, even if her mother had meant well. But, most surprisingly, Jenny found that in allowing all of her feelings toward her mother, positive and negative, she could maintain a more authentic tie to her, which eventually made for a much closer feeling than she'd ever known.

Jenny returned to her own journals from her tween years, where she described Sonya's talks about her bedroom troubles with Jenny's father (*touch tool*). Reading those words made Jenny see how her role as her mother's confidant interfered with her ability to feel sexually free, begin-ning then, in her teens. If Sonya couldn't enjoy her sex life, Jenny couldn't either. Reading these journal entries stirred a deep anger toward Sonya for sharing too much information about her sex life with her young daughter. This was a new point of reckoning for Jenny. However, as she looked at her anger, she used mindfulness and allowed it to be."

**Letting the Anger Be: Look at It Without Judging or Taking Action.** Jenny saw how her sex life suffered because of the self-image distortion she shared with Sonya, and because of the anger toward Sonya that she kept hidden. She noted that pleasurable sex was the trigger that led to her major symptom, a depressed feeling. Her sense of her mother image at those times beckoned her back to the pea pod, away from intimacy with another person. Jenny recalled a night in her teens when she came home from a fun time with a boy named Steve, whom she'd been hoping to date. Sonya asked questions with an anxious look, implying that she doubted that Steve was really attracted to Jenny (in the same way that she had doubted that a guy could be attracted to *her* at that age). "He didn't drive you home? You had to go home with your girlfriends?"

Jenny explored the idea that facing resentment toward Sonya meant first just letting the anger be, without judging it or doing something with it except to look at it and talk, think, or write about it. When she was able to accept the resentment, she didn't have to turn it against herself. When she came to this realization, her depression lifted. An insight followed: "I think I always feared that if I even thought about negative feelings toward my mom, they would harm her."

**Plumbing the Depths of Anger: Explore Hidden Anger Further.**
Jenny experienced her anger on an even deeper level when she happened upon her childhood scrapbook (*touch tool*). There were all the mementos she'd kept from places she and Sonya had enjoyed going to together when she was a child. That made her feel anger about the contrast in Sonya's manner toward Jenny after puberty. That was when she started focusing on Jenny's nose and hips, and made her feel that she had to choose: either stay in the pea pod with Mom or abandon her. Jenny realized that she had responded by hurting herself instead of Sonya, through self-loathing, even when others gave her strokes.

## Stage 3: Stirring Buried Love

Even while Jenny was facing her buried anger toward Sonya, she still felt held back from fully enjoying her sex life. She gradually came to see that other feelings lay beneath the surface. She returned to her journals from her tween years (*touch tool*) that had recently evoked anger toward Sonya, because Sonya had shared too many facts with Jenny about her own sex life. Jenny also recalled how close to her mother she'd felt when she played the role of confidant, even though mixed in with the warm feelings was a fear of rejection if she were to openly show her love. So the journal entries that had stirred buried anger now also stirred buried love.

## *thought link 3—sowing*

Here, you'll face the buried love for your childhood mother that ties you to her in unhealthy ways you may not recognize. The three phases of this thought link are *uncovering the love, letting the love be,* and *plumbing the depths of love.*

By allowing yourself the love for your childhood mother that you've unknowingly kept buried through the years because you feared that she would reject you if you showed your love, you then can look at it without judgment and without needing to take action. From there you can more fully explore it. After Jenny peeled away some of the layers of anger, she began to touch on feelings of love from early on in her childhood that she'd kept hidden to avoid hurt.

**Uncovering the Love: Face Hidden Love for the Childhood Mother.** Jenny recalled that as a child, when she showed open signs of love for Sonya, she felt she was exposing herself to potential hurt. As we'd done when she and I began exploring her buried anger, we first considered how scary it was to just feel the love, because it might open her up to feel Sonya's distancing: "My mother's distancing? But she's dead. How could she be distant from me if she's not here?" However, when she thought about it, she noted that she still had that fear, though it was now shrouded in her unconscious. While growing up, she had sensed Sonya's same scrutiny of Jenny's gifts as of her body, which felt like a rejection of Jenny herself: "Oh, there's a crack on it. Did they charge you full price?"

During this period, on a snowy December day, while baking Christmas cookies, Jenny suddenly recalled the good times she used to have as a little girl, doing the same thing with Sonya. She then put on some classical music that her mother used to play when they baked together, Prokofiev's *Peter and the Wolf,* Beethoven's *Pastoral Symphony,* and love songs from Broadway shows (*touch tool*). At her next session, she talked about her feelings of love for Sonya that she'd kept buried all these years. Now she saw that her love was based on a fuller appreciation of her mother, a mere mortal who'd tried her best.

She recognized that her relationship with Bill suffered because she hid love from him in the same way she'd hidden it from Sonya. Although when she was a child, concealing her love from her mother had given Jenny a sense of safety, it now blocked intimacy with her boyfriend. After gaining that insight, she no longer had to push Bill away when he acted tenderly toward her. As she looked at her love, she practiced mindfulness.

**Letting Love Be: Look at It Without Judgment or Action.** One day, while crocheting, Jenny decided to take her work outside. She gazed at her stitches and recalled Sonya's teaching her to crochet when she was a child (*touch tool*). That memory mingled with the blended scent of peonies and honeysuckle, two of her mother's garden flowers, and connected Jenny with the part of her mother she loved (*touch tool*). She thought about how the love seemed to come from a place she couldn't describe, a place deep within, where it had lain dormant. We talked about letting her love "just be" without doing anything about it.

Gradually, she was able to feel her early love for Sonya on an even deeper level by unearthing memories.

**Plumbing the Depths of Love: Explore the Love Further.** Jenny's feelings went from the love she'd felt for her mother to a memory of her scrutinizing her crochet work in the same way she scrutinized her nose. Jenny realized she'd buried her early love for Sonya in order to prevent hurt. Paradoxically, by avoiding the love, she stayed tied to Sonya: when she wasn't able to get that ideal maternal love from a female friend, because the need appeared as a demand others couldn't meet, she would return to the pea pod and the feeling that no one could replace Sonya.

As Jenny thought and talked about her fear of love, she gained more insight to build on what she'd begun through thought link 1. The more aware she became of her demanding ways with friends, the less she had to act on her needfulness. Because her behavior became more appropriate, her female relationships improved. And she opened up with Bill too, because she saw that he would stay with her even if she expressed loving feelings. Her buried fear of being hurt by her childhood mother lessened as it came more to the surface. After she spent time facing those issues, she and Bill began discussing a wedding.

## Treatment Stage 4: Tea for...Three?

After a few years of marriage, Jenny and Bill began planning for a baby. But then Jenny took a step back. She began worrying that a child of hers would have a body defect, since she and her mother both had one. While wondering if she'd have a daughter, she thought of Madeleine, the ideal daughter she'd imagined in childhood. Jenny pictured her baby, if a girl, at one of two extremes: she'd either have Madeleine's perfect aura, or Jenny's and Sonya's flawed looks.

## *thought link 4—sowing*

This thought link helps you face buried sadness that keeps you tied to your childhood mother in unhealthy ways you don't recognize. The three phases are *uncovering the sadness, letting the sadness be,* and *plumbing the depths of sadness.*

You need to touch the sadness about what you've missed with your childhood mother that you've kept buried through the years because you feared it might be too hard to take. Once you uncover it, you can then look at it and fully explore it. That allows for a healing process that comes from within you.

Jenny began to peel away layers of denial of sadness, which appeared as overblown positive statements about her earliest years. "My mother was the greatest cook. Her pasta dishes were outrageous; her homemade sauce was out of this world, her souffles were to die for." In truth, Sonya wasn't even a good cook.

**Uncovering Buried Sadness: Touch Hidden Sadness About What Your Childhood Mother Couldn't Give You.** Jenny had now let go of enough anxiety about her future child's defects to get closer to trying for a baby. She looked at family photo albums and unearthed a memory of Sonya's reacting to her as a twin pea in the pod (*touch tool*). One day she began crying while talking about when to try for a baby and couldn't pinpoint why. She then noted that she felt sad because she anticipated that Sonya would still be trying to pull her into the pod, and Jenny wouldn't give Sonya support while going through pregnancy, a sign of her growing up. As she looked at her sadness, she used mindfulness.

**Letting Sadness Be: Look at It Without Judging or Taking Action.** We talked about Jenny's first letting the sadness be, in the same way she'd let the anger and love she felt toward Sonya be. So she just thought and talked about it. While looking at an old family video, Jenny saw herself at age ten at her next-door neighbor's house, witnessing that mother, Joanne, adoring her newborn (*touch tool*). She realized now that she envied her neighbor's baby for getting more TLC than she herself was getting from Sonya at the time.

Jenny did become pregnant, and tragically, during the pregnancy Sonya died from an illness. In looking at her sadness and talking about it—while letting it be—Jenny gained more insight into the causes of her sadness. More emotionally separate now from Sonya she felt the full impact of her mother's absence during this new phase in her life. But she also knew full well that, because of her hard-earned insight and emotional growth, she would be able to take care of her own baby.

Jenny gave birth to a girl, Kaycee, who had Jenny's auburn curls. For the first two years, Jenny purely enjoyed her. But then there came a point when she began losing patience with her, and she noted that her impatience surfaced when she was focused on her daughter's face, wondering whether that face would one day have Jenny's nose. She also realized she felt some sadness in connection with these moments, but she couldn't pinpoint why. She began to call up her first memory of feeling scrutinized by Sonya: *(touch tool)* it was at age twelve, when she was getting dressed to go to school, and Sonya advised her not to wear her hair in a ponytail because it would highlight her nose.

**Plumbing the Depths of Sadness: Explore the Sadness Further.** At one of our sessions around this time, Jenny suddenly felt teary. When we talked about why she was sad, she realized she was crying because she'd never gotten from Sonya what Kaycee was getting from *her.* Jenny's dread of uncovering sadness came from a fear that it would lead to a never-ending ache that she felt helpless to relieve. We discussed the idea that as a child she *was* powerless to do anything about the pain, but now she could do something by facing it.

Later, on a rainy afternoon when Kaycee was napping, Jenny spied *Little Women* on her bookshelf. She'd loved this book as a preteen, and she decided to get cozy with it under an afghan. At times, as a little girl, she'd done the same with a book, sharing an afghan with Sonya while sitting on the couch on a rainy day. Jenny recalled how she'd wished she could be like Beth in the book, because she seemed perfect as a sister and daughter *(touch tool)*.

Rereading *Little Women* helped Jenny get in touch with her need to see Kaycee as the perfect daughter that Sonya had wanted *Jenny* to be. She realized that she was living through Kaycee and on some level also envying her for getting what Jenny had never gotten. Once Jenny felt that sadness, just as she'd felt the anger and love, she recognized that avoiding it was what had kept her hoping for approval from Sonya, and it perpetuated her self-image distortion, which resembled Sonya's.

By *uncovering the sadness, letting the sadness be,* and *plumbing the depths of sadness* repeatedly, Jenny found that her impatience with Kaycee decreased. She no longer felt resentful about what she hadn't gotten from her mother, and she could now more fully embrace her daughter.

## Stage 5, Part I

During the fifth stage of her treatment, Jenny went over the first four thought links many times. Three years after Kaycee's birth, she gave birth to a boy, Justin. This pregnancy had little of the anxiety she'd had in the first one. She ended therapy with a much more positive feeling about her life. But there were still trigger events that got to her, especially regarding anxiety about Kaycee's looks. She asked whether she could return to therapy in the future if troubles arose. Of course, she could.

Several years later, when Kaycee and Justin were in their teens, she called. She'd stored a good deal of insight that led to growth during her previous therapy experience, which allowed her to pick up where she'd left off years before.

## Stage 5, Part II

When Jenny entered treatment this time, at age forty-eight, she said she'd had a hysterectomy because of a fibroid tumor. Aside from feeling down about the end of her fertility, she was also feeling another surge of envy toward Kaycee, who now had a fifteen-year-old's firm yet supple body; long, wavy hair that had replaced her baby curls; and a classic beauty's nose like Nadia's.

## *thought link 5—reaping*

This thought link helps you shift from the carnival mirror to the truer mirror. The four phases are *blending, pinpointing, Zen focusing,* and *homing in.*

While you have been journeying through the previous thought links, there is a good chance that a shift from the carnival mirror to the truer mirror has been taking place within you. You may very well begin to see more overt signs of change when you begin *blending*: tying thought-link phases together to form seamless thoughts. Please note that if you don't recognize these signs, it doesn't mean you've failed the five thought links! It is a journey that takes place over time. You may return to parts of the journey in the future, or apply them in varying ways in daily life, or both. But the key point here is that your individual experience in which *enduring* growth comes with time.

**Blending: Form Seamless Thoughts.** Jenny aimed to form seamless thoughts out of previous thought links, because that increases our ability to apply the insights we've gained from the sowing phase to daily life, where changes occur in the reaping phase. You can find an analogy in the process of learning to drive a car, which may clarify how this process works. During your first lessons, you learn each step separately (sowing): how to turn on the engine, use the mirrors, know which gear to use when, parallel park, and so on. When you first go on the road, you may time yourself when you reach a stop sign and focus on which mirrors to look at when passing another car. But the more you drive, the more the steps flow together and become routine, until the whole process occurs without separate thoughts (reaping).

Here's the shorthand for learning to drive: learn separate cognitive steps, soak them up (internalize them) in a flow that connects with action, repeat the flow of cognitive steps while linked with the action, and the whole process becomes one seamless and more automatic routine. Similarly, here's the shorthand for learning the five thought links: gain separate insights, soak them up in a flow of thought to apply to trigger events in daily life, repeat the flow of thought when trigger events occur, and the whole process becomes more seamless and automatic.

There is one major difference between learning to drive a car and learning the five thought-link approach: the steps for driving are pretty universal, but the steps in the approach, while consistent from one woman to another, differ in the way you apply them, according to your needs. In the next section we'll see how forming a word chain helps you learn the phases, and forming a personal list helps you apply those phases to yourself and internalize them.

With an aim toward creating the chain and the list, Jenny bought a fountain pen with her favorite ink color—aqua—and a journal with handcrafted paper, and she sat at her preferred corner table in her local cafe. While sipping cappuccino and munching on a cinnamon scone, she began dipping the pen into the ink and *blending*, by forming a chain.

1.  **The Chain:** Write down all the phases, linked to each other, creating a word chain. Here's what it might look like:

    *exploring~stepping into mother's shoes~sifting
    out~uncovering anger~letting anger be~plumbing the
    depths of anger~uncovering love~letting love be~plumbing*

*the depths of love~uncovering sadness~letting sadness be~plumbing the depths of sadness~blending~pinpointing~ Zen focusing~homing in*

2.  **The List:** List the terms for the phases in the chain. Then attach your own buzzwords for personal examples (not full sentences), as shown in Jenny's example, below. Then, saying the terms in order without pausing, think of the buzzwords for each as you go. Repeat the latter step as many times as you need to internalize them. The buzz words will change as you gain a greater ability to apply the meaning of the phases to your own life.

    **Jenny's List**

    Thought Link 1

    > *exploring*: shared self-image, beauty equals worth
    > *stepping*: Mom inferior to Grandma
    > *sifting*: my worth, unlike Mom, more than beauty

    Thought Link 2

    > *uncovering*: anger, pea pod
    > *letting*: talk, think, write, anger
    > *plumbing*: anger, from puberty, self-loathing

    Thought Link 3

    > *uncovering*: love, pea pod
    > *letting*: talk, think, write, love
    > *plumbing*: love before puberty, hurt

    Thought Link 4

    > *uncovering*: sadness, pea pod, wish for mother substitute
    > *letting*: talk, think, write, sadness
    > *plumbing*: sidestep sadness, Kaycee perfect doll

    Thought Link 5 (Fill in the buzzwords below after you journey through this thought link.)

    > *blending:* _____
    > *pinpointing:* _____
    > *Zen:* _____
    > *homing:* _____

I like to think about the next phase, *pinpointing*, as making lemonade out of lemons; you use your symptom to get to a better place.

**Pinpointing: Tune in to Your Symptom and Connect It with a Trigger Event.** Jenny noticed her tendency to criticize Kaycee when she thought about her comments to her: "Don't you think you should fix your belt? It's uneven in the front. And why would you wear that bag? It looks beaten up." She worked to tune in to this symptom and understand that it was brought on by envy of Kaycee. Next, Jenny connected this symptom with a trigger event that had actually occurred: her awareness of Kaycee's lovely, developing body when she dressed up to meet her boyfriend. She noticed how Kaycee's beauty matched the ideal that Sonya had made Jenny so conscious of, and how it contrasted with Jenny's loss of muscle tone and thinning hair. Jenny later noted her mother image conveying Sonya's message that Jenny, like Sonya, was inferior to any woman with a more classic appearance; in this case the woman was Jenny's own daughter.

Now, Jenny used meditative tools to thwart her symptom and trigger event, and soften her mother image.

**Zen Focusing: Use Meditative Tools.** Zen focusing contains three meditative techniques based on Buddhist approaches that I've tied together, described by Mark Epstein (1995) in *Thoughts Without a Thinker*. Before applying them in the moment, of course, it's helpful to go over them through thinking and writing in a quiet space.

1. Use mindfulness. Let the feeling be. Don't judge or take action regarding the symptom.

2. Relax into your body. Loosen tight muscles.

3. Surrender to your breathing. Count breaths in time frames; observe where your breath goes when you exhale. Does it touch your nose? Can you feel your heart beating?

After an unpleasant episode where she found herself critizing Kaycee, Jenny thought and wrote about what had happened and how her stored insights might help her change her response. A few days later, when Kaycee was getting dressed for a dance, Jenny felt a hint of an urge to say, "What's wrong with your hair? Your part isn't straight. Your barrettes don't match the dress. And they're not symmetrical on your head."

In response, she stopped, sat down in a soft chair, took a breath, and began Zen focusing.

First, she let the feeling be. She thought, "Okay, I'm feeling envious of my daughter. Is that so bad? It comes from Mom's making me so aware of my flaws. I can forgive myself."

Second, she relaxed into her body. She felt the tightness in her neck and back, and pretended she was massaging the area. Then she imagined seeing her rigid muscles, and concentrated on relaxing them all the way to her feet.

Third, she surrendered to her breathing. As she focused on the waxing and waning of her breaths, she could hear her heart beating, in a dull, steady rhythm. She was then able to mute her envy by softening the mother image message that pulled her back into the pod with Sonya, making her feel inferior. Now she found herself able to feel excited for Kaycee. Zen focusing had helped her thwart the symptom and trigger event, and soften the mother image.

Homing in, the next phase, involves two parts: reflecting on how the recent symptom thwarts fulfillment, and selecting a thought link, or phases of it, that will best help you gain insight about the recent symptom.

**Homing In: Reflect and Select.** When examining her tendency to criticize when she felt envious of Kaycee, Jenny homed in on the thought link that would help her think through this symptom.

First, she reflected on how her envy held her back from embracing a fuller life; it deprived her of joy as a mother and deprived her daughter of a freer sense of self. Next, after she used Zen focusing, described above, she went over some autobiographical short stories she'd written for a high-school English class (*touch tool*). Rereading the stories jogged memories from her teen years, when she and Sonya were involved in struggles over how Jenny groomed herself. She remembered Sonya's saying her hair shouldn't be pulled back because that would magnify her nose, and that she should avoid wearing clingy pants because they'd highlight her too-wide hips.

Thinking about these memories, she saw that thought link 2 would be the most helpful to her in changing her responses in this type of situation. Selecting thought link 2, Jenny first uncovered the anger toward Sonya about the restrictions she'd placed on her that Jenny was not placing on Kaycee. She then let the anger be. That led Jenny to plumb the anger's depths to realize that Kaycee's blossoming reminded her of all that she had missed when Sonya held her back in her teens. Once Jenny could accept the anger toward Sonya, she didn't have to turn it against herself and then take it out on Kaycee. And her envy of Kaycee abated when she could stop beating herself up and accept her own beauty as a vibrant woman in her forties.

The farther Jenny traveled through thought link 5, the better she got at controlling her symptoms and anticipating trigger events, and softening the mother image. When she ended her period of therapy, she knew she would always have some rough spots, but she felt pretty comfortable with using the five thought links as an approach for working through them.

Gradually, Jenny's carnival-mirror self-image as a loser compared to other females shifted to a truer one: the fact that Sonya had let a physical flaw make her feel like a loser didn't mean that Jenny had to feel like a loser too. With a truer self-image, Jenny felt freer to enjoy her daughter. And she returned to practice law, her career before having kids. But instead of going back to administrative law, which had bored her in the past, she went into trial law. Although she'd always dreamed about entering that specialty, she'd never had the courage to attempt it before, because it involved competition with other attorneys, some of them female, and she'd dreaded losing out to them. Now that she had more comfort with herself, she could go into the field that intrigued her most and allow the excitement that it offered. Fulfillment began to creep into Jenny's life as a natural part of it, rather than as a hoped-for gift that rarely or never came.

## let's recap

This chapter's first section explored Jenny's carnival-mirror self-image, and that of her mother and grandmother. Each of the three women had made her appearance the measure of her worth, rather than viewing it as only a part of a whole picture of herself. The next section presented Jenny's four stages of therapy and the related four thought links.

The last section discussed Jenny's therapy stage 5 and thought link 5, with its four phases, blending, pinpointing, Zen focusing, and homing in. With blending, you aim to form seamless thought groups using the phases of thought links 1 through 4. With pinpointing you tune in to the symptom, connect it to the trigger event, and note the mother image. With Zen focusing, you let the feeling be, relax into your body, and surrender to your breathing. With homing in, you reflect on how the symptom thwarts you, and then you select a thought link or any of its phases that you feel will most deepen your insight about the cause of your symptom. As is the case with all the thought links, the more often you journey through thought link 5's phases, the more stored in memory they will be, and the more effective they'll be for change.

In the next chapter we'll explore how mothers can apply the five thought links in raising daughters from infancy through the teens. We'll also discuss how you can use the approach to improve your relationship with your adult daughter.

## A Note to Daughters and Mothers of Daughters

After journeying through the five thought links, you may be expecting to understand the reasons for your mother's influence on your self-image. And you may also be expecting to easily face your buried anger toward, and love for, your mother, as well as face sadness about what she didn't give you, view yourself more accurately, and feel liberated to enjoy life a whole lot more than you did when you started this book. Chances are that many of you will feel some of these ways, and many of you won't. If you're in the latter group, you may not recognize the ways in which you've changed! I recommend that over time you return to the parts of the five thought links that hit home most for you, go over them, repeat the steps, take breaks, and go over them again.

If you see the approach as a musical piece requiring practice that takes time but gradually leads to a release of the sounds of ever more beautiful harmonies, I believe you'll feel rewarded.

# Questions for Reflection

1.  Which thought link do you find most useful to ward off symptoms?

2.  How would you describe your most frequent sense of your mother image? What is the most frequent picture that you see?

3.  What was your most recent trigger event? How could you describe the symptom and mother image at that moment?

4.  What do you think is your most buried feeling toward your childhood mother? Is it anger, love, sadness about what you never got, or perhaps all of these?

# *Reading Touch Tool*

*The Joy Luck Club* and *The Bonesetter's Daughter,* by Amy Tan, reveal many hidden feelings and intertwined self-images in mother-daughter pairs. The following questions can help you see some of those elements in your relationship with your mother.

## The Joy Luck Club and
## The Bonesetter's Daughter, by Amy Tan

*   What examples in the books show the daughters' difficulty in expressing anger toward their mothers?

*   What signs were there that the mothers' self-image distortions affected their daughters' self-images?

*   What insight would the daughters gain from stepping into their mothers' shoes?

*   What situations show a daughter creating the pedestal mother or the sad-sack mother, and how might she have used that to avoid anger?

*   Choose one of the mother-daughter pairs in the books that most remind you of your and your childhood mother's self-image and sense of self.

*   Try freewriting about yourself and your mother as if you're another pair in one of the stories.

# for mothers: the truer mirror— for you, for your daughter

*I couldn't believe that after all that effort to become myself, as a mother I was back to reflecting her...I saw that separating myself from my mother wasn't enough. I needed to try to understand her.*

— "Connections," P. Hunter, O, *The Oprah Magazine*

*I still have a vivid picture of my maternal grandmother's apartment, though I haven't seen it since her death many years ago. The aroma of coffee from the percolator, with its discolored pattern on the lid, a lopsided star, meets me as I open the door. I rush into the kitchen to see her near the Hoosier with its tiny pewter box snug in the corner, filled with a neat pile of transparent tissue papers for rolling cigarettes. Near it sits the Delft canister stuffed with receipts pressed up against the wooden lid with the broken hinge that drops sawdust bits when raised, and its white flowers on the sides, a hairline crack on one stem. I can also envision her in the parlor chair, loosely slip-covered in ecru chintz dappled with antique-rose and indigo-blue pansies—some open, some shut—aside the oblong mahogany table covered with the yellowed crocheted doily, its edges curled.*

I think of my maternal grandmother as a rather quiet person. She and I didn't have many of the classic "Grandma moments," such as cooking or sewing together, or sharing secrets between the two of us. And yet when I'd walk into her apartment to visit almost every week during my childhood, her expression always told me how my presence by itself made her happy; anything else I did was icing on the cake. Her eyes smiled as she stretched her arms out toward me, forming a sanctuary where safety seemed forever.

Her touch stayed with me. And because I knew I had touched her, I felt that I mattered. For healthy development, at some point in infancy we must not only feel nurtured by our mothers but also sense that we can nurture them (Stern 1985). This need continues throughout childhood, and when it's gratified, we feel our worth. But for our mothers to let us know we affect them, they must be able to look beyond themselves enough to see us.

A piece by Alice Walker (1983), in *In Search of Our Mother's Gardens*, poignantly reveals how a mother's seeing her daughter allows her to feel her touch. Due to a childhood accident, the author lost vision in one eye. Ever since, she has called the scar from that accident a "blob."

> From the day of her baby daughter's (Rebecca's) birth, the author has feared that one day she'd realize that "her mother's eyes are different from other people's...Every day [Rebecca] watches a television program called *Big Blue Marble*. It begins with a picture of the earth as it appears from the moon. It is bluish, a little battered-looking but full of light with whitish clouds swirling around it....One day...she suddenly focuses on my eye. Something inside me cringes...all children are cruel about physical differences....I assume Rebecca will be the same. But no-o-o-o. She studies my face intently...even holds my face maternally between her dimpled little hands...she says...'Mommy, there's a world in your eye'...Yes indeed, I realized, looking into the mirror. There was a world in my eye. And it was possible to love it" (48–49).

For a mother like Alice Walker to be moved by her child, she needs to *see* her. But often, because we have so many of our own problems, it's difficult to do this. This mother and daughter have had publicized conflict during the daughter's adult life, which underscores that the early mother-daughter relationship is influenced by the daughter's experiences through the years that can change its quality—for better or worse.

# preoccupied mother sees daughter as self-reflection

Here, the word "see" has a connotation beyond the usual visual one. It means to recognize her unique ways, likes, strengths, and soft spots: to know her, take her in. Alice Walker's noting her daughter's "dimpled little hands" is an example of this. It's the kind of seeing that goes with cherishing, when a mother has tuned-in traits and builds the hug cycle during the daughter's infancy, as discussed in chapter 3.

As explored in chapter 4, preoccupied mothers can't see their children very clearly, because they have too many of their own problems. And they tend to see their daughters as a reflection of themselves. But it's easy to do this even for mothers who aren't so self-absorbed, because of the common thread of gender.

In *The Common Thread*, Martha Manning (2003) shows how easy it was for her to experience her daughter as an extension of herself. Because she and her husband both had acne as teens, she worried when she saw her daughter's first pimple.

> 'Is that a zit?' I ask gently.
>
> 'Thanks, Mom. Thanks a lot!' She slams down the newspaper.
>
> 'Are you mad at me? I'm just trying to help. You can hardly tell it's there.'
>
> 'Why don't you just draw a bull's-eye around it?'

Of course, some oneness between mother and daughter reflects healthy closeness, loving connection with freedom to be an individual. But what I'm referring to here instead promotes what I call the mother-daughter "stuck state," a rigid connection between the members of the pair. The stuck state thwarts the individuality of both, and blurs the daughter's sense of her own opinions, decisions, and feelings. And the daughter often learns that love is dependent upon being like Mom.

## The Mother-Daughter Stuck State

Eunice had a problem. As a child, if she burst out with an idea at the dinner table—where her two older brothers stood in the spotlight and her father was the gatekeeper for family decisions—her mother, Gloria, would often validate her sons' ideas and pass over Eunice's. Eunice discovered as an adult in therapy that Gloria had a similar situation growing up, in which males dominated the household.

In some ways, she viewed Eunice as a sister rather than a daughter, in order to feel bolstered as a wife and mother in the male-dominated household. In treatment, when Eunice tried to identify many of her feelings, she used what she called her "seek and ye shall find" process. Gloria had a carnival-mirror self-image—feeling loved by Mother is accompanied by feeling squelched—which easily passed to Eunice because of the mother-daughter stuck state.

In order to free ourselves and our daughters from the stuck state, we need to give them the opposite message: that not only will we survive but we'll also *thrive* if they thrive as individuals. I know, it's easier said than done, especially if we were in a stuck state with *our* mothers. Separating isn't a purposeful process. It's not something daughters choose in order to reject us but instead is something they naturally move toward when they feel our love. As Barbara Marcus (2004) writes, "a daughter...[has] the conflict between her need and desire both to identify with and retain her attachment to her mother, on one hand, and to differentiate and separate from her mother, on the other" (686).

Marcus's statement highlights the fact that our daughters' separation is a struggle not only for us but also for them.

## Separate Your Self, Help Your Daughter Separate Her Self

Often the root of the stuck state is our distorted self-image. That issue makes us need our daughters to play the role of sister, husband, best friend, mini-mama, or soul mate, and it causes us to cling to them. And, because the boundary between mother and daughter is blurred, the carnival mirror easily slides from us to them. If we shift from skewed to truer self-image, our need to cling is reduced, and we and our daughters are free to embrace our individuality.

Think of a mother, Miranda, reluctant to sing for others because she doesn't like her voice, which is actually quite lovely. Because she's journeyed through the five thought links, she knows she perceives her voice inaccurately. But because she recognizes her daughter's individuality, when her daughter Ramona asks for singing lessons, Miranda can encourage her without letting her own self-image issue intrude. After seeing Ramona blossom, Miranda is inspired to try singing lessons herself, and this opens up a path to more pleasure. Both mother and daughter have gained from the mother's ability to see herself accurately and allow her daughter's separation. This chapter will focus on how we can move ourselves and our daughters in that direction.

The chapter's first section discusses how to confront the burden of guilt many a mother takes on when she looks back and considers her role in passing a distorted self-image on to her daughter. The second section shows how to use the strategy to further your growing daughter's separation process and strengthen her truer self-image. The third section uses the fairy tale "Rapunzel" to illustrate how the five thought links can be used to help deal with your daughter's separation issues at the tweens stage. The fourth section discusses how the approach can help you address her separation obstacles at the teen stage. And the last section explores how the strategy can help you improve your relationship with your adult daughter.

# going on a mother-guilt trip? change course!

## You're Off the Hook

This is a good time to repeat the five mother mantras.

By its nature, the book's theme relieves you of self-blame: Unwittingly, your female forebears passed the carnival-mirror self-image down to you, and unwittingly, or unintentionally, you've passed it down to your daughter. (Many mothers may be sensitive to their influence on their children and still find themselves unable to change unwanted behavior.)

## Blame-Free Freckles, Blame-Free Mothering

You wouldn't blame yourself for the fact that your daughter inherited your freckles; similarly, there's no reason to blame yourself for passing on the carnival-mirror self-image, passed down from your grandmother to your mother before it got to you. We can't control genes that cause freckles. And we can't control those interactions with our daughters that we weren't or aren't aware of, influenced by the distorted self-image legacy.

One of the benefits of the five thought links is a way to heighten your insight in order to change your way of relating to your growing or grown daughter.

I didn't realize how difficult it is for parents to modify their interactions with their children until I became a mother and a therapist. Before I began those careers, I taught primary school for a number of years. At parent-teacher conferences I enjoyed guiding mothers and fathers toward helping their children grow. Looking back, however, I realize that, as I spoke with the parents during that pre-parental phase of my life, I often had thoughts that were biased toward the kids. "Mrs. A, how can you be so demanding of Ted when he seems to want to please everyone?" "Mr. B, you're putting too much pressure on Sally. Doesn't that sweet voice of hers win you over as it does me?" "Mrs. C, why can't you go easier on Abbey? She's such a cute kid." Without realizing it, I wasn't putting myself into the parents' shoes.

I didn't think about this child-biased viewpoint until I looked back after having my own children and then treating women who were mothers too. As a mother, I thought about the parents I'd met during my teaching career and, in retrospect, found myself cutting them breaks, just as I had to try to cut myself breaks (not always successfully) each time one of my maternal imperfections came to my attention. And, as a therapist who treated so many mothers with self-doubts about their mothering, I realized how the sayings about parenting I'd heard through the years had endured because they hold a universal truth: we can try what we believe to be our best, give what we believe to be the most, and love with what we believe is our all, and we still make mistakes and feel a loss of control.

## Is That *Really* How You Saw It Then?

Hindsight gives you stellar vision. This last point emerged from my personal and professional growth, and you need to recall this idea when you think about how you've acted with your child in the past. Many mothers have sat before me with a list of what they call their sins, screwups, or lost opportunities during their children's earliest years: mistakes that they fear may have caused eating disorders, allergies, nightmares, irregular bowels, lack of ambition, or poor choice of friends.

I tell them something like what I'll tell you: The chances are great that you had a different mindset when you raised them, with different circumstances, and a different or possibly no support system. You were not who you are now. You were younger, lonelier, inexperienced, upset a lot, overburdened, ill, anxious, down, trying too hard, lacking good modeling from your *own* mother, or afraid to seek help for reasons you couldn't control then. So try to get more into your own shoes as you were *then* and lift the guilt.

# daughters in childhood

This section first explores separation issues that come up between mothers and daughters in infancy and in later childhood. Next, it shows how to find a model of how to use thought link 5 when you feel you're in a knotty spot with your daughter in later childhood.

## Infancy

It's more difficult to think about your daughter as an individual in infancy than it is at any other stage, because this is such an amazing time of oneness—feeling the warmth of her body against yours, gazing at her while nursing, nestling her head in the crook of your neck, and feeling her fingers grasping your pinky. Yes, that closeness is wonderful for both of you. But her separation process is already occurring, just as her attachment to you is building.

Your feeling about the idea of separation, and your image of yourself as a mother, may be revealed in how long you let your baby cry before picking her up or how long you let her sleep in your bedroom. According to the most recent parenting theories, it's better to coddle than to deprive. But sometimes your coddling may occur more because of an inaccurate way in which you view yourself than because that's what your child needs in the moment.

Here's what I mean. Let's say you grew up feeling unable to "get it right" for your mother, even though you actually did many things well. So, unjustifiably, you've viewed yourself as inadequate. Now, as a mom with a daughter of your own, you continue to carry her at times when she can walk on her own. What is a likely reason that you do this? Because without awareness, you're trying to prove to your childhood mother—represented in your mother image—how supereffective you can be.

## Later Childhood

As she grows older, her natural development, and the world of peers, school, and outside interests, makes it even harder for you to boost your daughter's separation. Sure, on the surface you feel happy about her spreading her wings, but on another level it's not so clear.

In *You're Wearing That?* Deborah Tannen (2006) reports research from a study comparing the mother-daughter dyad to the other parent-child dyads (mother-son, father-son, father-daughter) in relation to the child's achievement. The results showed that more mothers of daughters had a reduced sense of self-esteem than the parents in each of the other pairs when the child was a high achiever. Of course, we don't view this evidence in any way as a conclusive statement about all mothers' reactions to all daughters' accomplishments. In fact, we're more familiar with the opposite reaction, that is, a mother's glee over her young daughter's feats (and often, pure glee is all she feels). But the results of the study do reveal that, for many women, beneath the thrill related to their daughters' individuality—whether in their achievements or in other markers of separateness—there's often a hidden mixed feeling that mothers don't recognize in themselves.

And there are other hidden feelings that can affect your ability to further your daughter's separation. If, as is frequently the case for mothers of girls, your daughter has acted as your soul mate to compensate for your husband's emotional inabilities, the fact of her moving out into the world will seem more difficult than it would otherwise be. That can cause you to send veiled messages indicating that growing up means leaving Mom behind.

That kind of shrouded communication can look like the following example: You let your daughter stay home from school too frequently because she has stomachaches from stress triggered by a school clique. The situation reminds you of one you experienced in sixth grade with cliquey girls who didn't let you "in." Your mother let you stay home frequently with colds that the doctor said must've been sparked by your emotional upset. Just as your mother did with you, rather than strengthening your daughter's self-esteem and guiding her in how to deal better with the group, you make it easy for her to stay home. That conveys to her the message that you doubt her ability to face the problem. In other words, you lead her to question her self-reliance just as you've questioned yours.

Now we'll see how a mother uses thought link 5 to help separate her ten-year-old daughter's experience from her own. She's recently used thought link 5's four steps (blending, pinpointing, Zen focusing, homing in). But since she's very familiar with blending, she skips it this time and goes straight to the last three phases.

## *pinpointing*

Loretta's daughter, Dale, had a fourth-grade teacher, Ms. Ayers, who said Dale had cheated on a test (Dale actually glanced at another girl's paper because of insecurity). Dale denied having cheated and said that the teacher didn't believe her. Without looking at Ms. Ayers's side of the story, Loretta immediately tensed up with anger when Dale gave hers. After tuning in to the anger, Loretta identified it as her symptom.

Ms. Ayers's rigidity had angered Loretta previously, because she reminded her of her childhood mother, who also acted rigid, like when she didn't want to hear Loretta's version of squabbles with her younger brother. She connected the symptom with her trigger event: because Loretta viewed Dale and herself as one, she felt as if Ms. Ayers had accused *her.* And she noted her mother image echoing her mother's "it's my way or the highway" style. So Loretta dismissed the teacher's input and focused on her belief that Dale had not cheated.

The next time Dale had an incident with Mrs. Ayers, Loretta was more prepared for her symptom and trigger event, and could use Zen focusing when they occurred.

## *zen focusing*

Dale showed Loretta homework that the teacher had marked in many places in red, offering no constructive input. Loretta felt undue resentment building. So she used the meditative steps: letting the feeling be, by not self-judging or taking action on the anger; relaxing into her body by loosening up her muscles; surrendering to breathing by noting the rise and fall of her diaphragm and the air going in and out of her nostrils and mouth. The anger subsided.

Loretta was then able to help Dale talk about what made her glance at another child's paper. She also told Dale that she would probably have to deal with other difficult teachers, and that she would have to adapt to them as best she could. And Loretta asked for a conference with Ms. Ayers to say that she did not excuse Dale's behavior but that they needed to discuss Dale's insecurity in math and figure out how she could help her get more on track. Though Ms. Ayers didn't lose her rigidity, the rest of the year was much improved for Dale.

Though Zen focusing helped Loretta soften the effects of the symptom and trigger event, she knew she needed to deepen her understanding of her over-the-top reaction. So she went to the next step, homing in.

## *homing in*

On a bright autumn day, Loretta sat under a brilliant-yellow sugar maple dropping one or two leaves at a time. The tree reminded her of sitting in her backyard as a child under the same type of tree to cool down after upsets with her mother *(touch tool)*. She reflected about how the symptom thwarted her now, in her present life: anger made her stressed out and unable to help Dale very well.

She then selected thought link 2, facing buried anger, and went to plumbing the anger's depths. She took out her journal and wrote: *(touch tool)* "When Ms. Ayers called, her voice reminded me of Mom's getting angry with me when it didn't feel fair. My mother image sent Mom's annoyed tone through me. I was afraid to face my own anger, because she'd get riled if I expressed it and acted as if Dale were me. I've kept it in for a long time, and maybe it came out against the teacher."

Because Loretta saw Dale too much as herself, she couldn't help Dale grow as a separate person. And Loretta's modeling for Dale included her self-image, distorted as less acceptable when angry. As a daughter enters the tweens stage, the mother-daughter separation issues intensify, because the mother's problem in dealing with her daughter's puberty and expanded social world can be as difficult as the daughter's struggle to let go of her earlier relationship with her mother.

# rapunzel mother, rapunzel tween

The fairy tale "Rapunzel" illustrates those and other issues uniquely connected with the tweens. The daughter who attempts to leave the

205

childhood mother's nest while trying to maintain the relationship with her could be called a "Rapunzel daughter," and the mother who's trying to cope with the situation, a "Rapunzel mother."

But first, a few notes of advice:

- Although the next section speaks to you as a mother of a preteen daughter, it's helpful to see yourself at the same stage and think about how being stuck could've made your mother's self-image distortion your own.

- In the next two sections, "puberty" is sometimes used interchangeably with the "preteen," "tween," or "teen" stages for clarity, but of course, it's not exactly a synonym for any of these stages.

- Many of the separation issues in the tweens could also be included in the teens. I've separated the two stages for simplicity, because at times the challenges do differ.

In *The Uses of Enchantment*, Bruno Bettleheim (1976) offers one view of the enchantress in the Grimms' "Rapunzel": as a mother who's having a hard time letting go of her daughter, who will soon enter puberty. He tells us that the sorceress isn't evil for wanting to keep her ward close, just as a mother isn't evil for wanting to keep her own daughter close. She doesn't want to lose her daughter to a new world and is usually unaware of how her reluctance to let go will cause problems for her daughter.

When we picture the sorceress, we can imagine Lisbeth, a mother with her eleven-year-old daughter, Amy, in a dressing room trying on clothes that, for the first time, entirely reflect her own taste. Up to now Amy has let her mother help shape her wardrobe, and mother and daughter enjoyed shopping trips together. But, recently influenced by other girls her age, Amy wants more clinging, shorter, and tighter clothes than Lisbeth would ever approve of.

To make matters worse, Amy swings between criticizing Lisbeth for not looking younger, like Amy's friends' mothers, and dressing too sexy. She goes from "Ma, don't cut your hair; you wouldn't look cool that way, and why can't you wear your skirts shorter?" to "That top shows too much of your cleavage, Mom." Lisbeth feels that she can't win, and she also mourns the loss of her little girl. But because she's not in touch with her feelings, she gets argumentative. Like the enchantress in "Rapunzel," Lisbeth knows that she can't stop her daughter's separation, although she won't let herself admit it.

## Stay with Me

The song "Stay with Me," in Stephen Sondheim's musical, *Into the Woods*, illuminates Bettleheim's ideas through a dialogue between the enchantress in "Rapunzel" and the young girl with the long, golden tresses, locked in a tower. The lyrics let us feel the sadness beneath the witch's harsh front, the kind of sadness felt by a mother who knows her little girl must soon leave.

The sorceress's tough front masks a vulnerability revealed in questions that she poses to Rapunzel in the lyrics of "Stay with Me." Don't you value me anymore after all these years I've cared for you? I know I'm old and unattractive. Are you ashamed of who I am? Are you going to replace me with a handsome guy? It's true that there are lovers for you in the dark woods, but it's dangerous and they can hurt you. If you stay a little girl with me by your side, I'll give you TLC you won't get in that murky unknown world beyond the tower.

When a preteen daughter and her mother are in a stuck state, both mother and daughter have to experience a letting go of the daughter's little-girl stage. Before we discuss that situation further, let's first see how a smoother separation process might look.

## A Daughter's Smoother Tween Path

Note: The following scenario gives a too-good-to-be-true version of a mother-daughter interaction, but it can act as a framework for what works.

When twelve-year-old Debby enters puberty and wants to stay out at a party later than she has in the past, it's hard for Vivian to tell if Debby's being pushed by older kids. When she was a teen, Vivian's mother's leniency led Vivian to get into drinking by going along with the crowd. So Vivian made a vow to herself that if she ever had a daughter, she'd be ready to set more guidelines during her teen years than her own mother had set with *her.*

But since Vivian sees herself and her daughter as separate enough, she realizes that what's happening to Debby isn't exactly the same thing that happened to her at the same age. So Vivian talks about the group's influence in a way that allows Debby perspective on the decision: "Dad and I will think about this. But you should think, too, about whether you'd be doing this because you want to feel accepted by the group or because you want to do it for fun."

## Rapunzel's Bumpy Path to Separation

Now, we'll explore three issues in this stage that frequently interfere with the Rapunzel daughter's separation: the daughter's developing body, the mother's sadness about having to let go of her little girl, and, sometimes, the daughter's eating disorder.

### *the changing body*

Leslie, aged ten and a half, just got her period and her breasts have begun to develop. She feels self-conscious in school, because the older boys frequently stare at her chest. She tries to hide it with shapeless shirts, but that doesn't lessen her dread of facing "the macho staring packs." Her mother, Jacqueline, also went through puberty a bit on the early side and had a rough time when friends said things like, "The boys only want you for your boobs."

Jacqueline struggled then, and her daughter struggles now, with a key theme for this age: the body is changing in its unique way, while the peer group puts an emphasis on conformity, which is rooted in insecurity that encourages body comparisons. The halls of any middle school transform into a stage where every difference in height, weight, and breast size is scrutinized by the audience of schoolmates. A thick thigh, a stray facial zit, an unshaved underarm, a wayward flabby stomach—any noticeable physical feature is observed by the social clan's vigilant eye.

Because Jacqueline never got help with her problem as a young teen, she grew up with the carnival-mirror self-image formed during that period: believing she was valued for her body, not her inner beauty. She can't help her daughter deal with a similar problem now, because that will cause her to confront her past turmoil. And because Jacqueline doesn't realize she's not treating Leslie as separate enough, she can't help her any better than *her* mother helped *her* during the same stage: she's a Rapunzel mother with a Rapunzel daughter. And she unwittingly passes the carnival mirror on to Leslie, who believes its reflection is true into her teens.

The next issue that stalls separation is the Rapunzel mother's need to cling to her little girl.

## *no more bubble baths?*

A daughter's changing body and blossoming sexuality alerts the mother to the impending loss of a phase in her own life. The mother's closeness with her little girl's body through bathing it, healing it, and soothing it will now be replaced with distance from it as the body of a developing, sexual woman. She will no longer be the mother of a young child; that phase of her life, with all the worry, love, frustrations, and joys that accompany it, will now be over, for better or for worse. She'll be faced with the challenge of figuring out how to be the parent of a teenager and, soon, a young adult.

Another separation-related problem that often arises around the time of puberty is an eating disorder.

## *eating disorders: glue for the stuck state*

The young teen's feelings expressed through an eating disorder include anger, a wish for control, or the fear of losing a little girl's body (especially with anorexia). All of these emotions put obstacles in the way of separation. An added roadblock emerges when the daughter feels that her moving on will leave her mother in the dust. In *The Hungry Self,* Kim Chernin (1994) writes that, when the first women's movement announced that women could be anything they wanted to be, an eating disorders epidemic along with the generation gap. Why? If teens with all the new possibilities had mothers who were unfulfilled, then achieving success could make the daughters feel as if they were abandoning their mothers. A key cause of an eating disorder is the daughter's fear of moving forward and the resulting need to stay back with her childhood mother.

In *The Body Betrayed*, therapist Kathryn J. Zerbe (1995) relates eating disorders to separation problems in a different way. She shows how the illness passes from mother to daughter through generations, similar to the way the carnival-mirror self-image heirloom is passed down. Zerbe writes about an adult patient looking back at her teen's eating disorder. "Natalie pointed out that at least three generations of women in her family had been obsessed with thinness. This obsessiveness had worsened over the years....Her mother's desire for Natalie to achieve academically and socially (by having a slender figure) was derived from dictates passed down from her own mother. This intergenerational pattern intensified Natalie's eating disorder all the more" (69–70).

As tweens enter their teens, they reach what Carol Gilligan (1990) calls "the crisis of connection."

# teens' crisis of connection

"Connection" here means the tie between the childhood years and the teen testing ground, with its new demands on a girl's assertiveness, on her ability or willingness to compete with boys, and on her sense of direction. The mother-daughter tie is tested too. In *Reviving Ophelia*, Mary Pipher (1994) writes that, besides the teen storms created by bodily changes, there are also the crises created by a ramped-up rivalry with boys in sports and academics. Many girls fall back in those areas, because they retreat to a false sense of little-girl safety with Mom, unable or unwilling to face that competition.

I've chosen three areas where I find the crisis of connection most visible and the chances of the mother's handing down the carnival mirror most possible. They create challenging issues in the tweens stage, but in adolescence they intensify.

## Three Grounds of Separation

A teen's body image, sexuality, and relationships are prime areas for separation problems and the easy handing off of the carnival mirror. Though body image and sexuality issues overlap, I'm treating them separately for clarity.

### *body image*

When a teen's figure develops into a woman's, she naturally compares it to other females' bodies, including her mother's, whose body she may view as superior or inferior to her own. And if her mother's view of her own body causes competition with her daughter, the separation process will show it.

**Ingrid:** Ingrid's mother, Beatrice, had grown up with a distorted self-image that made her believe that beauty was equal to her whole worth. So that issue entered into Ingrid's separation experience.

210

During Ingrid's teens, Beatrice let Ingrid know, in subtle and obvious ways, that Ingrid's looks were inferior to her own. "I was a teen model. I had perfect proportions. The men still look at me. You resemble the women on Dad's side of the family. You have their larger bones, you know." Ingrid's separation from her mother was affected by the competition: she transferred her view of Beatrice's body as superior to her own onto other women's bodies, which kept her feeling inferior to those women—and kept her back socially.

**Cara:** Cara's mother, Estelle, had the same distorted self-image as Beatrice—believing that beauty equates with worth—but the way it played out in Cara's separation experience was different. At twenty-six and in therapy, Cara said she felt self-conscious about her body, even though she was very attractive. She'd wear dull colors and unrevealing tops. She recalled that in her teens her body developed into one her mother said she wished she had: long, graceful legs and a flat stomach. Her mother called her own legs "stubby" and her stomach "flabby." On top of that, on some level Cara felt guilty because her father became flirty with her. As an adult she realized that her body shame came from teen guilt related to her mother.

Even natural competition (there's usually some, even if we don't know it) between mother and daughter during the daughter's teens is not helped by our culture. As Nancy Friday (1999) notes in *Our Looks, Our Lives,* when a daughter reaches her teens, for the mother she's "the girl...now recognizable as society's beauty icon, the model wearing the clothes that mother admires in her favorite magazine" (298). And what makes it worse is what the author calls an "ugly denial of mother-daughter competition" (298) during the daughter's teens, which our culture encourages.

She writes that since envy is one of the seven deadly sins and our culture holds on to a "joined at the hip" image of the mother-daughter relationship, mothers' envy of their teen daughters is something they can't face. But what's a mother—with a distorted self-image dictating that worth is based on appearance—supposed to feel, if the culture puts youth and beauty on a pedestal and the teenage girl has more of both? As you can see, it's not surprising that competition would creep into a mother-daughter relationship.

Concern for her daughter is also a natural thing for a mother to feel. But how do we differentiate concern from competition? Sometimes the two get muddled around the issue of girls' revealing clothes. That questioning tone when the daughter wears a halter that's more revealing than a bra, a skirt that looks like a shrunken piece of fabric wrapped around her waist, or a pair of extremely low-cut jeans that reveal her underwear and show off her navel might be a sign of appropriate concern, of course. But it might also convey a message that says, "Don't have more fun than I do."

Whatever the cause, daughters' body-image issues lead to sexual issues (and vice versa) that interfere with separation and allow the carnival-mirror legacy to continue.

## *sexuality*

Competition between mother and daughter can also be stirred by the sexual issues that interweave with body issues. Let's now look at one more issue that surfaces during the teens and interferes with separation: mothers' discomfort with the subject of sexuality, especially when relating with their daughters.

**The sex-talk taboo.** Often there's an unspoken agreement between mother and daughter that talking about sex or, let's say, acknowledging that the daughter experiences it is off limits. Analyst Rosemary Balsam (2005) noted that, because sinful Eve lured Adam with words, the woman who differs from Eve—"chaste, silent, obedient"—is our culture's ideal. That concept, ingrained in women's psyches, has caused many mothers to be uncomfortable when even speaking about sex appropriately with their daughters. The silence sends an implicit message not to go there. Daughters wind up confused about how to view themselves and their sexuality: they're not sure if they should trade on their sexuality because they're only valued for their looks, or if they should take control of it as independent young women, or if they're really supposed to avoid it altogether, being chaste and silent. This uncertainty, like eating disorders, interferes with their separation from their mothers.

Besides the teen daughter's body image and sexuality issues, relationship issues reveal a lot about her separation. In chapter 6 we discussed the subject of how the carnival mirror affects women's choices of partners. In this section we'll show how some of those relating issues affect separation in the teen years.

## *relationships*

Relating patterns begin in infancy with the hug or boomerang cycle, and they develop through the teens, when they form a springboard for adult interactions. When a Rapunzel mother–Rapunzel daughter relationship has thwarted the daughter's separation, that relationship reawakens in her later relating with partners and as a mother with her own child.

**Romeo, Romeo, wherefore art thou—*Mom*?!** Often, a woman who can't find the right partner is amazed to find that the guy she chooses is a man on the outside but resembles her mother on the inside. It's fine to "marry your mother" if you had a pretty healthy relationship with her that allowed you your individuality. But if it squelched your separation, you can wind up with a husband who's really your mother in disguise—and pass that pattern on to your teen daughter.

Sophia sat in my office and talked about her difficulties with dating. After I mentioned the possible connection between her problem with dates that don't work out and her relationship with her mother, she said, "But my mom is short with blond hair and blue eyes, and I usually date tall guys with dark hair and brown eyes." At first glance, they're two very different images. But the deeper sense of her mother more closely matches the guys she chooses than she realizes. Her mother let her know, from childhood on, that no one would love her the way she did. From Sophia's teens on, she was drawn to guys who made her feel that no one could love her as they did, and then they'd act possessive. She wound up leaving them to find her own space.

Daughters' separation troubles also affect another kind of relationship: the one they have with their children when they're mothers themselves.

**Am I my mom as a mom?** Bertie was a lonely wife with a workaholic husband. So she needed her daughter, Margot, to act as a soul mate who would echo Bertie's opinions and ideas. By the time she reached her teens, Margot lacked many of her own ideas and interests. Later, as an adult with a daughter of her own, Ava, she still felt she needed her mother to make major decisions, because she'd never developed a separate-enough self.

At age nine, Ava asked Margot if she could sleep over at her friend Penny's house that night. Margot's mind wandered, and she couldn't respond. The last two times Ava had slept over at Penny's, she'd gotten

213

almost no sleep, because Penny's father was an alcoholic who yelled at his wife, and her mother couldn't draw limits for anyone. The right response was obvious: it wasn't a good idea, especially on a school night. But just the smell of a decision sent Margot mentally back to her mother. So she waited for her husband, a stand-in for Bertie, to give the answer.

In order to recognize our children's needs as separate from ours, we must have a separate sense of ourselves. But if we're like Margot, in a stuck state with our childhood mother, it means we still have little-girl needs we hope she'll fill. And those wishes make us focus on ourselves a bit too often when our child expresses needs.

Another problem that the stuck state creates is our inability to "get it" with our adult daughters, causing conflict that could be avoided.

# getting it with your adult daughter

*I went into the attic and saw Joan's high-school yearbook. Dust particles swirled in the air as I pulled it off the shelf. I looked at the photo of her with that gorgeous smile and thought, where did my little girl go? I think it started when she married Eddie and his opinions seemed more important to her than mine. Salt fell on the wound when she didn't need my input in raising Carolyn. I miss feeling closer but don't know how to get there.*

Ilona and her daughter, Joan, grew apart after Joan and Eddie had their kids. Ilona recalled her last time with them, when Joan seemed too loose with her eight-year-old daughter, Carolyn. Ilona told Joan to be more aware of details in Carolyn's life: how she brushed her teeth, cleaned her room, used her allowance, and so on. After that visit, Joan communicated with her mother less often. Ilona felt bad and realized she'd been uptight a lot recently when she saw Joan with Carolyn and acted as if *she* were the mother, not Joan. So she went to thought link 5 to try to change in a way that would improve her relationship with Joan.

## Traveling Through Thought Link 5

Ilona felt that she'd pretty well internalized the first three phases of this thought link. So now she just briefly went over them: blending, pinpointing, Zen focusing. Here's how she journeyed through her fourth phase, homing in.

It was early summer, and Ilona sat on a park bench to write and think near a rose garden. She alternated between looking at her thoughts and looking at the roses in clusters of white, yellow, and red, framed by the stone walls around them. She began reflecting on how her symptom—loss of control when seeing her daughter interact with her granddaughter—reduced fulfillment. That was easy. It kept her from having a closer relationship with her daughter and more fun with her granddaughter.

Then she selected a phase from thought link 1 that she felt would best offer her understanding of her symptom: sifting out. She thought and wrote about the connection between her distorted self-image and her mother's. Her mother, Aileen, had grown up with the carnival-mirror self-image. She viewed herself as sloppy, when she was actually a free-spirited kid who didn't care about order. She passed the carnival mirror to Ilona by giving her signals to be the opposite, a neatnick. So when Ilona raised Joan, she got involved with every detail, wanting to know how often Joan used the bathroom, exactly what she ate at school, and whom she played with outside.

Joan, showing some rebel modeling, appeared laissez-faire as a mother with Carolyn, which made Ilona feel uptight. Deep down, she still needed to win approval from the mother image representing Aileen by being a neatnick. Ilona, in a stuck state with Aileen, had trouble seeing Joan as too different from herself, which is why she was overly involved with Joan regarding her mothering of Carolyn.

Ilona returned to the park bench a number of times throughout the summer and alternated thought links. While gazing at a potpourri of fallen rose petals, she sifted out her self-image from the mother-daughter mix. During situations of conflict, she used Zen focusing and improved her relationship with Joan. By giving Joan more space to be her own self as a mother, she opened up a space of mother-daughter closeness that Joan could enter.

# let's recap

We've explored how the mother who didn't have enough of her own childhood needs met is often too self-absorbed to meet her own child's needs, one of them being separation. So, if the mother has a distorted self-image, her daughter will easily gain one of her own. We also discussed a model of how the five thought links can help you move your growing daughter toward a truer self-image.

We also explored two particularly difficult stages that test the mother-daughter relationship. During the tweens or preteen stage, the daughter's changing body provokes previous difficulties in the mother-daughter relationship, at times leading to an eating disorder. And in the teens, body image, sexuality, and relationship issues are heightened and slow separation. And we discussed using the five thought links to lessen conflict with your adult daughter.

## A Note to Mothers

If you're feeling as if you'll never gain a truer self-image in order to help your daughter have a truer one because following the strategy is too hard or complicated, think about the idea that the five-thought-links approach is a journey over time. And you don't move in a straight line to reach your destination. Instead, you take the unexpected turns in the path and see where they take you, retrace your steps in places, or return to the starting point. Most likely, you won't know that you're seeing yourself more accurately until after you feel freer, which may be reflected in your daughter's eyes.

# Questions for Reflection

1. If you're a Rapunzel daughter still tied in some way to your Rapunzel mother, what childhood needs did you have that she couldn't notice?

2. How does the tie between you and your childhood mother appear in your daily life, and how does your mother image keep it alive?

3. How might you repeat the above patterns with your growing daughter, and use thought link 5 to change it?

# *Reading Touch Tool*

We've discussed how the fairy tale "Rapunzel," by the Brothers Grimm, reveals how the mother's distorted self-image can thwart the daughter's separation. If you read the tale, you can use the following questions to understand how your own skewed self-image might connect with your daughter's separation, now or in the future.

## "Rapunzel," by the Brothers Grimm

• What feelings of the enchantress might you share regarding your "tween" daughter?

• How might your tween daughter's feelings about you resemble yours at that stage with your own mother?

• Try relating your own separation from your mother to the fairy tale, or freewrite, taking on the role of Rapunzel in the tower. Next, freewrite, taking on the role of your mother at the time.

# appendix

## suggestions for *my mother, my mirror* groups

You may find it helpful to start or join a group of women who are also working to shift their view from a carnival-mirror self-image to a more accurate self-image. Below are suggestions for a book group, and a "creativity group" based on themes from *My Mother, My Mirror.* They include ideas for topics to focus on, discussion questions to ask, and books to read. For further ideas or information, see my website, www .mymothermymirror.com.

### *My Mother, My Mirror* Book Groups: New and Established

- Read *My Mother, My Mirror* in parts. While reading each part, keep key concepts in mind for discussion afterward, such as those listed below:

     **Part I:** Truer self-image, distorted self-image, mother-image, freer self, thwarted self, hug cycle, boomerang cycle, rebel modeling, Narcissus, Echo daughter, mind-body moments, trigger events, fantasy, unconscious, watersheds, finding yourself lost, symptoms.

> **Part II:** Exploring; stepping into Mother's shoes; sifting out; not-loss experience; uncovering; letting it be; plumbing the buried anger, love, or sadness.
>
> **Part III:** Blending, pinpointing, Zen focusing, homing in, Rapunzel mother, Rapunzel daughter, stuck state, mindfulness.

+ Use Questions for Reflection and Reading Touch Tools at the ends of chapters and in The List, later in this appendix, as a starting point for discussions.

+ As a springboard for discussions, identify yourself and your childhood mother in the mother-daughter archetypes of celebrity women and their mothers in chapter 4.

## *My Mother, My Mirror* Creativity Groups

The group might alternate the following activities from one month to the next, or stay with an approach and see where it takes the group.

### *spark the creative experience*

+ Read: *My Mother, My Mirror,* and use Questions for Reflection, and Reading or Writing Touch Tools to open up discussions. Collect ideas in a group journal.

+ Read: *The Artist's Way,* by Julia Cameron (1992). Follow the "tasks" suggestions at the ends of chapters that most evoke your creative feelings.

+ Hear music: Listen to musical recordings that stir feelings from the past while you're engaged in a creative activity.

+ Write: Freewrite using the group's ideas, which you've collected. Use the material to create memoirs, mother-daughter stories, or poems, or a group freewriting activity.

+ Use hands-on art: Draw, paint, or make a collage to create designs that reflect themes discussed.

- Do craftwork: Knitting, crocheting, weaving, embroidering, or quilting: Create designs reflecting themes such as mother-daughter, self-image, sense of self, female fulfillment.

- View films: Watch movies related to our themes (see The List, later, for titles), and discuss.

- View art: Explore mother-daughter themes in paintings of Mary Cassatt and Berthe Morisot that are discussed in art books, museums, or the Internet (google "images").

## *when and where to seek therapy consultation*

If at any time it seems that you or another group member might want or need the help of a therapist, it's best to consult with a trained analytic clinician. Below are several websites that offer information, referrals, or both:

American Association for Psychoanalysis in Clinical Social Work: www.aapcsw.org

Division 39 of the American Psychological Association: www.division39.org

American Psychoanalytic Association: www.apsa.org

# the recommended reading, listening, and viewing list

The books, plays, music, and films listed below include themes that touch on those discussed in *My Mother, My Mirror*. They can be used to further the process of any of the groups suggested, or to enrich your experience of reading the book.

## Fiction

*Bastard Out of Carolina,* by Dorothy Allison

*The Red Tent,* by Anita Diamant

*Love Medicine,* by Louise Erdrich

*White Oleander,* by Janet Fitch

*Pearl,* by Mary Gordon

*The Secret Life of Bees,* by Sue Monk Kidd

*Annie John* and *Lucy,* by Jamaica Kincaid

*The Bean Trees,* by Barbara Kingsolver

*Beloved* and *The Bluest Eye,* by Toni Morrison

*A Leak in the Heart: Tales from a Woman's Life* and *And the Bridge Is Love: Life Stories,* by Faye Moskowitz

*One True Thing,* by Anna Quindlen

*Snow Flower and the Secret Fan,* by Lisa See

*Anywhere but Here,* by Mona Simpson

*A Tree Grows in Brooklyn,* by Betty Smith

*The Kitchen God's Wife, The Bonesetter's Daughter,* and *The Joy Luck Club,* by Amy Tan

*Divine Secrets of the Ya-Ya Sisterhood,* by Rebecca Wells

*Losing Battles,* by Eudora Welty

*Crazy Ladies,* by Michael Lee West

*The Land of Women,* by Regina McBride

*Postcards from the Edge,* by Carrie Fisher

## Nonfiction

*Necessary Losses,* by Judith Viorst

*Daughters of Madness,* by Susan Nathiel

*How I Learned to Cook,* by Margo Perin

# Memoirs

*I Know Why the Caged Bird Sings,* by Maya Angelou

*Her Mother's Daughter: A Memoir of the Mother I Never Knew and of My Daughter, Courtney Love,* by Linda Carroll

*In My Mother's House,* by Kim Chernin

*Wild Swans: Three Daughters of China,* by Jung Chang

*Circling My Mother,* by Mary Gordon

*Fierce Attachments,* by Vivian Gornick

*The Liar's Club,* by Mary Karr

*The Woman Warrior: Memories of a Girlhood Among Ghosts,* by Maxine Hong Kingston

*Daughter of the Queen of Sheba,* by Jacki Lyden

*Tender at the Bone: Growing Up at the Table,* Ruth Reichl

*Her Last Death: A Memoir,* by Susanna Sonnenberg

*Wishful Drinking,* by Carrie Fisher

*Mothering Mother,* by Carol D. O'Dell

*My Life So Far,* by Jane Fonda

# Mythology

*Demeter and Persephone*

# Plays

*August: Osage County,* by Tracy Letts

*The Beauty Queen of Leenane,* by Martin McDonagh

*Mourning Becomes Electra,* by Eugene O'Neill

*The Glass Menagerie,* by Tennessee Williams

## Films

*Georgia Rule*

*I'll Cry Tomorrow*

*The Joy Luck Club*

*Mildred Pierce*

*The Mirror Has Two Faces*

*One True Thing*

*The Piano Teacher*

*Terms of Endearment*

*Divine Secrets of the Ya-Ya Sisterhood*

*Postcards from the Edge*

## Music

"Stay with Me," from *Into the Woods*, by Stephen Sondheim

# glossary

Note: The term "mother" as used herein refers to the mother as she was during the daughter's childhood, the childhood mother. If there was another primary caregiver, like a father or grandmother, the term "mother" is used to refer to that person. Similarly, if an adoptive mother was the primary caregiver, "mother" refers to her.

**Adrift Daughter:** The daughter with a self-image distortion influenced by a mother who was absent, abusive, or neglectful due to death, illness, or mental health problems (see *out-at-sea mother*).

**Affect Regulation:** Mother's management of the infant's difficult emotions, which builds security and carries over to later relationships.

**Attachment Theory:** Evidence shows that our style of getting our needs met in relationships is established in infancy, when we learn that certain ways of relating to our mothers are more likely than others to elicit their care. According to this theory, mothers who create the hug cycle would raise more securely attached babies (see *hug cycle*), while mothers who create the boomerang cycle would raise less securely attached babies (see *boomerang cycle*).

**Boomerang Cycle:** A pattern established in infancy beginning with the baby's frustration and tears of rage. The tuned-out mother can't calm the baby, so she remains frustrated, which leads to an insecure attachment. Adult signs of the boomerang cycle include insecurity, erratic relationships, difficulty expressing anger constructively, and turning anger against the self.

**Carnival-Mirror Self-Image:** A view of the self that doesn't further the innate self's free growth (also called "distorted," "skewed," "inaccurate" self-image). Since we all have self-image distortions, we call it the carnival-mirror self-image when it is skewed enough to hinder the freer self (see *thwarted self*). It is handed down, without awareness, from mother to daughter through family generations.

**Childhood Mother:** Your mother when she raised you.

**Echo Daughter:** This type of daughter resembles the nymph Echo, in the myth, *Narcissus*. Like the caregiver of this type of daughter, the hero in the tale can't see or know Echo because he's too self-absorbed. The Echo daughter winds up keeping emotions to herself and often feels lonely or displays aloof or remote qualities.

**Encoding:** Mind-body patterns based on responses to the mother's input that become set into the forming of the brain's memory. They reawaken later in life when situations resemble the early ones that set off the responses.

**Fantasy:** What the mind makes of actual events. Much of fantasy is in the unconscious. Use of fantasy is healthy when it helps us get through difficult times or stirs creativity, and it is unhealthy when it carries us too far away or too often from reality.

**Female Watersheds:** Puberty, pregnancy, and menopause. During these stages the body's dramatic changes trigger a woman's responses that echo the earliest mind-body moments with her primary caregiver (see *mind-body moment*).

**Finding Yourself Lost:** Feeling immersed in a creative process (see *transformative experience*).

**Flowing Traits:** The mother's qualities that emerge from her freer self and don't weigh on her baby's innate self.

**Freewriting:** Writing without focusing on grammar, structure, or punctuation, to help stir feelings and creativity. It often leads to other kinds of writing.

**Freer Self** (includes some aspects of Winnicott's "true self"): A sense of self formed when the innate self is allowed to thrive because of the mother's flowing traits. A truer self-image leads to a freer self.

**Healthy Modeling:** Identifying with the mother who has a truer self-image and freer self. It involves internalizing her traits and emulating her.

**Healthy Narcissism:** A state of being able to fulfill oneself and therefore notice the needs of others. Mothers with healthy narcissism are tuned in to their children's needs and further their individuality (see *healthy separation*).

**Healthy Separation:** A process occurring over many years of growing up that involves the development of separateness combined with a healthy attachment to the mother. The child's individuality grows out of the mother's recognition of her need to separate (see *healthy narcissism*).

**Hug Cycle:** Pattern established in infancy beginning with the baby's frustration and tears of rage. The tuned-in mother soothes the baby, so she's no longer frustrated, which leads to a secure attachment. Adult signs of the hug cycle include security, tamed anger, and healthy relationships.

**Imposing Traits:** The mother's qualities that impose themselves on her baby's innate self (see *thwarted self*).

**Innate Self:** The self we are born with, including qualities and traits. The innate self becomes the freer self when allowed to grow without undue influence from the parents' issues.

**Internalization:** Process that begins when the brain forms, involving mind-body imprinting of responses to primary caregivers' input. Although those earliest patterns (see *encoding*) in memory are most powerful, internalization goes on throughout life involving other relationships.

**Little-Girl Mother:** The mother who, because of a distorted self-image, gives her daughter unconscious cues to be caregiver to the mother (see *mini-mama daughter*).

**Jealous Queen Mother:** The mother who, because of a distorted self-image, resembles the stepmother in the fairy tale, "Snow White." She views her daughter (or stepdaughter, in the tale) as a rival (see *Snow White daughter*).

**Mind-Body Moment:** A moment early in life with the primary caregiver, when the body expresses emotion before words can do it (a primal mind-body moment). It is echoed in adulthood when an event reminds the daughter, on some level, of the early interaction (a revived mind-body moment).

**Mini-Mama Daughter:** The daughter given unconscious cues by her mother, who has a distorted self-image, to act as the mother's caregiver beginning early in life (see *little-girl mother*).

**Mother Image:** Ongoing positive or negative sense of the childhood mother, mostly in the unconscious. It includes aspects of who she actually was during your childhood and what your fantasies made of her. The mother image differs from a specific *memory* of the mother, because it's an overall sense of her that comes through as an image: vocal tone, verbal message, or manner of feeling touched.

**Narcissistic Extension:** The mother's inability to see her child as separate from her, with her own needs and desires. This concept often implies that the child represents a shining reflection of the mother for the world to see, because the mother lacks self-worth.

**Not-Loss:** An emotional void created while parents are alive, due to a lack of, or the wrong kind of, attention.

**Out-at-Sea Mother:** The mother, who, because of a distorted self-image, abuses or neglects her daughter through physical or emotional absence or mental or physical illness. (see *adrift daughter*). The mother's absence due to death falls into this group, but the issue for the daughter in that case is a sense of abandonment rather than abuse or neglect (it gets fuzzier if the mother was abusive or neglectful before she died).

**Pedestal Mother Image:** Idealized view of the mother that the daughter uses unawares, to avoid anger toward her.

**Rapunzel Daughter:** Named after the "tween" in the tale "Rapunzel," kept in a tower by an enchantress who replaced the mother; she is the daughter who can't separate easily while keeping a warm attachment to her childhood mother.

**Rapunzel Mother:** The mother of the Rapunzel daughter, who has trouble with her daughter's separation. The mother's self-image distortion easily flows to her daughter because of the fluid boundaries between mother and daughter.

**Reaping:** Feeling change in daily life during the later phases of the five thought links, as a result of building insight during the earlier phases of the approach.

**Rebel Modeling:** The daughter's identification *against* the mother, negating her with so much passion that, paradoxically, the daughter stays tied to her mother and defeats herself; the tie makes her unconsciously act in ways that harm her.

**Sad-Sack Mother Image:** A view of the mother as vulnerable that the daughter unwittingly takes, in order to avoid anger toward the mother.

**Self-Image:** The view of the self that includes qualities, traits, and sense of worth.

**Showgirl Daughter:** The daughter who is given unconscious cues by her mother, who is self-absorbed because of her own issues, to act as the mother's shining reflection from early on in life (see *stage mother*).

**Snow White Daughter:** A daughter whose mother consciously wants her to do well. But when she does, if the achievement doesn't reflect well on the mother, she rejects the daughter. And if the daughter supersedes the mother, she envies the daughter.

**Sowing:** The internalizing of insight gained in the earlier phases of the five thought links.

**Spirit-Dampened Daughter:** The daughter whose ego is deflated because of her *spirit-dampening mother*'s hurtful ways.

**Spirit-Dampening Mother:** The mother, who, because of her own issues, is verbally hurtful to her daughter; she can't help it (see *spirit-dampened daughter*).

**Stage Mother:** The mother, who, because of her own issues, is self-absorbed and puts her daughter in the spotlight so the light will shine on the mother (see *showgirl daughter*).

**Stuck State:** A rigid connection between mother and daughter that thwarts the individuality of both. The daughter often learns that love is dependent upon likeness with Mom, which slows separation.

**Symptom** (as defined for the purposes of this book): A physical expression of difficult emotions; it is *not medically related*. A symptom echoes the earliest mind-body moments (see *mind-body moment*). It emerges when an event upsets us in adulthood because it awakens an early upsetting event with the mother (see *trigger event*). Adult symptoms flow from self-image distortions and are used in the five thought links approach as signs that lead to change.

**Thwarted Self** (includes some aspects of Winnicott's "false self"): A sense of self that results when the innate self is affected by the mother's imposing traits. The distorted self-image leads to the thwarted self.

**Touch Tools:** Approaches that stir the senses to gain insight about your female forebears' self-image issues (including your mother's) while raising their daughters (includes you).

**Transformative Experience:** This term, created by Christopher Bollas, means the inner sense of stability and calmness that first occurs when a frustrated infant is soothed by the mother and finds herself in a more secure state than before. Later, we have a transformative experience when we're creative.

**Transitional Object:** This term, created by D. W. Winnicott, applies to the security blanket (and sometimes the thumb). It's the first thing outside the baby that she makes her own without her mother's direct input, but with security in her presence. Use of the transitional object spawns creativity.

**Trigger Event:** A situation that sets off an upsetting mind-body moment in the form of a symptom that's intensified by the negative mother image.

**Truer Self-Image:** A view of the self that reflects what the innate self could be if allowed to grow freely.

**Tuned-In Traits:** A mother's healthy self-focus and freer-self qualities that let her soothe her baby (see *hug cycle*).

**Tuned-Out Traits:** A mother's self-absorbed and thwarted-self qualities that make it difficult for her to soothe her baby (see *boomerang cycle*).

**Unconscious:** The part of the mind described by Freud that is beyond awareness. The unconscious contains the images in dreams, fantasies, art, and jokes, and our deeper aggressive and sexual wishes. The mother image, composed of real and fantasized aspects of our childhood mother, resides in the unconscious (see *mother image*). The unconscious influences relationships, feelings, and actions throughout life, without our knowing it. Although many of Freud's theories are often challenged today, many cognitive scientists agree that most thinking occurs in our unconscious, an area of the brain where early memory sets in while neural pathways are shaped.

**Unhealthy Narcissism:** A state of preoccupation that keeps a mother from enjoying life and tuning in to her child's needs. Mothers with unhealthy narcissism have difficulty furthering their children's separation.

**Unhealthy Separation:** A process involving a clinging attachment to the mother that thwarts separation. The problematic connection is influenced by the mother's need to see her child and herself as one (see *unhealthy narcissism*).

# references

Alexander, P. 2003. *Rough Magic*. 2nd ed. New York: Da Capo Press.

American Heritage Dictionary. 2000. *American Heritage Dictionary of the English Language*. 4th ed. Boston: Houghton Mifflin.

Audy, J. R. 1981. Man, the lonely animal: Biological routes of loneliness. In *The anatomy of loneliness*, ed. J. Hartog, J. R. Audy, and Y.A. Cohen. New York: International Universities Press.

Balsam, R. 2005. A language of silence: Remarks on the history of the female body in psychoanalysis. Paper presented at the New York Academy of Medicine, October, 17. New York.

Bateson, M. C. 2001. *With a Daughter's Eye*. New York: Perennial.

Beebe, B. 2002. *Infant Research and Adult Treatment*. Hillsdale, NJ: The Analytic Press.

Begley, S. 2008. *Train Your Mind, Change Your Brain*. New York: Ballantine Books.

Benjamin, J. 1988. *The Bonds of Love*. New York: Pantheon Books.

Bettleheim, B. 1976. *The Uses of Enchantment*. New York: Alfred A. Knopf.

Bollas, C. 1987. *The Shadow of the Object*. New York: Columbia University Press.

Brown, T. 2007. *The Diana Chronicles*. New York: Doubleday.

Cameron, J. 1992. *The Artist's Way*. New York: Penguin Putnam.

Chernin, K. 1994. *The Hungry Self*. New York: HarperPerennial.

————. 1994. *In My Mother's House.* New York: HarperPerennial.

————. 1998. *The Woman Who Gave Birth to Her Mother.* New York: Viking.

Clarke, G. 2000. *Get Happy.* New York: Dell Publishers.

Cook, B. W. 1993. *Eleanor Roosevelt,* vol. 1: 1884-1933. New York: Penguin.

Cozolino, L. 2006. *The Neuroscience of Human Relationships.* New York: W. W. Norton & Company.

Cross, J. 2006. *Secret Daughter.* New York: Viking.

Edelman, H. 2006. *Motherless Daughters.* New York: Da Capo Press.

Epstein, M. 1995. *Thoughts Without a Thinker.* New York: BasicBooks.

Finstad, S. 2001. *Natasha.* New York: Three Rivers Press.

Fonda, J. 2006. *My Life So Far.* New York: Random House.

Friday, N. 1999. *Our Looks, Our Lives.* New York: HarperCollins Publishers.

Fuerstein, L. A. 1992. Females in bondage: The early role of mother and father in the woman's tie to abusive men. In *Psychoanalytic Perspectives on Women,* ed. E. V. Siegel. New York: Brunner/Mazel.

————. 1997. The tell-tale heart: Responding to a patient's somatic language. In *Mind-body problems,* ed. J. Finell. Northvale, NJ: Jason Aronson Publishers.

Gilligan, C. 1990. Teaching Shakespeare's sisters: Notes from the underground of female adolescence. In *Making connections,* ed. C. Gilligan, N. P. Lyons, and T. J. Hammer. Cambridge, MA: Harvard University Press.

Goldberg, N. 1986. *Writing Down the Bones.* Boston, MA: Shambhala.

Graham, K. 1998. *Personal History.* New York: Vintage Books.

Gutwill, S. 1994. Women's eating problems: Social context and the internalization of culture. In *Eating Problems: A Feminist Psychoanalytic Treatment Model,* ed. C. Bloom, A. Gitter, S. Gutwill, L. Kogel, and L. Zaphiropoulos. New York: BasicBooks.

Hamilton, E. 1942. *Mythology.* New York: New American Library.

Howard, J. 1989. *Margaret Mead.* New York: Ballantine Books.

Hunter, P. 2007. Mother's nature. *O, The Oprah Magazine* (May), 283-88.

Jackson, L. C., and B. Greene, eds. 2000. *Psychotherapy with African American Women.* New York: The Guilford Press.

Jong, E. 1973. *Fear of Flying.* New York: Henry Holt & Company.

Karen, R. 1998. *Becoming Attached.* New York: Oxford University Press.

Kavaler-Adler, S. 1993. *The Compulsion to Create.* New York: Routledge.

Kernberg, P., B. Buhl-Nielson, and L. Normandin. 2007. *Beyond the Reflection.* New York: Other Press.

Kidd, S. M. 2002. *The Secret Life of Bees.* New York: Penguin Books.

Kohut, H. 1977. *The Restoration of the Self.* New York: International Universities Press.

Lamott, A. 1995. *Bird by Bird.* New York: Anchor Books.

Lawson, C. 2000. *Understanding the Borderline Mother.* Northvale, NJ: Jason Aronson.

Leaming, B. 1998. *Marilyn Monroe.* New York: Three Rivers Press.

———. 2002. *Mrs. Kennedy.* New York: Touchstone.

Levitin, D. 2007. *This Is Your Brain on Music.* New York: Plume.

Llerena-Quinn, R., and M. P. Mirkin. 2005. Immigrant Mothers. In *Psychotherapy with Women.* New York: The Guilford Press.

Love, S. M. 1995. *Dr. Susan Love's Breast Book.* 2d rev. Cambridge, MA: Addison-Wesley.

Lyden, J. 1997. *Daughter of the Queen of Sheba.* New York: Houghton Mifflin.

Manning, M. 2003. *The Common Thread.* New York: HarperCollins.

Marcus, B. 2004. Female passion and the matrix of mother, daughter, and body: Vicissitudes of the maternal transference in the working through of sexual inhibitions. In *Psychoanalytic Inquiry,* ed. J. Lichtenberg. New York: Analytic Press.

Mayes, F. 1996. *Under the Tuscan Sun.* New York: Broadway Books.

McClanahan, R. 1999. *Word Painting.* Cincinnati, OH: Writer's Digest Books.

**233**

McGoldrick, M., J. Giordano, and N. Garcia-Preto. 2005. *Ethnicity and Family Therapy*. New York: The Guilford Press.

McWilliams, N., 2004. *Psychoanalytic Psychotherapy*. New York: The Guilford Press.

Mead, M. 1972. *Blackberry Winter*. New York: William Morrow.

Miller, A. 1981. *Prisoners of Childhood*. New York: Basic Books.

Milner, M. 1990. *On Not Being Able to Paint*. Madison, CT: International Universities Press.

Morrison, T. 1994. *The Bluest Eye*. New York: Plume.

Morton, A. 1998. *Diana*. New York: Simon & Schuster.

Northrup, C. 2001. *The Wisdom of Menopause*. New York: Bantam Books.

———. 2005. *Mother-Daughter Wisdom*. New York: Bantam Books.

Orbach, S. 1986. *Hunger Strike*. New York: Norton.

Pipher, M. 1994. *Reviving Ophelia*. New York: Ballantine Books.

Reichl, R. 1998. *Tender at the Bone*. New York: Broadway Books.

Roosevelt, E. 1992. *The Autobiography of Eleanor Roosevelt*. New York: Da Capo Press.

Rose, G. J. 1992. *The Power of Form*. Madison, CT: International Universities Press.

See, L. 2005. *Snow Flower and the Secret Fan*. New York: Random House.

Shabad, P. C. 1990. Vicissitudes of psychic loss of a physically present parent. In *The problem of mourning and loss,* ed. R. Dietrich and P. C. Shabad. Madison, CT: International Universities Press.

Siegel, D. J. 1999. *The Developing Mind*. New York: Guilford Press.

Smith, B. 1943. *A Tree Grows in Brooklyn*. Philadelphia, PA: The Blakiston Company.

Solms, M., and O. Turnbull. 2002. *The Brain and the Inner World*. New York: Other Press.

Spoto, D. 2000. *Jacqueline Bouvier Kennedy Onassis*. New York: St. Martin's Press.

Stern, D. 1985. *The Interpersonal World of the Infant*. New York: Basic Books.

Tannen, D. 2006. *You're Wearing That?: Understanding Mothers and Daughters in Conversation.* New York: Ballantine Books.

Von Drehle, D. 2004. *Triangle.* New York: Atlantic Monthly Press.

Walker, A. 1983. *In Search of Our Mother's Gardens.* New York: Harcourt Brace Jovanovich.

Wallin, D. J. 2007. *Attachment in Psychotherapy.* New York: The Guilford Press.

Wells, R. 1997. *Divine Secrets of the Ya-Ya Sisterhood.* New York: HarperPerennial.

White, M. T., and M. B. Weiner. 1986. *The Theory and Practice of Self Psychology.* New York: Brunner/Mazel.

Williams, T. 1971. *The Glass Menagerie.* In *The Theatre of Tennessee Williams,* vol. 1. New York: New Directions Books.

Winnicott, D. W. 1986. *Playing and Reality.* New York: Penguin Books.

———. 1994. *The Maturational Processes and the Facilitating Environment.* Madison, CT: International Universities Press.

Zerbe, K. J. 1995. *The Body Betrayed.* Carlsbad, CA: Gürze Books.

**Laura Arens Fuerstein, Ph.D.**, has worked as an analytic therapist for more than thirty years. She is a popular speaker at conferences about love, sexuality, and women's issues, and has written many articles on those subjects. As a senior faculty member at the New York Center for Psychoanalytic Training and the Institute for Psychoanalysis and Psychotherapy of New Jersey, Fuerstein has trained many clinicians in her approach to psychotherapy. She leads supervision groups and maintains a private practice in Highland Park, New Jersey.

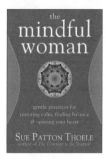

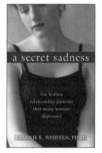

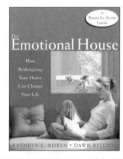